James Oglethorpe
FATHER *of* GEORGIA

CARL & SALLY GABLE FUND
for Southern Colonial American History

James Oglethorpe

FATHER *of* GEORGIA

A FOUNDER'S JOURNEY *from*
SLAVE TRADER *to* ABOLITIONIST

Michael L. Thurmond

The University of Georgia Press
Athens

Published in part with generous support from the Carl and Sally
Gable Fund for Southern Colonial American History

Published by the University of Georgia Press
Athens, Georgia 30602
www.ugapress.org
© 2024 by Michael L. Thurmond
Designed by Melissa Buchanan
Printed and bound by Sheridan Books
The paper in this book meets the guidelines for
permanence and durability of the Committee on
Production Guidelines for Book Longevity of the
Council on Library Resources.

Most University of Georgia Press titles are
available from popular e-book vendors.

Printed in the United States of America
24 25 26 27 28 C 5 4 3 2

Library of Congress Cataloging-in-Publication Data
Names: Thurmond, Michael L., author.
Title: James Oglethorpe, father of Georgia : a founder's journey from
slave trader to abolitionist / Michael L. Thurmond.
Other titles: Founder's journey from slave trader to abolitionist
Description: Athens : The University of Georgia Press, [2024] |
Includes bibliographical references and index.
Identifiers: LCCN 2023040797 | ISBN 9780820366043 (hardback) | ISBN
9780820366029 (epub) | ISBN 9780820366012 (pdf)
Subjects: LCSH: Oglethorpe, James, 1696–1785. | Slaveholders—
Georgia—Biography. | Abolitionists—Georgia—Biography. |
Governors—Georgia—Biography. | Equiano, Olaudah, 1745–1797—
Influence. | Diallo, Ayuba Suleiman, 1701–1773—Influence. |
Georgia—History—Colonial period, ca. 1600–1775. | Slave trade—
Great Britain—History. | Royal African Company.
Classification: LCC F289.O37 T48 2024 |
DDC 975.8/02092 [B]—dc23/eng/20230831
LC record available at https://lccn.loc.gov/2023040797

Image on page v courtesy of the Library of Congress

CONTENTS

ILLUSTRATIONS

FOREWORD

IT IS MY HONOR TO offer an endorsement to the first in a series of publications devoted to deepening our appreciation for early Georgia history. Created to recognize the passion of Carl and Sally Gable for history in general, and specifically that of Georgia's passage from colony to state, these books aim to cast new light on the significance of Georgia's role in shaping our country, from the colonial era through the era of the new republic.

Michael Thurmond is ideally qualified to be our inaugural author in the series—a man whose contributions to the social betterment of our state are well known. Currently the CEO of DeKalb County, Georgia, in 1986 Mr. Thurmond was the first African American elected to the Georgia Assembly from Athens/Clarke County since Reconstruction. The son of a Georgia sharecropper, Mr. Thurmond earned a BA degree in philosophy and religion at Paine College, in Augusta, a juris doctorate at the University of South Carolina School of Law and training in the Political Executives Program at the John F. Kennedy School of Government, Harvard University. As the former director of Georgia's Division of Family and Children Services and commissioner of the Georgia Department of Labor, he is credited with shaping initiatives that helped tens of thousands of Georgians move from unemployment into the workforce.

Even this brief overview of Thurmond's political career suggests why he has long maintained an interest in Georgia's founder, James Edward Oglethorpe. Widely credited as a man at the leading edge of the humanitarian wave of the eighteenth century that would bring attention to the misery of the poor wrought by the closure of the commons and rise of industrial wage labor, Oglethorpe, along with the Trustees for Establishing the Colony of Georgia in America, founded the colony of Georgia as a remedy. They explicitly prohibited the institution of slavery to encourage self-reliance and egalitarian uplift among the newly settled working poor of England and Scotland, which certainly supports the humanitarian dimension. Yet this progressive aspect has been criticized as patronizing to the poor and racist in its not-so-subtle goal of excluding Blacks from the landscape. Oglethorpe's membership among the Trustees of the Royal African Company, which enslaved and transported to the Americas more African women, men, and children than any other organization during the era of the Atlantic slave trade, also undercuts the humanitarian position. It is impossible to believe that Oglethorpe did not understand the business of the RAC. He somehow ignored its activities even as he enjoyed the profits born of bloody exploitation.

Thurmond argues, however, that a close reading of Oglethorpe's life reveals the capacity for an awakening in the man that would lead him, finally, to become a pioneer abolitionist. He attributes this to personal relationships that Oglethorpe formed with two victims of the Atlantic trade, Ayuba Suleiman Diallo and Olaudah Equiano, both of whom found freedom from bondage and who devoted themselves to sharing their stories in the antislavery cause. As a result, Oglethorpe would divest his stock in the RAC and resign his trusteeship. Oglethorpe also attempted to model, Thurmond believes, more respectful relationships with Indigenous neighbors than had the Virginia or Carolina colonies, and he devoted himself to a better diplomacy with the Yamacraw leader Tomochichi through the linguistic and diplomatic skills of Mary Musgrove, a mixed-descent woman who became wealthy and influential in the interstices of Indigenous and colonial affairs.

This reinterpretation of Oglethorpe, I would suggest, accords well with Thurmond's own experience as an advocate for progressive solutions to social problems in a politically conservative state. His success has depended on his personal warmth and genuineness, his commitment to a common good, and a keen ability to pursue social transformation through well-grounded, practical programs. It is perhaps too early for the judgment of history in Thurmond's case, but we can now understand what, he writes, underlies this book: "If Oglethorpe voiced moral opposition to the transatlantic slave trade, the history of abolitionism would become more firmly rooted in Georgia's red clay. If Georgians were exposed to a more enlightened view of our founder's values and philosophy, perhaps current and future state leaders would chart a more inclusive and progressive course. If any or all these questions could be answered in the affirmative, had generations of Georgians been denied the opportunity to emulate and celebrate Oglethorpe's original vision for our state?"

James F. Brooks
Gable Chair
University of Georgia

ACKNOWLEDGMENTS

WHILE RESEARCHING AND WRITING THIS book, I have benefited from the knowledge and counsel of many colleagues and friends who have graciously assisted my efforts.

I would like to thank preeminent Oglethorpe scholar Edwin L. Jackson for encouraging Georgia governor Zell Miller to appoint me to the James Oglethorpe Tercentenary Commission. It was during the commission's 1996 visit to Oglethorpe's grave site in Cranham, England, that my interest in examining his role in shaping Georgia's unique antislavery heritage was engaged. The associations, relationships, and friendships established with my fellow delegates have withstood the test of time.

Professor John C. Inscoe graciously invited me into his home, read early drafts of the book, and provided invaluable criticism and advice. I am honored to have been a recipient of his private tutelage. A personal debt of gratitude is owed to Professor John H. Morrow Jr. for being an inspiring role model, and to several other distinguished historians whose research and writings formed the intellectual foundation of this book: Phinizy Spalding, Betty Wood, Harvey H. Jackson, Charles Grant, Thomas H. Wilkins, Thomas D. Wilson, Judge Leon Higginbottom, F. N. Boney, Charles Wynds, Kenneth Coleman, Milton L. Ready, Edward J. Cashin, Buddy Sullivan, Marion E. Anthony, Rubye M. Jones, Amos A. Ettinger, and Thaddeus M. Harris.

Words of gratitude are extended to Professor James Brooks for his insightful foreword, and to Charles and Sally Gable for their generous contribution that helped underwrite the costs of publication.

For assistance and access to their collections, I would like to acknowledge the archivists, librarians, and administrators of the University of Georgia Main Library, the Paine College, Collins-Calloway Library, the Richard B. Russell Building, Hargrett Rare Book and Manuscript Library, the Atlanta University Center, Robert W. Woodruff Library, Oglethorpe University, Philip Weltner Library, Emory University, Candler School of Theology, Pitts Theology Library, the University of South Carolina, South Caroliniana Library, the DeKalb County Public Library, the Athens-Clarke County Library, Heritage Room, the Atlanta-Fulton County Public Library System, Auburn Avenue Research Library on African American Culture and History, the Georgia Archives, the Georgia Historical Society, the Athens Historical Society, the Susie King Taylor Women's Institute and Ecology Center, the Association for the Study of African American Life and History, the Carl Vinson Institute of Government, the American Baptist History Society, the Florida Museum of Natural History, the National Museum of African American History and Culture, the British Library, and the National Portrait Gallery, London.

I am especially grateful to Lisa Bayer, director; Nathaniel Holly, acquisitions editor; Jon Davies, assistant director for editorial, design, and production; and the entire staff at the University of Georgia Press for their assistance and support in the publication of this work, as well as to their collegial reviewers whose thoughtful and well-reasoned assessments elevated the historical narrative and sharpened my reasoning. Any errors or omissions in the text remain my own. Deirdre Mullane also provided invaluable editorial and publishing assistance during this process.

Lifelong friends Denny and Peggy Galis have been a constant source of encouragement, and I am grateful as well for the assistance of James Grande, Hermina Glass-Hill, Rev. Thurman N. Tillman, Van Johnson, Todd Groce, Maria Saporta, Annette Johnson, and Michelle Hasty.

Finally, to my wife Zola and our daughter Mikaya, thank you for traveling with me on this sometimes-challenging journey. Without your unwavering love and support, the publication of this book would not have been possible.

INTRODUCTION

GRAY BRITISH SKIES GREETED OUR afternoon arrival at the venerable Parish Church of All Saints, in the picturesque village of Cranham, located on the northeastern outskirts of London. Led by Georgia governor Zell Miller, our fifty-seven-member delegation had journeyed there from across the pond to celebrate the three-hundredth birthday of General James Oglethorpe, Georgia's founding father. This final stop of our four-day itinerary, on October 7, 1996, was to be drenched in pomp and circumstance, not an intellectual twist—or so I thought.

A palpable sense of history filled the seven-hundred-year-old church. Bright red carpet running between two elevated choir stands overlaid the final resting place of General Oglethorpe: he and his wife Elizabeth are entombed beneath the floor of the sanctuary. Our presence that day was owed to the efforts of the irrepressible Dr. Thornwell Jacobs, who oversaw the reopening of Oglethorpe University, in DeKalb County, Georgia, in the early twentieth century after it had been shuttered during the Civil War. Following his selection as president of the university in January 1915, Jacobs became the "driving force" behind its revival and subsequently led the archeological team that located the long-lost Oglethorpe burial site in October 1923. Fortunately, Jacobs's quixotic plan to exhume and reinter the general's remains on his campus was rebuffed by British and Savannah officials.

Following a brief memorial service, we placed a wreath at the site and our British guides ushered us toward an adjacent meeting hall for a reception hosted by local dignitaries. But I lingered behind to study a large white marble plaque overlooking Oglethorpe's tomb, its text repeating the narrative familiar to me and any Georgia middle schooler: Oglethorpe sought to alleviate the plight of England's debtor prisoners by offering them a fresh start in the New World. But one intriguing sentence on the memorial plaque now riveted my attention: "He was the Friend of the oppressed Negro."

As a Georgia native, public official, and historian, I had never heard our state's founder described in this way. Oglethorpe is portrayed as a passionate advocate for poor and persecuted white Christian colonists. Prevailing historical narrative concludes that Oglethorpe and his fellow Georgia Trustees prohibited chattel slavery in their experimental colony solely to protect the moral and physical well-being of Europeans.

Although Oglethorpe's desire to create a "Zion in the wilderness" is widely known, any advocacy on behalf of enslaved Blacks was news to me. As I stood motionless in the now quiet chapel, one question took center stage in my mind: Had essential elements of Oglethorpe's humanitarian legacy been overlooked, marginalized, or possibly hidden?

———

Among the elected officials, historians, educators, business leaders, and other prominent citizens on that trip, I was the only African American representative. My unexpected participation, if not an act of Providence, had risen from the ashes of a divisive, racially charged political debate in Georgia regarding recent changes to federal welfare programs.

Two years before, Governor Miller had asked me to serve as director of the Georgia Division of Family and Children Services. DFCS, pronounced "dee-fax," is a massive state agency responsible for administering a multitude of human service programs designed to uplift destitute Georgians. And a major shift was underway: historic federal and state welfare reform legislation had eliminated "entitlement" to cash assistance, and able-bodied welfare recipients were now required to seek and maintain employment to qualify for benefits.

Hoping to boost employee morale, I invoked the spirit of Oglethorpe, Georgia's champion of the poor and unemployed, as I began to oversee the new guidelines. Oglethorpe was the anointed patron saint of DFCS, his portrait proudly displayed in county offices, and overworked and underpaid social workers claimed the motto of Georgia's founders, *Non sibi, sed aliis* (Not for self but for others). In response, some skeptical employees cleverly nicknamed their novice director James Michael Thurmonthorpe!

While my rebranding strategy failed to reshape public opinion, Oglethorpe's persona did influence the outcome of Georgia's contentious welfare reform debate. Governor Miller first proposed a draconian "tough love" regimen for job-seeking welfare recipients. After I broached Oglethorpe's concern for the "less fortunate," the governor, a lifelong Oglethorpe admirer, endorsed a more compassionate strategy that we called Work First: welfare reform without the meanness. As with Oglethorpe's vision for jobless Georgia colonists, the long-term unemployed were offered a second chance to earn self-sufficiency. Surprisingly, the revised plan won bipartisan support from legislators and lobbyists.

With unprecedented investments in childcare for the working poor, transitional medical coverage, and job training, Georgia's welfare rolls steadily declined. Following a recommendation from Oglethorpe scholar Edwin L. Jackson, I received a gubernatorial invitation to join the Oglethorpe Tercentenary Delegation's pilgrimage to England. As our Delta flight soared into the evening skies over Atlanta on October 3, I was unaware that my understanding of Oglethorpe's vision for Georgia would soon be brought into question and, in time, fundamentally altered.

A well-known Georgia origin story prefigured our trip: in the last of the so-called thirteen original British colonies to be established in North America, Oglethorpe and his fellow Trustees envisioned a place where England's "worthy poor" and Christians fleeing persecution would earn a "comfortable subsistence" exporting goods produced on small farms. And, in marked contrast to their colonial neighbors, the social reformers viewed chattel slavery as an insurmountable obstacle on this path to self-sufficiency. They feared that importation of enslaved Africans would encourage idleness and economic inequality among white colonists. But while Oglethorpe diligently worked to establish a slave-free colony, the consensus among contemporary historians is that Georgia's ban on slavery lacked concern for the plight of enslaved Blacks.

Proslavery colonists called the "Malcontents" argued that banning the importation of enslaved laborers would result in the fledgling colony's economic ruin. The slavery prohibition drew intense controversy, and Oglethorpe, the only Trustee to reside in Georgia, bore the brunt of fierce and determined opposition. Despite his antislavery stance, historians and critics castigate the enigmatic Oglethorpe for affiliating with the Royal African Company, a notorious British slaving enterprise, and for allegedly exploiting enslaved Black laborers on a South Carolina plantation. All but a few Europeans of the era, considered dark-skinned Africans and their descendants to be subhuman beasts of burden, so it seemed far-fetched that Oglethorpe would have acknowledged the humanity of downtrodden Blacks, much less befriended them. The royal family, British elites, businessmen, insurers, and investors pioneered the transatlantic slave trade and transformed it into a brutally efficient and lucrative international enterprise.

Considering this reputation, the eight words chiseled on the marble plaque commissioned by Oglethorpe's widow were extraordinary, but were they factual? Did Oglethorpe truly befriend oppressed Blacks? Or was he a self-serving hypocrite, publicly opposing slavery while privately profiting from human trafficking? Although my skepticism was pervasive, I was acutely aware that providing forthright answers to these seminal questions could rewrite Georgia's origin story.

If Oglethorpe was indeed a friend of free and enslaved Blacks, if his empathy for the "worthy poor" transcended racial boundaries, that evidence would necessitate a reevaluation, and possibly a revision, of his humanitarian legacy. If Oglethorpe voiced moral opposition to the transatlantic slave trade, the history of abolitionism would become more firmly rooted in Georgia's red clay. If Georgians were exposed to a more enlightened view of our founder's values and philosophy, perhaps current and future state leaders would be inspired to chart a more inclusive and progressive course. If any or all these questions could be answered in the affirmative, had generations of Georgians been denied the opportunity to emulate and celebrate Oglethorpe's unique vision for our state?

———

You may wonder why I, the great-grandson of Harris Thurmond, who in 1865 was enslaved on the Harris Thurman plantation in Oconee County, Georgia, would devote more than two decades of research to answering these intriguing questions. Let me share some additional details regarding my family history. After emancipation, successive generations of my ancestors were share-croppers, including my parents, Sidney and Vanilla Thurmond, who joined the Black flight out of Oconee and Walton Counties following the infamous lynching of four African Americans near the Moore's Ford Bridge in 1946. The shocking, still unsolved murders of George W. and Mae Dorsey and Roger and Dorothy Malcom occurred only a few miles from where my parents were living. Thus, I was born and raised in Sandy Creek, an isolated rural area of northeastern Clarke County near the college town of Athens.

Even though he could not read or write, my father valued education, which led him to purchase a set of World Book Encyclopedias "on time" when I was a third-grade student in the county's racially segregated public school system. In the early 1960s I was introduced in those pages to "traditional" Georgia history, which included only a few precious details regarding the achievements and contributions of Black Georgians. Today, the dog-eared "G" volume is a treasured literary possession that summons memories of my adolescence, when I was seduced by history's irresistible lure of knowledge, insight, and enlightenment.

My lifelong affection for Georgia history, buttressed by a desire to document the contributions and achievements of Black Americans, helped pry open the door to public service, bestowing me with political insight illuminated by historical scholarship. One of the more salient realities of American history is that long-standing conflicts involving race, class, gender, and gender affiliation still roil our political discourse. As I write, full-blown "history wars" are raging over the meaning and political implications of Lost Cause mythology, critical race theory, and the 1619 and 1776 Projects. Especially as southerners, we share a heritage and history that is controversial, painful, and conflicted. If we can somehow summon the courage to earnestly examine or reexamine our collective history, the better we will understand ourselves and how we became who we are. While reading Oglethorpe's memorial plaque, I felt compelled to resolve the vexing contradictions that shadow his life and legacy. The implication that Georgia's founding father advocated on behalf of oppressed Blacks deserved a thoughtful vetting; our state deserved no less.

And so, I returned to the first step on my journey: a solemn pledge to my known and unknown ancestors, to objectively pursue the facts wherever they might lead. I have faithfully kept that pledge while racially charged, sometime violent confrontations over our history have unfolded in Georgia's Stone Mountain Park, my own backyard. As long-simmering tensions erupted from Ferguson to Minneapolis and here in my home state, where we grieved the deaths of Ahmaud Arbery and others, the more relevant Oglethorpe's humanitarian legacy became.

What I discovered, through an extended period of research, analysis, rumination, and finally, revelation, is a far more complex view of Georgia's founding father than we have previously allowed. Though James Oglethorpe died believing the ambitious Georgia social welfare experiment had failed, his willingness to forge interracial alliances informed and shaped the prehistory of the antislavery and abolitionist movements. Oglethorpe came to reject outright proslavery Christian theology based on the belief that enslaved Blacks were subhuman, docile, and preordained to eternal damnation. He was among a small group of eighteenth-century white evangelical Christians and Quakers who acknowledged what all but a few of his European contemporaries were loath to admit: Black men, women, and children possessed the God-given right to live as free people. In addition, Georgia's principal founder repeatedly warned slaveholders that enslaved Blacks would fight and, if need be, die for the right to live free from perpetual bondage.

Critically, Oglethorpe did not come to embrace abolitionism on his own accord. As I would learn, his philosophical and moral journey was propelled by two Black men who had endured the degradation and brutality of chattel slavery. One young man, Ayuba Suleiman Diallo, a Muslim African who had been kidnapped and enslaved in British colonial America, wrote a letter that inspired Oglethorpe to arrange for his passage to England. Dr. Henry Louis Gates quipped that Diallo literally "wrote his way out of slavery," became a "roaring lion" of British society, and galvanized early eighteenth-century antislavery sentiments. The other was Olaudah Equiano, a self-emancipated African living in England and author of the only surviving account of the harrowing Middle Passage prior to the American Revolutionary War. Oglethorpe facilitated Equiano's introduction to his friend Granville Sharp, a tireless antislavery activist, and the two men subsequently formed a unique interracial partnership that spurred the birth of the formal abolitionist movement. The general's enlightened advocacy emphasized the agency of Black people, amplified long-muffled voices that bore the yoke of bondage, and affirmed their humanity.

Oglethorpe's interactions with Diallo and Equiano revealed to him how the enslavement of human beings dehumanized both the enslaved and the enslavers. Far from the racist stereotypes harbored by the great majority of eighteenth-century Europeans, Oglethorpe was a scholar and admirer of ancient African civilizations that predated the rise of the British Empire. The intellectual connection between the founder of Georgia and these two influential Black men has not previously been fully acknowledged or explored.

Oglethorpe also inspired emerging Black and white abolitionists to prosecute the fight against chattel slavery until abolition was realized in England. It is not hyperbolic to conclude that the largely unheralded efforts of the man buried beneath the floor of the Parish Church of All Saints helped breathe life into the international crusade that ultimately broke the chains of Anglo-American slavery. During the American Civil War, echoes of Oglethorpe's antislavery rhetoric resounded in the jubilation of eighteen thousand newly freed Black Georgians who joined General William T. Sherman's devastating march from Atlanta to Savannah and his apocalyptic vision of providential retribution for America's embrace of chattel slavery reverberated in President Abraham Lincoln's second inaugural address.

I expect that some readers will resist the notion of a more inclusive origin story for Georgia, no matter how meticulously documented. It will not surprise me if other readers push back against a Black historian's attempt to revise the reputation of a long-dead white founding father, especially one whose legacy includes questionable affiliations with those who enabled and profited from the trafficking of human beings. I welcome all perspectives. The publication of this book is not intended to be a full-length account of Oglethorpe's life nor an exoneration of his sometimes-enigmatic behavior regarding the transatlantic slave trade. Hopefully, it will spur honest dialogue and respectful debate among the inheritors of his legacy and, more importantly, additional research by historians more skilled than I am.

At this critical juncture in the history of our nation, "We the People" appear to be hopelessly divided along racial, political, and economic fault lines. Thus, General James Oglethorpe's life and legacy are worthy of our reckoning. The historical record affirms that Oglethorpe demonstrated empathy, and respect for others, no matter their skin color or legal status. The fact that he befriended early Black antislavery activists demonstrates the indomitable and redemptive power of human agency and reaffirms our duty to improve ourselves and the world around us, even in the face of seemingly insurmountable odds. But readers should carefully ponder what I believe is the most compelling aspect of Oglethorpe's long and consequential life: his strident opposition to slavery evolved over several decades. He, like all human beings, deserves historical judgment based on not a snapshot in time but an objective, full accounting of one's achievements and shortcomings.

Now more than ever, as once-venerated statues and monuments are defaced or removed from public spaces, we must summon the courage to objectively examine authentic examples of individuals—regardless of race, political persuasion, or gender affiliation—who pressed to guarantee liberty and justice for all. Oglethorpe's words and deeds instruct us not to be bystanders to our lives. Both his moral rectitude and his character flaws are important for Georgians of all ages, especially our youth, to study. The willingness to listen, learn, and evolve, to courageously address personal and societal shortcomings, to glean insight through self-examination and public engagement—these are the essential ingredients of enlighten proactive leadership. It is the inspiring, protracted process through which General James Oglethorpe changed himself and, more importantly, helped change the course of world history.

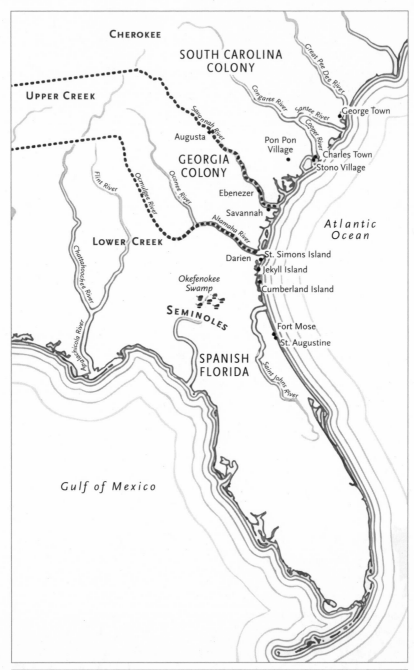

Map of the southeastern region of North America, ca. 1734.

(Julie Witmer Custom Map Design)

I

"No Common Slave"

In the Land of Christians

IN FEBRUARY 1730 AYUBA SULEIMAN DIALLO, the son of Solomon, a wealthy and influential Wolof Muslim cleric who lived in what is now Senegal, traveled to the mouth of the Gambia River on Africa's Atlantic coast. Solomon had directed Diallo to trade two enslaved Africans to British slave merchants in exchange for paper and other desirable commodities. However, he warned his twenty-nine-year-old son not to venture across the Gambia River into territory controlled by the fearsome Mandinka tribe, their long-standing enemies.[1]

Shortly after his arrival on the coast, Diallo tried to negotiate a trade with Captain Stephen Pike, commander of the slave ship *Arabella* and an agent of the Royal African Company (RAC), a British slave-trading enterprise. When the two men failed to strike a bargain, Diallo, ignoring his father's stern instructions, hired an interpreter named Loumein Yoas and crossed the Gambia in search of a more willing trading partner. After making a deal with an African slave trader, he began the difficult two-week journey back home.[2]

During the return trip, Mandinka warriors surprised Diallo and his interpreter, taking them captive and seizing about twenty cattle in their possession. Warring tribes often sold or traded prisoners of war to European slavers for weapons and other valuables, and the new prisoners' heads and beards were shaved so that they would appear to be captives taken in battle. Ironically, on February 27, 1730, Diallo and Yoas were sold to Captain Pike, the same man Diallo had negotiated with earlier.[3]

Fluent in several African languages and literate in Arabic, Diallo tried to convince Pike that he had been kidnapped and was not a slave. With the assistance of an African interpreter, Diallo promised a lucrative ransom to the captain in exchange for his freedom. Motivated by the possibility of an unexpected financial windfall, Pike dispatched a messenger to inform Solomon of his son's dire predicament. The desperate father sent a rescue party with several enslaved Africans to be traded for Diallo, but the ship sailed before they arrived on the coast.[4]

Imprisoned in the hold of the crowded, disease-ridden slave ship, Diallo endured the arduous eight-week Middle Passage across the Atlantic Ocean to the New World. In Annapolis, Maryland, he was sold at auction by Vachell Denton, an RAC agent to a Chesapeake Bay slaveholder named Tolsey who put Diallo to work cultivating tobacco, but he struggled to endure the back-breaking manual labor. His enslaver subsequently assigned him to the less strenuous task of tending cattle.[5]

Whenever the opportunity arose, the devout young Muslim secretly withdrew into the woods, where he engaged in various Islamic rituals and prayer. After being discovered by a young white boy who mocked and ridiculed his piety, Diallo briefly regained his freedom by escaping from the plantation, only to be captured and incarcerated in the Kent County, Maryland, jail. News of a mysterious freedom seeker who spoke and prayed in a strange tongue quickly spread throughout the region.[6]

In June 1731 Diallo was visited in prison by the Reverend Thomas Bluett, a lawyer, judge, and missionary affiliated with the Society for the Propagation of the Gospel (SPG), an Anglican organization working with limited success to Christianize free and enslaved Blacks and Native Indians. Regarding his visit with Diallo, Bluett writes, "Upon talking and making signs to him, he wrote a line or two before us, and when he read it, pronounced the words Allah and Mahommed." After Diallo refused to accept a glass of wine, Bluett and his associates concluded that the young man was a "Mahometan," but they were unable to "imagine of what country he was, or how he got thither." (Roughly 15 percent of the 12.5 million African captives transported to the Americas prior to 1865 were Muslims.)[7]

Because of his "affable carriage, and easy composure of his countenance," Bluett and his companions all agreed that the freedom seeker was "no common slave." An "old Negroe Man" who spoke the Wolof language, which Diallo understood, was then summoned to serve as an interpreter between the freedom seeker and his captors, and the prisoner was able to explain who he was, how he became enslaved, and the place of his enslavement. The jailer subsequently sent a message to Tolsey, who came to the jail, claimed possession of Diallo, and transported him back to the tobacco plantation.[8]

Typically, an enslaved person caught attempting to flee enslavement would have suffered severe punishment, but Bluett claims that Tolsey was

Dressed in traditional West African attire, Ayuba Suleiman Diallo, the son of a wealthy Muslim cleric, was kidnapped by African warriors and sold to British slave traders.

During his enslavement in the Maryland colony, Ayuba Suleiman Diallo wrote a letter to his father in Africa. Written in Arabic, the letter was couriered across the Atlantic Ocean and placed in possession of James Oglethorpe.

(Courtesy of the British Library)

in fact "kinder" to Diallo after his failed escape and provided "him a place to pray . . . in order to make slavery as easy as possible." Despite these concessions, Diallo refused to accept the drudgery and dehumanization of perpetual servitude and somehow convinced Tolsey to allow him to write a letter acquainting his father "with his Misfortunes and, hoping he [Solomon] might find Means to redeem him."[9]

Written in Arabic, the letter passed through the hands of several white men during its improbable four-thousand-mile journey across the Atlantic from America to England. Diallo's letter was given to Vachell Denton with the expectation that he would deliver it to Captain Pike, who would then courier the document to Diallo's father in Africa. But the slave ship captain had already sailed for England, so the letter was turned over to Pike's employer, Captain Henry Hunt, who promised to deliver it to Pike in England so that he could take it to Africa on his next slaving voyage. Unfortunately, Pike had already sailed for Africa before Hunt arrived in England, so he decided to keep the letter until the "proper opportunity" arose for Diallo's letter to be delivered to his heartbroken father. As fate would have it, during the summer of 1732 the letter was placed in the possession of James Oglethorpe, then a member of the British Parliament, who was also serving as the deputy governor of the RAC and chair of a charitable organization whose primary mission was to Christianize enslaved Africans. This serendipitous turn of events would have far-reaching consequences for Diallo, Oglethorpe, and the nascent British antislavery movement.[10]

Worldly Servitude and Spiritual Freedom

BORN IN LONDON ON DECEMBER 22, 1696, James Edward Oglethorpe was the youngest of ten children of Theophilus and Eleanor Oglethorpe, a landed family from Surrey. The Oglethorpes, like Diallo's family, were not a part of the ruling nobility, but they were wealthy and influential members of their respective country's elite societies. Eleanor was a dedicated Jacobite, a term derived from Jacobus, Latin for James, used to describe British subjects who remained loyal to King James II after he was forced from the throne into exile in 1688. According to one modern source, "The Oglethorpe family believed it was their duty not only to serve the nation's royalty, which they had done for generations, but also to support and represent working-class [subjects] who depended on them for their livelihood."[1]

Oglethorpe was only six years old when his father died in 1702, leaving his doting mother, who was intimately involved in British politics, to shape the lives and careers of her children. When family members, friends, and acquaintances predicted success for the precocious little boy they fondly called "Jamie," she sought to engineer his quick ascension to a position of influence.[2]

Eleanor leveraged the family's political connections to enroll her youngest child in the prestigious Eton College boarding school, then later secured for him the plum assignment of ensign in Her Majesty's First Regiment of Foot Guards. Oglethorpe was soon promoted to the rank of lieutenant in the celebrated unit. In 1714, at the age of seventeen, he exited the British military and followed in the footsteps of his two older brothers by enrolling in Corpus Christi College at Oxford University. He studied there off and on for two years, developing what would become a lifelong interest in the great civilizations of the antiquities, especially classical Greek, Roman, and African history. In January 1716 he left Oxford to attend a French military academy and subsequently joined the Army of the Holy Roman Empire under the command of the Habsburg Prince Eugene of Savoy. While serving as the aide-de-camp

James Edward Oglethorpe was a member of Parliament who sought to alleviate the plight of debtor prisoners by establishing a colony in the New World for impoverished and persecuted colonists.

(Gen. James E. Oglethorpe, woodcut, from *The History of Castillo de San Marcos and Fort Matanzas: From Contemporary Narratives and Letters*, by the National Parks Service [Washington, D.C.: U.S. Government Printing Office, 1945], 23, on behalf of the Department of the Interior)

to Prince Eugene, he distinguished himself in battle at the siege of Belgrade in 1717, during the Austro-Turkish War against the Ottoman Empire.[3]

In 1719 Oglethorpe returned to his family's estate at West Brook Manor in Haslemere, England. Two years later he continued another Oglethorpe family tradition by announcing his candidacy for a seat in the House of Commons of the British Parliament. Standing over six feet tall, the handsome young war hero was primed for a distinguished career in politics. However, two violent confrontations threatened to upend his bright political future.

The first altercation, in March 1722, began with an exchange of heated words and then quickly evolved into a "Scuffle" involving drawn swords between the hot-tempered Oglethorpe and two men on the streets of Haslemere.

According to the March 27, 1722, edition of the *London Daily Journal*, the brief duel resulted in non-life-threatening injuries to Oglethorpe's adversaries. A few weeks after winning election to the House of Commons, a second, more serious encounter occurred at six o'clock in the morning on April 24, at a "Night-House of evil Repute" after a drunken Oglethorpe accused another patron of stealing a piece of gold. Swords were drawn again, and during the ensuing duel Oglethorpe killed the man who challenged him. The aspiring young politician was arrested, charged with murder, and jailed. Following five months of incarceration, the charges were summarily dropped, and the embarrassing publicity did not prevent Oglethorpe from taking a seat in Parliament later that year.[4]

While Oglethorpe's early years in the House of Commons were unremarkable, his political career received a much-needed boost after he became acquainted with Dr. Thomas Bray. Born in 1658, Bray had studied at Oxford University and earned the patronage of "wealthy and influential men" who promoted his "clerical career and his missionary and philanthropic schemes." Bray put his considerable energy into creating a missionary organization to educate and convert poor white children, and in 1689 he established the Society for Promoting Christian Knowledge (SPCK). In 1697 Bray authored *A General Plan of the Constitution of a Protestant Congregation or Society for Propagating Christian Knowledge*, which detailed his vision for deploying missionaries throughout the British Empire, with a focus on educating and converting enslaved Black and Native Indian children in the New World. In June 1701 he founded the SPG, with which Reverend Bluett was serving when he met the ill-fated captive Diallo.[5]

In 1723 Bray's charitable work received a significant infusion of revenue when Sieur d'Allone, the private secretary of England's King William III, bequeathed a tenth of his estate and a portion of his unpaid pension to establish schools for Christianizing Black children and their "inclineable" and "desirous" parents enslaved in far-flung British colonies. The following year Bray formed a third missionary organization called the Associates of Doctor Thomas Bray specifically dedicated to providing religious instruction to enslaved Blacks, creating parochial libraries, and distributing books to slaveholders so they could educate and convert their enslaved. Initially, the Associates traveled from plantation to plantation to evangelize Blacks in and around their slave quarters. By the 1750s the Bray Associates had established "schools" for enslaved children and adults in several British colonies, including Georgia.[6]

Although Bray was apparently genuinely committed to improving the spiritual welfare of Black people, he was not opposed to slavery itself. In fact, he considered Blacks to be "barbarous and heathen" and expressed no interest in liberating enslaved Blacks from bondage. Bray's concern was limited to freeing the "immortal souls" of enslaved Blacks from damnation, not changing their "temporal condition" under slavery. Bray and his associates therefore adhered to the antithetical proposition that slavery could be "confined within the boundaries of Christian, civilized behavior." Within the contours of their zealous outreach, no inherent moral contradictions existed between "worldly servitude and spiritual freedom."[7]

Unwittingly, Church of England dogma did provide one unanticipated benefit for enslaved Christians. The Anglican missionaries believed that Christianization was a time-consuming educational experience, a tedious process rather than a single act of spiritual conversion. Prior to baptism, free and enslaved worshippers were required to learn prescribed religious tenets or catechisms, which necessitated the development of basic literacy skills. Thus, the Bray missionaries inadvertently armed enslaved Black converts with a powerful weapon that would come to be leveraged against their enslavers: the ability to read and write.[8]

The proselytization of enslaved Blacks would eventually create difficult moral and religious issues for Christian slave traders and slaveholders. A small minority of white Christians embraced the concept of manumission by baptism, the belief that one Christian could not enslave another, and the proposition that enslaved Blacks who converted to Christianity were entitled to freedom. Some white Christians believed that conversion conferred on enslaved Christians certain privileges such as observance of the Sabbath and the taking of communion. Other white Christians were more pragmatic and supported Christianization because they were convinced that enslaved converts were more subservient and less likely to engage in violent acts of retribution or rebellion against slaveholders.

Christian slave traders and slaveholders also rationalized their involvement in the trade by asserting that Christianization of the enslaved fulfilled a providential purpose. They argued that the cruelties of perpetual bondage notwithstanding, so-called heathen Africans ultimately benefited from exposure to the civilizing principles of Christianity. But the most controversial aspect of the Bray Associates' evangelism, by far, was the belief that redeemed souls of white and Black Christians would be granted equal access to the kingdom of God.[9]

Nonetheless, the great majority of proslavery Christians were, ultimately, categorically opposed to any attempt to modify or reform the institution of slavery, and they espoused biblical scriptures that could be interpreted to justify the institution. Relying on strained exegesis of Genesis 9:24–27, for example, they argued that dark-skinned Africans were descendants of Ham, son of Noah, who was cursed for observing his father's naked body.

According to this proslavery theology, Blacks were therefore preordained to be enslaved, incapable of spiritual redemption and irrevocably condemned to eternal damnation.[10]

Unlike the missionaries, slaveholders themselves seemed to grasp the long-term consequences associated with exposing converted Blacks to the concept of racial equality before the Throne of Grace. Despite vehement slaveholder opposition to the idea of religious equalitarianism and Church of England ambivalence, the Associates remained steadfast in their conviction that enslaved Blacks would be spiritually enriched by exposure to Christianity. This ideology aligned with the advocacy of antislavery Quaker leaders such as George Fox, William Edmundson, John Woolman, Benjamin Lay, and, most famously, Anthony Benezet, who sought to ameliorate the brutalities of enslavement by welcoming free and enslaved Blacks as equals into the Quaker faith. Benezet is widely recognized as the "founding father" of the antislavery "movement in the Atlantic World." Benezet's family migrated from France to England and then to the Pennsylvania colony in 1731, and he was twenty years old and living with his parents when Oglethorpe founded the slave-free Georgia colony in 1733.[11]

For their part, enslaved Christians often rejected concerted efforts by white Christians to indoctrinate them with what they derisively called "slave religion." One skeptical potential Black convert recalled that the ultimate purpose of slaveholder-inspired Christianization had little to do with heavenly salvation. According to him, enslaved worshippers were forced to sit in the back of the church or balcony and listen to supposedly edifying sermons like "Don't steal your master's chickens or his eggs and your backs won't be whipped." Meanwhile, enslaved Christians began to formulate a Christianity that combined African religious traditions and biblical scriptures that emphasized temporal concepts of freedom and justice. Led by semiliterate lay preachers, Black Christians would "Steal away, steal away, steal away to Jesus!" and conduct secret worship services in bush arbors or nearby swamps. The same master who sought to Christianize enslaved Blacks would often punish with the lash those caught worshipping at these clandestine meetings.[12]

Whatever the intended purpose, one of the more enduring African American transmutations of Christian scripture was the belief that a living God would hear the cries of His chosen people. Enslaved Black Christians drew powerful parallels between their enslavement and Old Testament scripture, taking inspiration from God's deliverance of the Hebrews from Egyptian slavery in the book of Exodus. Likewise, they believed God would deliver them from enslavement just as He delivered the Children of Israel from bondage.

Second in inspirational value only to the Exodus narrative of enslavement, deliverance, and conquest was the Jubilee prophecy chronicled in Leviticus 25:10. According to biblical text, God commanded a Year of Jubilee that required the liberation of all Hebrew slaves, restoration of alienated land to former owners, and omission of land cultivation. Devoutly religious but mostly illiterate enslaved Christians liberally interpreted the scripture to mean that on the "Day of Jubilo" the sounding of a trumpet would "Proclaim Liberty throughout the land, and to all the inhabitants thereof." To generations of free and enslaved Black Christians, these Exodus and Jubilee prophecies conveyed powerful and inspiring messages of hope, human agency, and providential favor.[13]

The significance of Christian evangelism based on the radical proposition that enslaved Blacks possessed immortal souls cannot be overstated. If the Bray Associates and other evangelists maintained that the immortal souls of enslaved people were redeemable, then "heathen" Blacks, despite their enslaved status, could not be soulless beasts of burden. By seeking to save the souls of enslaved Blacks, the missionaries, intentionally or not, also acknowledged the humanity of Black worshippers. The pursuit of "spiritual equality" by enslaved Black Christians would ultimately feed their desire to seek "corporal equality" under the laws of man, and the Christianization of enslaved Blacks would become a subtle antislavery strategy and important precursor of the abolitionist movement.

The genesis of the Georgia colonization scheme can be traced to the merger of two early eighteenth-century social welfare reform initiatives—the Christianization of enslaved Black people and alleviating the plight of England's debtor prisoners. Dr. Bray and Oglethorpe would both become known throughout the British Empire for their evangelization of enslaved Blacks and advocacy on behalf of imprisoned debtors. Thus, England's two most prominent humanitarians were "fortuitously" brought together at a critical juncture in the evolution of the Georgia social welfare experiment.

CHAPTER THREE

"Asilum of the Unfortunate"

ALTHOUGH ENGLAND ENJOYED UNPARALLELED PROSPERITY during the early eighteenth century, economic dislocations and political indifference had plunged thousands of debtors into poverty and prison. At the time, established British legal precedent gave creditors the right, which they frequently exercised, to sue for the imprisonment of Britons unable to pay their debts. Along with his desire to proselytize enslaved children and adults, Thomas Bray also evangelized thousands of inmates languishing in debtor prisons. Through his missionary outreach, Bray ultimately exposed horrible living conditions at the Whitechapel and Borough Compter prisons, which sparked public outrage and demands for reform. On February 25, 1729, the House of Commons established a Committee on Jails, chaired by Oglethorpe, charged with the responsibility of investigating the administration of the Fleet, Marshalsea, and King's Bench prisons and recommending relief measures for indebted inmates.[1]

Oglethorpe possessed personal knowledge of the horrendous conditions within Fleet Prison. A close friend, Robert Castell, had died of smallpox on December 12, 1728, while incarcerated due to numerous unpaid debts, including those that accrued when his self-published book failed to sell enough copies to cover publication costs. During the parliamentary proceedings, committee chair Oglethorpe conferred with several religious leaders regarding relief strategies that might help destitute prisoners. The investigation documented deplorable living conditions at the prisons and rampant corruption among prison officials, transforming the thirty-three-year-old Oglethorpe into a national hero. Parliament subsequently passed a 1729 statute titled "An Act for the Relief of Debtors," which authorized the release of ten thousand indebted Britons. But if the relief measure eased the overcrowding that plagued the prisons, at the same time it added to the mass of unemployed, homeless beggars who slept on the streets of London and other cities. Undaunted, the ever-resourceful Oglethorpe sought to solve the dilemma

Doctor Thomas Bray founded the Associates of Dr. Bray, a charitable Christian organization whose primary mission was to evangelize enslaved Blacks. He also worked to address the horrible living conditions that existed in England's debtor prisons.

(From *The Founders: Portraits of Persons Born Abroad Who Came to the Colonies in North America before the Year 1701*)

of impoverished British subjects set adrift on a sea of prosperity. He began marshaling support for the establishment of a charity colony in America for England's "miserable wretches" and "drones."[2]

Meanwhile, "Bray, in poor health and with only a few months to live," writes one historian, "was then casting about for some way to enlarge the number and increase the scope of his organization to ensure that it would survive his passing." During a bedside meeting with Oglethorpe in December 1729, the feeble humanitarian implored his visitor to embrace the Bray Associates' evangelical efforts to Christianize enslaved Blacks and establish a debtor colony in America.[3] Historians disagree over how much, or even if, Bray influenced Oglethorpe's specific decision to found the colony of Georgia, but there is little doubt that the two men were committed to reforming England's debtor prisons. Bray and Oglethorpe were convinced that establishing a debtor colony in the New World would help alleviate British poverty and unemployment.[4]

On January 15, 1730, Bray relinquished authority over the Associates with the understanding that Oglethorpe would reorganize and enlarge its board. He also granted Oglethorpe permission to use the organization as a base for soliciting funds to support the debtor colonization scheme. Oglethorpe's newly minted affiliation with the Bray missionaries was mutually benefi-cial. The Associates gained the expertise of a charismatic, skillful leader, and debtor colony proponents benefited from the imprimatur of the respected organization. Oglethorpe immediately began recruiting well-known British social reformers, politicians, and clergymen to join the society. The member-ship expanded from four to thirty members that included several Bray evan-gelists, ten members of Parliament, and four Anglican ministers. As a result of these important developments, the loosely defined colonization scheme would evolve quickly into what became known as the "Georgia Plan."[5]

Bray died exactly one month after his transfer of power to Oglethorpe, on February 15, 1730. His legacy, the "little charitable society" he originally devised to provide religious instruction to enslaved populations and establish parochial libraries, would now include a third imperative. According to an early Bray biographer, "From these two designs of founding libraries, and in-structing the Negroes, a 3rd was now added, which tho' at first view appears to be a different nature, has a perfect coincidence with them. . . . And therefore, out of the same charitable regard to the bodies and Souls of Men, a design was form'd of establishing a Colony in *America*."[6]

A few weeks after Bray's death, Oglethorpe informed John Viscount Per-cival, a fellow member of Parliament and a Bray Associate, of the existence of a trust established by the late Joseph King, a wealthy haberdasher. The sole purpose of the 1,500-pound trust was to support the Christianization of enslaved Blacks. Nevertheless, the King trustees promised Oglethorpe they would contribute 500 pounds to support the Georgia colonization effort, contingent on the funds being administered by an existing charity. "The best-known and most-effective charitable organizations were those created by the [late] Reverend Thomas Bray."[7]

On March 21, 1730, Oglethorpe was elected chair of the reorganized As-sociates of Doctor Bray. Realizing that the newly selected members were primarily interested in advancing the Georgia plan, Oglethorpe created three committees, the Trustees for Instructing of the Negroes in the Christian Religion, the Committee of the Associates for Parochial Libraries, and the Trustees for Establishing the Colony of Georgia in America, which allowed each member to focus on his primary interests. During Oglethorpe's chair-manship the most active committee was the one dedicated to the establish-ment of the Georgia colony, and he himself became the undisputed leader of the colonization effort. He immersed himself in the time-consuming tasks

of securing political support for the proposed colony, raising charitable dona-
tions, vetting the qualifications of potential colonists, purchasing provisions
for the Atlantic voyage, and warehousing supplies needed to establish the
colony. While the Associates initially sought to resettle a hundred former
debtor prisoners in the New World, as the colonization plan evolved the men
decided not to limit the charitable venture to debtors and instead sought to
help as many poor and persecuted people as possible.[8]

Despite a growing list of challenges associated with establishing a new
colony, Oglethorpe also devoted time and attention to the primary mission
of the Bray Associates: educating and converting enslaved Blacks. On July 30,
1730, he informed the committee of "Trustees for Instructing of the Negroes
in the Christian Religion" that RAC officials had requested a meeting with
the Associates. According to the minutes of that meeting, the slave-trading
company offered to contribute financial assistance to help promote the
Christianization of enslaved Africans and other missionary objectives.[9]

The minutes also revealed that RAC officials had become preoccupied with
a communication sent to their employees at Cape Coast Castle on the western coast of Africa. Located in present-day Ghana, Cape Coast Castle was
the headquarters and principal slaving factory of the RAC. Described by a
British governor as "the grand emporium of the British slave trade," the castle could hold approximately one thousand Black captives in its loathsome
labyrinth of underground dungeons. Behind the walls of the sprawling fortress, tens of thousands of African captives were systematically processed,
marketed, and shipped to the Americas after passing through the infamous
"Door of No Return." Dr. Bray had previously shipped a library of books to
the castle, and company officials promised the Associates they would conduct an inquiry regarding the status of the library and presumably determine
whether the books were truly used to evangelize Africans.[10]

This episode sheds new light on a perplexing aspect of Oglethorpe's humanitarian legacy: his affiliation with one of England's principal slave-trading
enterprises. Oglethorpe's ties to a company that transported, between 1662
and 1730, approximately 212,000 Africans to the Americas has sparked a
damning critique of Oglethorpe by biographers and state historians. Was
Oglethorpe seeking to advance the evangelical mission of the Bray Associates to Christianize enslaved Blacks? Or was he a hypocrite who publicly
opposed slavery in the new colony he would oversee while earning profit
from the brutal but lucrative transatlantic slave trade?

In September 1730 the Associates of Doctor Bray officially presented a petition to King George II requesting a charter to establish the Georgia colony, which would be named in his honor. The document contained several provisions designed to prevent the development of an economy dependent on slave labor. According to the charter, all persons "who shall at any time hereafter inhabit or reside within our said province, shall be, and are hereby declared to be free." Although usage of the words "slave" or "slavery" were avoided by the Trustees, this language clearly implies that the importation of enslaved Black laborers was prohibited. However, the clause left open the possibility that "free" Blacks might be offered the opportunity to migrate to the colony. There was also no legal requirement for the establishment of a colonial legislature. Initially, this insulated the Trustees in London (only Oglethorpe would live in the new colony) from political pressure generated by the proslavery lobby in Georgia. Unique conflict-of-interest restrictions also forbade the Trustees from profiting, directly or indirectly, from investments in the colony. Thus, they were less likely to be influenced by the possibility of personal gain associated with the enslavement of Africans. The hope was that these policies would buttress their fidelity to the charitable organizations' official motto, *Non sibi, sed aliis* (Not for self, but for others).[11]

The charter also stipulated that all but a nominal percentage of landholdings would be restricted to small tracts. By implementing this "Strict Agrarian Law," the Trustees sought to prevent the proliferation of large rice plantations, which they feared would concentrate the colony's wealth in the hands of a few wealthy slaveholders. The document also specified that silk, flax, hemp, wine, and spices would be the primary staples produced in Georgia, none of which, they argued, required the use of enslaved Black laborers.[12]

Finally, the Georgia charter promised "there shall be a liberty of conscience allowed in the worship of God" in the colony; this privilege, however, was not extended to members of the Catholic faith. The prohibition against the migration of papists to Georgia grew out of a fear that Catholic colonists would cast their lots with Spain during times of military conflict. In January 1733 the Trustees subsequently voted to prohibit the migration of Jews into their colony. According to Trustee Thomas Coram, a vocal antisemite, without the prohibition Georgia would "soon become a Jewish colony," and all the Christian inhabitants would "fall off and desert it, as leaves from a tree in autumn."[13]

The revolutionary colonization plan would establish the Georgia colony as a groundbreaking social welfare and economic experiment. The colony was envisioned as a place where England's "worthy poor" could earn a "comfortable subsistence" exporting goods produced on small farms. Most significantly, unlike her sister colonies, Georgia was envisioned as a sanctuary that would be free from the evils of the transatlantic slave trade. The Trustees were convinced that widespread economic vitality could not be achieved in a society dominated by slave labor. James Oglethorpe, Georgia's principal founder, would be among the first white men in North America to advocate against chattel slavery.[14]

On April 21, 1732, the king granted the Georgia charter to twenty-one Trustees, including Oglethorpe. Although the charter did not contain a specific prohibition of slavery, supporting documents submitted by the Trustees provided pragmatic arguments justifying their opposition to the institution. One anonymous article titled "Appeal for the Georgia Colony" published in the *London Journal* on July 29, 1732, established the philosophical foundation for the proposed colony: "If they give Liberty of Religion, establish the People free, fix an *Agrarian* Law, prohibit within their Jurisdiction that abominable and destructive Custom of Slavery, by which the Laboring Hands are rendered useless to the Defence of the State . . . If they go upon the glorious Maxims of Liberty and Virtue, their Province, in the Age of a Man, by being the Asilum of the Unfortunate, will be more advantageous to *Britian* than the Conquest of a Kingdom." Historians have concluded that the author of this bold vision was most likely Oglethorpe himself.[15]

From the point of view of defense, the Trustees were certain that enslaved Blacks would pose a constant threat to white women and children because of individual acts of defiance or organized insurrections. They also argued that in the case of an enemy invasion, white male slaveholders would choose to remain on their farms and plantations to guard against slave rebellions rather than serve in the colonial militia. Finally, Oglethorpe warned that without a ban against slavery, Georgia, like neighboring South Carolina, would find that the disproportionate number of enslaved Blacks to whites placed the colony "in great danger of being lost in case of a war" with Spain or France. The Trustees also believed that the presence of Blacks in Georgia would allow South Carolina freedom seekers to blend into the colony's enslaved population until they reached Spanish-controlled Florida.[16]

Turning their attention to economic concerns, the Trustees argued that should slavery flourish, poor white farmers would be enticed into mortgaging their farms to purchase enslaved Blacks, a circumstance guaranteed to keep them in the impoverished condition they were trying to escape. Lastly, Georgia's founders claimed that the presence of enslaved Blacks would encourage idleness and economic inequality among the colony's white population, which would ultimately defeat the purpose of their grand experiment.[17]

During the spring and summer of 1732, during preparations for his pending voyage across the Atlantic, Oglethorpe puzzled over the mysterious letter that had been placed in his possession. Although he was a respected scholar of ancient civilizations, Oglethorpe was unable to translate the Arabic document that had been written by the enslaved African, Ayuba Suleiman Diallo, now languishing in captivity in the Maryland colony. Still, his inability to comprehend the contents of the letter did not prevent him from grasping the broader implications of the document. Interpretation and authentication of Diallo's letter could undermine one of the principal European justifications for the transatlantic slave trade: removal of the so-called veil of ignorance that shrouded the eyes of supposedly illiterate, heathen dark-skinned Africans.

To understand the document more fully, Oglethorpe sent the letter to John Gagnier, the Laudian Chair of Arabic at Oxford University, for translation. Numerous historians have relied on Bluett's contention that Diallo's letter was a desperate plea for help and Oglethorpe's intervention was solely driven by "compassion." However, a modern English translation of the letter reveals that the author of the letter was not consumed by hopelessness, despair, or loss of agency. Rather than a desperate plea for help, Diallo's letter is a testament to his unwavering devotion to family and faith.[18]

The letter begins by detailing the Jalla family lineage, which served to eliminate any doubt that it was authored by Ayuba Suleiman Diallo. The proud husband of two wives and father of three sons and a daughter, Diallo implored the women not to remarry because he was confident of someday being reunited with his family. Despite the myriad of trials and tribulations to which he had been subjected, Diallo dutifully affirmed his faith, saying that he prayed and fasted daily. Throughout, he expressed praise and devotion to Allah, "the most compassionate, the most merciful, and ... the most generous." And the young man astutely avoided criticizing, insulting, or provoking those who enslaved him. However, he did offer one cryptic observation: "There is no good in the land of the Christians for a Muslim."[19]

One early biographer of Diallo asserts that the sorrowful details of the translated letter had a profound effect on Oglethorpe, who "took Compassion" on Diallo and in May 1733 entered into an agreement with Tolsey to purchase the enslaved young man for forty-five pounds and reimburse the cost of his passage, on Diallo's safe arrival in England. Numerous historians have previously argued that Oglethorpe was moved solely by "compassion," but there is likely a more intriguing rationale for his intervention. According to Henry Bruce, a nineteenth-century Georgia historian, Diallo's "history" played a critical role in the evolution of Oglethorpe's "ideas" about slavery. Prior to reading the translated letter, Oglethorpe had previously argued in an anonymous 1728 publication *The Sailor's Advocate* that the Royal Navy's practice of "impressing," or forcing British subjects to serve at sea for irregular compensation, was itself a form of slavery that violated their human and legal rights. "Wages are the motive upon which Freemen give their service," Oglethorpe asserted, "but if men are forced to serve without their consent, they are Slaves not Freemen."[20]

Diallo's letter had clearly pricked Oglethorpe's conscience and marked an important milestone in the evolution of his aversion to human bondage. He realized that regardless of race or color, evidence of literacy, the practice of monotheism, and devotion to family were recognizable traits of civilized behavior.

On December 21, 1732, Oglethorpe sold his stock in the RAC, resigned from the deputy governor's position, and severed official ties with the slaving company. Although he left no written explanation for his actions, in retrospect Oglethorpe had taken the first tentative steps on his protracted journey from awareness of the consequences of slavery to antislavery activism and abolitionism. Eventually, Oglethorpe's hardening opposition to the transatlantic slave trade would set the stage for a historic debate in Georgia and England regarding the economic, military, and moral expediency of chattel slavery.[21]

A Scene of Horror

THE GEORGIA TRUSTEES' PLAN TO establish a slavery-free colony in North America was a radical departure from prevailing eighteenth-century British economic and political theory. To fully appreciate the uniqueness of the Georgia colonization scheme, one must visualize a period in human history when, as one historian writes, "personal bondage was the prevailing form of labor in most of the world. . . . Freedom, not slavery, was the peculiar institution."[1] During this distressing era, slavery, debt bondage, or serfdom was considered the natural state for millions of impoverished laborers on every continent as men, women, and children toiled in the most miserable conditions.

Although slavery existed on the African continent centuries before the first European explorers arrived, forced labor in Africa was different from British chattel slavery. Generally speaking, the enslavement of Africans by Africans could best be described as being de facto feudalism. According to Olaudah Equiano, who was enslaved by British slaveholders and later an Oglethorpe acquaintance, forced bondage in his African homeland, which encompassed present-day Nigeria, differed significantly from British slavery. The British and later American legal systems of enslavement designated Black human beings and their offspring as property that could be bought, sold, and owned in perpetuity. In his remarkable autobiography, *The Interesting Narrative of the Life of Olaudah Equiano, or Gustavus, the African*, first published in 1789, Equiano provided the following explanation. "With us, [enslaved Africans] do no more work than other members of the community, even their masters: their food, clothing and lodging were nearly the same as ours. (Except that they were not permitted to eat meat with those who were born free); and there was scarce any other difference . . . than a superior degree of importance which the head of a family possesses in our state. Some of these slaves even have slaves under them as their own property, and for their own use." More importantly, the status of Africans enslaved by other

Africans was generally not inheritable—children of enslaved women were born free—while the children of mothers enslaved by the British were born into slavery, severing their biological relationship with Black or white fathers, and all rights to enslaved children were vested in slaveholders (*partus sequitur ventrem*). Another obvious distinction was that African slavery was not based solely on race or skin color.[2]

In 1556 the Portuguese pioneered the transatlantic slave trade when they transported enslaved African laborers to Spanish sugarcane plantations located in present-day Brazil. In 1562 Captain John Hawkins and his cousin Sir Francis Drake undertook the first British slaving voyage to Africa. With the financial support of Queen Elizabeth I, Hawkins made three additional voyages during the next six years. He purchased and abducted approximately twelve hundred Africans and sold them to Spanish colonists in the Caribbean islands.[3]

In 1660 England's King Charles II devised a plan to seize control of trade along Africa's west coast by chartering the RAC. The king granted RAC officials the exclusive right to exploit Gambian gold fields and supply British colonies in the New World with enslaved Africans. During the early decades of the eighteenth century, the RAC instituted a brutal and highly profitable strategy that established England as the dominant slave-trading nation. The other major slave-trading nations were Portugal, Spain, France, and the Dutch Empire.[4]

A survey of British slave-trading documents, banking records, and insurance company ledgers—along with maritime shipping logs—shows the merciless transformation of the enslavement of Africans into a booming international enterprise. Approximately 95 percent of British slaving voyages originated from the bustling seaports of London, Liverpool, and Bristol. Lured by the prospect of unlimited riches, businessmen, slave merchants, and investors developed what became known as the triangular slave trade.[5]

The first leg of the triangle involved the export of highly prized manufactured goods such as textiles, rum, guns, and ammunition from Europe to Africa. These items were used to purchase African captives from tribal leaders and African slave merchants. African intermediaries formed a critical component of the burgeoning transatlantic slave trade as they exchanged prisoners of war, convicted criminals, debtors, and other captives for European products.[6]

Bloody tribal and ethnic wars were, in fact, regularly instigated and supported by Europeans to increase the number of captives available for purchase. When intratribal conflicts failed to produce enough prisoners of war to meet slave market demands, European slavers dispatched African slave raiders to kidnap adults and children outright. Ambitious tribal leaders seeking to increase their wealth and influence also condemned political enemies, ethnic minorities, and religious dissidents to enslavement. Other enslaved Africans were purchased individually or in smaller groups directly from African slave merchants.[7]

Despite lucrative inducements, there are also numerous examples of African rulers who resisted European colonization and the enslavement of Africans, including Queen Nzinga Mbande, who ruled from 1624 to 1663 in what is present-day Angola, and King Agaja of Opobo, the ruler of a vast territory (1718–1740) that encompassed present-day Nigeria. Born into a ruling family, Queen Nzinga received advanced education and military training as a child. Following the death of her father and brother, she ascended to the throne, subsequently expanded her queendom, offered sanctuary to freedom seekers, waged a fierce struggle for independence against Portuguese colonizers, and earned a mythical reputation for being a skilled diplomat and negotiator. Agaja, while still in his youth, was purchased by British slave traders and subsequently sold to the chief of the Opobo people. The precocious young boy displayed unusual talents and leadership abilities, endearing himself to his royal master and eventually rising to the position of chief. King Agaja fiercely defended the independence of his adopted tribe and manifested a deep-seated hatred for Black and white slave traders.[8]

Fearing attack by indigenous warriors and deadly tropical diseases, European slavers rarely ventured into the African interior to purchase or capture Africans. Thus, African slave merchants would often march their captives hundreds of miles to the Atlantic coast where they were imprisoned in large castles or barracoons called factories. Men, women, and children, both young and old, were sometimes imprisoned in these slaving factories for days, weeks, or months, while slave ships would sail up and down the African coast until the holds of their ships were filled, often beyond capacity, with what was deemed "cargo"—not human beings. The more Africans that could be packed below deck, the greater the potential profits for slave traders and investors. Furthermore, captains and crewmen were often compensated with commissions and bonuses once their captives were sold.[9]

The second leg of the trade triangle was the dreaded five-thousand-mile

Queen Nzinga Mbande, a monarch who ruled what is present-day Angola, meets with
Portuguese governor Joao Corria da Sousa, 1622. While many African leaders aided the
slave trade, Queen Mbande resisted pressure from Europeans to enslave Africans.

(From Giovanni Antonio Cavazzi, *Istorica Descrizione de' Tre Regni Congo, Matamba, et Angola,* 2nd ed. [Milan: Nelle Stampe
dell'Agnelli, 1690], 437; courtesy of Fotosearch/Getty Images)

Middle Passage across the Atlantic Ocean, to the Caribbean Islands and
North America. The crossings usually took from four to twelve weeks de-
pending on the weather, prevailing currents, and the navigational skills of
slave ship captains. For the Africans shackled below deck, the harrowing experience could only be described as a living hell, as some committed suicide,
suffocated, or died from lack of sanitation and disease in the packed holds. A
typical eighteenth-century slave ship was constructed and outfitted to transport 150 to 600 African captives; it was little more than a floating prison
manned by thirty to forty heavily armed crewmen.[10]

Equiano provides a rare first-person account of the horrors endured by
millions of enslaved Africans prior to the American Revolutionary War. At
the age of eleven, he and his sister were kidnapped by African slave raiders.
During the next six or seven months, the siblings were purchased and resold
by several different African slaveholders. After being permanently separated

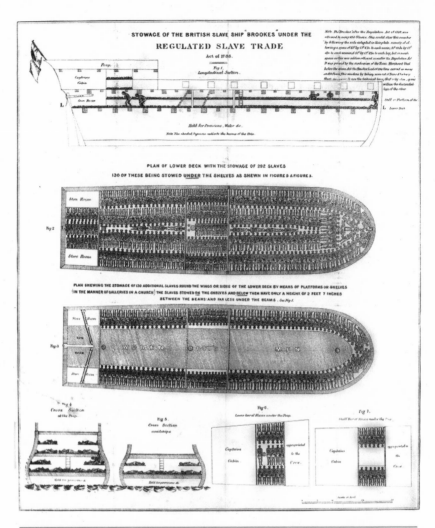

The Brooks slave ship diagram shows the tight packing of enslaved Africans during the Middle Passage to the Americas. In the British slave trade, enslaved people were regarded as cargo, not human beings, and millions died during the voyage to the New World.

from his "dear sister," Equiano was among a small group of captives who were marched to the Atlantic coast and sold to British slavers.[11]

Confused and terrified by his surroundings, Equiano noted, "The first object which saluted my eyes when I arrived on the coast was the sea, and a slave ship, which was riding at anchor, and waiting for its cargo." Convinced that he had "gotten into a world of bad spirits," the young boy was fearful that the "men with horrible looks, red faces, and loose hair" were cannibals. When Equiano was forced to board the ship, he encountered "black people of every description chained together . . . their countenances expressing dejection and sorrow." Overcome with "horror and anguish," young Equiano fainted. After he regained consciousness, Africans working for his captors tried to relieve Equiano's distress by offering him liquor and assurances that he would not be eaten.[12]

After being severely whipped for refusing to eat, Equiano was ordered below deck into the ship's windowless hold where his nostrils were repulsed by the "loathsomeness of the stench." He saw scores of Africans chained right ankle to left ankle, each prisoner left with "scarcely room to turn himself." According to Equiano, the stifling tropical heat, lack of fresh air, unsanitary conditions, and horrible smell created an insufferably "pestilential" environment. "This produced copious perspirations," he vividly recalled, "so that the air soon became unfit for respiration, from a variety of loathsome smells, and brought on a sickness among the slaves, of which many died. This wretched situation was aggravated by the galling chains, now become insupportable; and the filth of the necessary tubs, into which the children often fell, and were almost suffocated. The shrieks of the women, and the groans of the dying rendered the whole a scene of horror almost inconceivable."[13]

The cramped living conditions on slave ships were the perfect breeding grounds for the spread of infectious diseases such as diarrhea and dysentery ("the bloody flux"). The proximity and interaction between crewmen and African captives invariably resulted in high mortality rates among captors and captives. The mortality rate for captives is estimated to have been between 13 and 19 percent. Some crewmen claimed that so many dead or dying Africans were dumped into the ocean that sharks would alter their migration patterns to follow slave ships on their voyages to the New World.[14]

The financial benefits that could be derived from improved survival rates should have fostered more humane treatment of African captives. However, as one source put it, "One important, but overlooked, risk mitigation device that facilitated the growth of the slave trade in the eighteenth century was the increasing availability of insurance for ships and their human cargoes." The profit imperative for slavers was enhanced by the growing practice of purchasing marine insurance by ship owners, slave merchants, and investors.[15]

Standard insurance policies issued by the Lloyds of London insurance market compensated policy owners for the value of African captives who died due to "perils of the sea," which came to include Africans who died from natural causes as well as those killed during slave ship insurrections. Insurers were not liable for the deaths of Africans who committed suicide by jumping overboard, starved themselves to death, or died from lack of food and water due to inclement weather or poor seamanship. By 1731 approximately 42 percent of marine insurance policies sold by the London Assurance Corporation underwrote slave ships and the Africans they transported.[16]

A half century later, in 1781, the "destruction" of 130 Africans by crewmen on the *Zong* slave ship and ensuing legal dispute between the ship's owner and his insurers over a "property" loss insurance claim riveted the attention of the British public. An elderly James Oglethorpe would play a critical but little-known role in the transformation of this Middle Passage atrocity into a galvanizing moment for the British abolitionist movement.[17]

On most slave ships women and children were separated from the men in an area between the decks. Children made up roughly 26 percent of the African captives transported to North America and were a valuable "commodity" because they could be purchased at a lower cost and enslaved for the entirety of their natural lives. Sometimes the women and children were chained together, while on other ships they were allowed more freedom of movement. For African women and girls, this slight concession also exposed them to rape and sexual exploitation by crewmen. John Newton, the slave ship captain, author of the hymn *Amazing Grace*, and eventual abolitionist, matter-of-factly recalled that serial rape was a common occurrence on most British slave ships.[18]

Sickness and death from disease were a major concern for slave ship crewmen but paled in comparison to the omnipresent fear of violent resistance by African captives. Therefore, African men remained chained and under constant watch during the duration of the voyage. If the seas were calm, small groups would be brought on deck for one to two hours during the day for feeding, cleaning, and exercise. While on deck they were forced to dance, jump, and even sing songs in order to exercise their bodies.[19]

Despite around-the-clock vigilance by crewmen, individual acts of resistance and organized rebellion by African captives were not uncommon occurrences on British slave ships. Groundbreaking research is shedding new light on the frequency and seriousness of onboard revolts. Utilizing insurance company records and shipping logs, historians have conducted an extensive analysis of the circumstances surrounding the loss of 1,053 British slave ships between the years 1689 and 1807. "Of the 1,053 vessels, 679, or 64.5 percent of the total," it was found, "were taken by the enemy in wartime; 188, or 17.9 percent, were wrecked at sea outside the African coast; and 186, or 17.7 percent, were lost as a result of insurrection by African captives, conflict with coastal Africans and wrecks on the African coast."[20]

Although slave ship revolts rarely ended in kidnapped Africans returning to their homeland, the documentation of their occurrence undercuts "the myth of slave docility and quiescence." The most dangerous time for slavers was while slave ships were anchored off the African coast. Apparently, captives understood that their chances of escape were greater if they could jump into local waters and swim back to shore. Also, shore-based "free" Africans sometimes aided and supported escape attempts by Africans imprisoned on ships anchored offshore. Rebellious Africans who led or participated in unsuccessful revolts suffered swift and brutal retribution. They were summarily executed or subjected to severe punishments that included merciless beatings and amputations of arms, hands, legs, or feet.[21]

Africans who survived the harrowing Middle Passage were auctioned like cattle to the highest bidders in bustling slave markets in the Caribbean islands; New York; Boston; Philadelphia; Charleston; Newport, Rhode Island; and later Savannah. The final leg of the triangular trade involved using profits generated from the sale of Africans to purchase slave-produced goods such as sugar, rice, tobacco, molasses, indigo, rum, and cotton. These high-demand raw materials and products would be transported back across the Atlantic, where they were sold at a premium to wholesalers and consumers.[22]

According to the *Trans-Atlantic Slave Trade Database* edited by Emory University professors David Eltis and David Richardson, roughly 12.5 million Africans were crowded on European slave ships during the three-hundred-year period between the sixteenth and nineteenth centuries. It is estimated that two to five million captives lost their lives during the Atlantic crossings. Millions of other Africans died during slave raids and forced marches, while imprisoned in slaving factories and in Caribbean "seasoning camps."

Between 1619 and 1787 British ships conducted some eleven thousand transatlantic voyages, transporting more than three million Africans to colonies in the Caribbean islands and North America. Approximately four hundred thousand African captives shipped to the New World arrived in the thirteen British American colonies.[23]

How, when, or where Oglethorpe and Olaudah Equiano eventually become acquainted is not known; however, by the latter half of the eighteenth century the self-emancipated man would be recognized as the most prominent Black person in the British Empire and an influential member of Oglethorpe's ever-widening circle of antislavery activists and acquaintances. Equiano's gut-wrenching first-person accounts of his enslavement and manumission would have been familiar to Oglethorpe, and no doubt informed and propelled his evolving opposition to British chattel slavery.

"The Labour of Negroes"

GREAT BRITAIN'S DOMINANCE IN THE international trafficking of human beings meant that every aspect of its early eighteenth-century economy benefited, directly or indirectly, from the transatlantic slave trade. Prominent slave traders, like the British merchant and member of Parliament (MP) Edward Colston, amassed huge fortunes, constructed opulent mansions, and built prosperous businesses such as Lloyds of London and Barclays Bank, which survive to this day. Colston also served as deputy governor of the RAC from 1689 to 1690, a position that James Oglethorpe would briefly hold some four decades later.[1]

Among those who profited from the slave trade, there was no ambivalence as to its myriad benefits. James Houston, an employee of one eighteenth-century British slave-trading firm, no doubt spoke for many when he expounded on the importance of the slave trade: "What a glorious and advantageous trade this is. . . . It is the hinge on which all trade of this Globe moves."[2]

In 1718 William Wood, a British trade analyst, observed that "the Labour of Negroes is the principal Foundation of our Riches from the Plantations" and "the greatest Value to this Kingdom, if we consider the Number of Ships annually employed in it, the great Export of our Manufactures, and other Goods to that Coast." Similarly, Malachi Postlethwayt, an accountant, concluded, "The African trade is so very beneficial to Great Britain, so essentially necessary to the very being of her colonies, that without it, neither could we flourish, nor they long subsist."[3]

The growing demand for enslaved Black workers was fueled by severe labor shortages throughout British colonial America. Most European colonists sought to establish their own farms on inexpensive and widely available land, but many of the colonists in the New World did not possess the work ethic, physical stamina, or skills needed to support themselves and their families. The demand for additional workers was especially acute in the southern colonies because most white colonists were unwilling or unable to endure the arduous labor required to grow, harvest, and process rice, indigo, and other cash crops, in harsh semitropical conditions.[4]

Initially, British colonists tried to solve the daunting labor crisis by capturing and enslaving Native Indians. However, many enslaved Natives died in large numbers from the backbreaking work or Old World diseases such as smallpox and influenza, or they resisted enslavement by escaping into familiar terrain. Wealthy landowners gradually shifted their focus from enslaving Native Indians to recruiting white indentured workers from England and Ireland. The men, women, and children who contracted to become indentured workers were usually poor whites, persons with criminal histories, fugitives from justice, or social outcasts. Employers would pay for the indentured workers' passage across the Atlantic and provide food, clothing, and shelter during their indenture. The indentured worker repaid the employer's financial investment by working for a period of four to seven years.[5]

Bound workers who survived the challenging working conditions and fulfilled their contractual obligations, were granted "freedom dues," which sometimes included land, seed to plant their own crops, or weapons. Often, poor white indentured servants were forced to start a new indenture because they still lacked the financial resources needed to become self-supporting. Not surprisingly, indentured servitude proved to be unpopular with poor white workers because of the difficult work and lack of economic opportunity. In addition, landowners disliked the fact that indentured workers retained their legal rights even while in service and were contracted for only a limited time.[6]

In 1607 Virginia became the first British colony to be founded in what is now the United States of America. Within a span of forty-six years, numerous other for-profit proprietorships or colonies were established along the Eastern Seaboard of North America. Many of these ventures failed outright or were subsequently reconstituted as part of more successful business enterprises. More than fifty years would pass between William Penn's founding of Quaker-controlled Pennsylvania, the twelfth so-called original colony, in 1681, and Oglethorpe's founding of Georgia, the thirteenth colony, in 1733.[7]

The first documented arrival of enslaved Africans in the British American colonies occurred "about the latter end of August" in 1619, at Point Comfort on the Virginia coast. Although they were not legally classified as slaves,

Dutch slavers sold the "20 and odd Negroes" to the Virginia governor and a local merchant. Chattel slavery—the legal status whereby a human being becomes the personal property of another—quickly became the cornerstone of the rapidly expanding New World economy. By the mid-seventeenth century disenchanted British colonial leaders had all but abandoned indentured servitude and embraced the enslavement of Black people as the preferred source of labor. The rationale undergirding the preference for enslaved Blacks was multifaceted, but the primary driver was the singular pursuit of profit and wealth.[8]

Unlike Native Indians, Africans were enslaved far from their homelands, which made escape and survival extremely difficult. British chattel slavery also carried the sanction of generational bondage because the children of enslaved mothers inherited their mother's status. This legal provision was necessary because of the ever-increasing number of mixed-race or mulatto children being fathered mostly by white males. The entrenchment of slavery also had the effect of mitigating class conflicts between poor and wealthy white colonists by allowing both groups to embrace the shared status of racial superiority over enslaved Blacks.[9]

Blatant racism as well as perceived genetic, cultural, and religious differences also played a role in the evolution of chattel slavery in the British American colonies. The great majority of white Christian colonists considered Blacks to be genetically inferior and divinely ordained to be enslaved. But despite the alleged inferiority, they also believed that enslaved Blacks possessed greater tolerance for semitropical climates, which allowed them to toil in intense heat for longer periods of time and gave them a group immunity to malaria and other infectious diseases. On a more practical level, dark-skinned enslaved people were easily distinguishable from the white population for purposes of surveillance and control.[10]

Massachusetts was the first British colony to codify the enslavement of Black people in 1641. However, slavery did not become the primary source of labor in the New England colonies of Massachusetts, Rhode Island, Connecticut, and New Hampshire. Although the percentage of slave laborers was relatively small, enslaved Blacks worked as shipbuilders, dockworkers, sailors, craftsmen, and domestic workers, as well as on small farms.[11]

In the Middle Colonies of New York, New Jersey, Pennsylvania, and Delaware, large amounts of wheat and corn were cultivated and exported, but these cash crops did not require the labor of large numbers of enslaved Blacks.

ESTIMATED FREE AND ENSLAVED BLACK AND WHITE
POPULATIONS IN THE THIRTEEN BRITISH COLONIES, 1740

	Black	White	Total
(1) Virginia	60,000	120,440	180,440
(2) South Carolina	30,000	15,000	45,000
(3) Maryland	24,031	92,062	116,093
(4) North Carolina	11,000	40,760	51,760
(5) New Jersey	4,366	47,007	51,373
(6) Massachusetts	3,035	148,578	151,613
(7) Connecticut	2,598	86,982	89,580
(8) Rhode Island	2,408	22,847	25,225
(9) Pennsylvania	2,063	83,574	85,637
(10) New York	1,200	62,465	63,655
(11) Delaware	1,035	18,835	19,870
(12) New Hampshire	500	22,756	23,256
(13) Georgia	500	1,521	2,021
Total	142,736	762,827	905,563

Still, in the major urban trade centers of Boston, New York, and Philadelphia, enslaved laborers constituted between 20 and 25 percent of the population. Enslaved urban Blacks were also employed as domestic servants, artisans, sailors, dockworkers, laundresses, and coachmen.[12]

Enslaved Blacks were the primary source of labor, wealth, and prestige in the southern colonies of Maryland, Virginia, and Carolina. The Carolina colony was founded in 1663, when King Charles II of England granted a charter to eight "Lord's Proprietors," and subdivided into North Carolina and South Carolina in 1729. Thousands of enslaved Blacks also worked on tobacco plantations in the Chesapeake Bay area of Virginia and Maryland and in North Carolina.[13]

"The Debatable Land"

IN NORTH AMERICA, SOUTH CAROLINA was the wealthiest British American colony; not coincidentally, it was also its slave-trading capital. More than 40 percent of all African captives transported to the American colonies disembarked at slave markets in Charles Town (later Charleston) and Georgetown. South Carolina was also the only British colony where the number of enslaved Blacks outnumbered the white population.[1]

Around 1670 Carolina slaveholders began purchasing highly valued African captives from the Senegambia region of coastal Africa, where rice had been cultivated for more than three millennia. In 1680 enslaved Blacks, who cultivated, harvested, and processed "Gold Seede," a variety of African rice, on low-country plantations, made up 17 percent of the colony's population, and by 1720 that share had grown to 67 percent. Property titles held on enslaved Blacks and revenue generated by commercial rice production quickly became the primary sources of white wealth in the southernmost British colony.[2]

According to Peter H. Wood, South Carolina's rice "plantations" could be more accurately described as "slave work camps" or "gulags." During the early 1700s enslaved Black laborers drained low-country swamps and cleared fields that were infested with alligators, poisonous snakes, and disease-carrying mosquitos. This was especially true on low-country rice plantations where tidal cultivation, a complex system of levees, ditches, culverts, floodgates, and drains, was constructed to regulate the flow of fresh water onto and off the fields.[3]

The harsh and deadly environment forced absentee rice plantation slaveholders to utilize the "task system" whereby enslaved foremen or "drivers" assigned specific tasks and directed the cultivation and processing of rice, with limited slaveholder oversight and intervention. Thus, Blacks enslaved on isolated rice plantations took full advantage of this limited freedom through the retention of African culture, spirituality, and language. The cultural inheritance of these uniquely skilled enslaved South Carolina and later Georgia rice growers can still be found in their Gullah-Geechee descendants today.[4]

That South Carolina's lucrative rice economy was totally dependent on the knowledge, skills, and labor of enslaved Blacks forced white slaveholders to confront a vexing dilemma. Black slave laborers were the key to their economic well-being, but they also posed a clear and present danger to the safety and security of white colonists. For more than sixty years, beginning with the founding of their colony in 1663, the Carolinians had been harassed and threatened by Spain, which claimed ownership of land far to the north of Saint Augustine.

On September 26, 1526, more than 130 years before the British established the Carolina colony, Spanish explorer Lucas Vázquez de Ayllón founded San Miguel de Gualdape, the first European settlement in what is now the United States. Although the exact location remains a mystery, historians theorize the settlement was located on present-day Georgia's Atlantic coast near Sapelo Sound in McIntosh County, Georgia, where they were plagued by disease, starvation, and dissension. Included among the Spaniards were enslaved Africans who carried out the first recorded slave revolt in North America when they rebelled, burned several encampment structures, and allied themselves with Native Indians.[5]

Although Spain was a major participant in the transatlantic slave trade, according to Spanish law, "slavery was not a natural state for any race. It was a state of war by which victors enslaved rather than killed their enemy." Persons enslaved by Spanish slaveholders possessed legal rights, "including the right to own property, sue in courts, keep families together, and purchase freedom." On November 7, 1693, King Charles II of Spain from his palace in Madrid issued an edict commanding Spanish officials in Florida to offer sanctuary to all Black people enslaved by the British if they "accept the sacraments and the advocacy of the [Catholic] church." Thus, covert operatives were regularly dispatched northward from Saint Augustine to encourage enslaved Blacks to rise up in rebellion against their British oppressors or escape to freedom in Florida. Huge financial losses associated with the escape of freedom-seeking Blacks and their military alliance with Spain spread fear and trepidation throughout the southern British colonies.[6]

During the twenty-year period preceding the founding of the Georgia colony, Spain stepped up its long-standing efforts to destabilize the majority Black Carolina colony. For security and economic reasons, desperate South

Carolinians enthusiastically supported the plan to establish a buffer colony on their southern frontier. They were certain a British colony, garrisoned with well-trained soldiers, situated between the Savannah and Altamaha Rivers would protect them from further Spanish depredations. South Carolina slaveholders were also convinced that British settlement of "the Debatable Land" would stem the tide of freedom seekers who were fleeing south.[7]

The South Carolinians also believed a long-hoped-for buffer colony would provide additional security from the Native Indians who literally surrounded them—proud nations of Yamasee, Muscogee, Cherokee, and Seminole. Ever-shifting relations with these tribes, coupled with their ferocity on the battlefield and their skill in the fur trade, challenged the courage and ingenuity of British colonists.

Finally, and most importantly, profit-hungry slave traders and rice plantation owners supported Oglethorpe's colonization plan because they wanted to replicate South Carolina's slave-based economy farther south along the southeastern seaboard. Following several failed British attempts to colonize the strategic territory, the South Carolinians were hopeful the Georgia Trustees might succeed where lesser men had failed. Notwithstanding Oglethorpe's desire to establish a slave-free "Zion" in America, ambitious and cunning men were determined to export chattel slavery into his proposed colony.[8]

On November 17, 1732—following four years of intense planning and preparation—Oglethorpe and approximately 114 original Georgia colonists set sail from Gravesend, England, on what would be an eighty-eight-day voyage across the Atlantic Ocean. All but a few left behind lives of poverty and religious persecution in favor of a new life in the New World.

It is important to note that the establishment of a slave-free colony was an antislavery strategy, not an effort to abolish British chattel slavery. Much of the confusion surrounding Oglethorpe's humanitarian legacy can be largely attributed to the usage or misusage of the terms "antislavery" and "abolitionism." The words are often used interchangeably, but they describe distinct moral, philosophical, and political perspectives.

Simply stated, Black antislavery actions or Black agency included armed resistance, onboard ship revolts, malingering, suicide, infanticide, sabotage, escape, rebellion, military alliance with the enemies of their enslavers, learning to read and write, entrepreneurship, self-purchase, and conversion to Christianity. Manisha Sinha observes, "Black resistance to slavery was the essential precondition to the rise of abolitionism." Also falling within the antislavery sphere were efforts, primarily by whites, to "civilize" or mollify slavery through Christianization, regulation of slavery, manumissions, colonization of freed Blacks, and prohibiting the spread of the institution into new territories or jurisdictions. Most significantly, white antislavery advocates also asserted what was then a radical proposition: dark-skinned Africans and their descendants were members of the human family. The formal abolitionist movement originated in England in 1787 and subsequently migrated to the United States. Moderate abolitionists argued for the gradual emancipation of enslaved Blacks, while radical or "immediatist" abolitionists advocated for the immediate and unconditional abolition of slavery. Leading up to and after the founding of the Georgia colony, Oglethorpe was not an abolitionist—little wonder, since the formal British abolitionist movement would not be born for more than fifty years—but he was a vocal antislavery activist, and prohibiting the importation of enslaved Blacks into Georgia was a groundbreaking *antislavery* strategy.[9]

Definitional distinctions notwithstanding, the untamed wilderness that greeted Oglethorpe and the original colonists abounded with stark realities that would not yield to philanthropic idealism. The southeastern region of the North American continent hosted a complex mix of competing nations, warring races, and ever-shifting economic imperatives. Often overlooked is one critical fact: the land on which Georgia was founded was not uninhabited. The elderly chief Tomochichi and his band of two hundred Yamacraw occupied the bluffs overlooking the Savannah River a few years prior to Oglethorpe's arrival. Tomochichi's permission to establish a British colony, as well as the critical support and assistance of his people, had to be earned and maintained. Far removed from the stately courts of England, where well-mannered men plotted the course of Georgia's early development, this hostile environment would constantly test the resolve and moral fiber of European colonists.[10]

Georgia's early history is therefore replete with inconsistency regarding the use of enslaved Black laborers. Although the importation of Black people into the colony, slave or free, was prohibited, at least one enslaved man was already in the area when the colonists disembarked at Yamacraw Bluff on February 12, 1733. He was enslaved by Indian traders John and Mary Musgrove, who lived on Pipemakers Creek, near the future site of the Savannah settlement. Ironically, the Black man was named Justice.[11]

Enslaved Blacks toiled in Savannah from the settlement's earliest days, de-

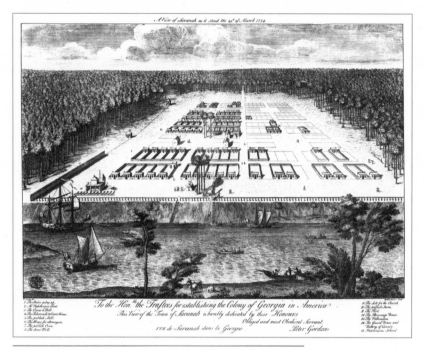

The Savannah Settlement, c. 1734, was built in part by enslaved Black laborers despite Georgia's slavery prohibition.

(Courtesy of Library of Congress Prints and Photographs Division)

spite the prohibition. In fact, a Mr. Bryan of the South Carolina colony brought four Black men to help saw trees and build houses in Savannah during its infancy. In the winter and spring of 1733, twenty enslaved Blacks—their labor donated by William Bull, a South Carolina slaveholder—helped Oglethorpe and the colonists clear forty lots for house construction, and they assisted in the delineation of the town squares and streets. "They [the colonists] worked hard indeed," wrote an observer, "in building some houses in town, but they labor'd in common, and were likewise assisted by Negroes from Carolina, who did the heaviest work." In this instance and numerous others during Georgia's embryonic stages, Oglethorpe conveniently ignored the presence of enslaved Black laborers. Nevertheless, his opposition to slavery soon hardened, as did the opposition of his fellow Trustees in England.[12]

The harsh realities of life in the North American wilderness also forced Oglethorpe to circumvent the prohibition against the migration of Jewish colonists into Georgia. During the spring and summer of 1733, approximately sixty Georgia colonists had fallen ill with fever and twenty died, including

Noble Jones, the colony's only doctor. Amid this spiraling health crisis, the *William and Sarah* arrived unexpectedly and dropped anchor in the Savannah River on July 11. Onboard were forty-two Jewish migrants, who prior to the January 1733 vote by the Trustees to prohibit Jewish migration had set sail from England on their voyage to the Georgia colony.[13]

Oglethorpe was informed that a respected physician, Dr. Samuel Nunes, was among the Jewish migrants. He invited Dr. Nunes to disembark and care for the sick colonists, but Oglethorpe refused to allow Nunes's family and the other Jewish migrants to exit the ship. Dr. Nunes rejected Oglethorpe's offer and declared that he would not offer medical assistance unless his family and coreligionists were permitted to settle in the Georgia colony.[14]

Oglethorpe requested a legal opinion from British lawyers in Charles Town regarding the legality of allowing Jews to migrate to Georgia. The attorneys reasoned that the group could stay because "the charter did allow religious freedom for all non-Catholics." With the impasse resolved, Nunes went about the task of caring for those who had fallen ill. Oglethorpe later reported to the Trustees in London that this "doctor of physic . . . immediately undertook our people and refused to take any pay for it. He proceeded by cold baths, cooling drinks and other cooling applications. Since which the sick have wonderfully recovered, and we have not lost one who would follow his prescriptions." Without consulting his fellow Trustees, a grateful Oglethorpe allowed fourteen Jewish men to purchase land in the colony. In July 1735 Georgia's original Jewish colonists founded Mickve Israel (Hope of Israel), "the third-oldest Jewish congregation in America and the Oldest in the South."[15]

Having resolved the health crisis, Oglethorpe turned his attention back to enforcing the prohibitions against slavery and consumption of rum. On May 14, 1733, he prematurely reported to his fellow Trustees: "I have brought all our people to desire the prohibition of Negroes and rum, which goes against the grain of the traders in the commodities in this town." He also offered a stark warning: "But if either of them are allowed our whole design will be ruined." Later that summer, Oglethorpe visited Charles Town, where South Carolina slaveholders tried to persuade him to open Georgia to rum, chattel slavery, and thus the plantation system. These proslavery British colonists were amassing influence and wealth through the cultivation of rice on coastal plantations, and they were certain that similar profits could be generated along the Georgia coast, if slavery was legalized. The frustrated

South Carolinians even offered Oglethorpe a bribe in return for his support, but he angrily rebuffed their overtures and departed the colony determined to maintain Georgia's slavery prohibition.[16]

What Oglethorpe witnessed on his return to Savannah only served to strengthen his resolve. Entering the settlement, he discovered the colonists had grown "very mutinous and impatient of labour and discipline." Blaming their laziness on the presence of enslaved Black laborers loaned from South Carolina and the widespread consumption of rum, Oglethorpe reported to the Trustees that he "sent away the Negroes for . . . our men were encouraged in idleness by their working for them." In a fit of anger, Oglethorpe then destroyed every barrel of rum he could find and threatened to withhold provisions from anyone caught distilling or selling spirits.[17]

Diallo Is a Free Man

IN APRIL 1733, WHILE OGLETHORPE was struggling to prevent the proliferation of slavery in Georgia, Ayuba Suleiman Diallo, the young man he rescued from enslavement in America, arrived in London. During his voyage across the Atlantic, Diallo had been accompanied by Thomas Bluett, the SPG missionary who befriended him while he was incarcerated in Maryland. Bluett had spent time teaching Diallo the rudiments of the English language and would continue to provide instruction during their twelve months together in England.[1]

Assuming the new name "Job ben Solomon," Diallo quickly ingratiated himself to admiring and influential Britons and became known as a "roaring lion" of British society. Described as being of "fine figure," lean, straight limbed, and standing about five feet, ten inches tall, Diallo possessed a narrow face dominated by piercing eyes and curly, Afro-styled hair. His countenance was described as "exceeding pleasant, yet grave and composed," and according to Bluett, Diallo exhibited "a solid judgement, a ready Memory, and a clear Head." Most remarkably, considering the virulent racism that permeated eighteenth-century England, Britons who met Diallo marveled at the "Acuteness of his Genius."[2]

Diallo's navigation of London's elite society was aided by his own highborn lineage and advanced education. His grandfather Abraham founded the city of Bunda during the reign of Abubeker, a former king of Futa, located in what is modern-day Senegal. As a high priest, Abraham exercised sole authority over the religious and political affairs of the thriving city. When Abubeker died, his brother the prince Jelazi ascended to the throne. The new king placed Samba, his eldest son, in the care of Diallo's father, who tutored Diallo alongside the young prince in Arabic and the Koran. Diallo became a close companion to Samba, who was later crowned king of Futa after his father's death.[3]

Among his many interactions with British elites, Diallo assisted Sir Hans

Sloane, whose store of historical artifacts formed the basis of the British Museum, in arranging and interpreting a large collection of Arabic manuscripts. Sloane was so impressed by Diallo's intellect and acumen that he subsequently orchestrated the honorary induction of the young African into the prestigious Spalding Gentlemen's Society. Diallo was subsequently introduced at the royal court of King George II and Queen Caroline. He also developed close relationships with the Duke of Montague and other members of the royal family.

Diallo's British hosts were especially intrigued by his devotion to Islam. He amazed them by reciting the Koran from memory and writing three copies of the sacred book without "so much as looking to one of those three when he wrote the others." Several members of the Spalding Gentlemen's Society sought to introduce Diallo to Christianity by presenting him with a copy of the Bible. The society's minute book contains a notation dated June 26, 1733, logging that a Bible was presented to the "Poor Mahometan Black redeemed by order of Mr. Oglethorpe." Diallo's patrons were surprised to learn that he was well versed in the historical aspects of the Christian religion and considered Jesus Christ to be a "very great Prophet." However, his steadfast "Belief in one God" led him to reject any "Notion of the Trinity" because he could not find one word in the Bible that referenced "three gods." Despite their Christian overtures, Diallo remained devoted to the religion of his ancestors.[4]

During moments of meditation Diallo often compared himself with Joseph, the youngest and favorite son of Jacob, whose story is told in the Bible and Koran. Joseph was blessed with the ability to interpret dreams and was sold into slavery by two of his jealous half-brothers. He used his talent to successively impress his enslaver, jailer, and later, the pharaoh of Egypt. The gracious pharaoh showered Joseph with expensive gifts and appointed him to an exalted leadership position in Egypt. Later a deadly famine forced Joseph's half-brothers to seek food and refuge in the land where their youngest sibling enjoyed royal status. Without revealing his identity, Joseph saved his family from starvation and forgave them for their transgressions. Joseph's story conveyed a powerful message to Diallo: what was intended to do harm can be transformed by God to achieve a preordained purpose. Diallo believed divine Providence had delivered him to a "strange land" to fulfill God's will. Like Joseph, he forgave the Mandinka who kidnapped and sold him into slavery and his British enslavers who had kept him in bondage. Diallo somewhat similarly "interpreted" the economic dreams of his RAC benefactors, by providing them with detailed knowledge of the abundant natural resources existing along Africa's west coast.[5]

The budding British celebrity was also encouraged by his admirers to sit for William Hoare, the leading portraitist of eighteenth-century England. Diallo initially refused to be painted for religious reasons, as the Koran prohibited the depiction of living forms, but he relented on the condition that "he be drawn in his own Country Dress" rather than European clothing. Hoard did not know what that clothing looked like, so Diallo described his native attire to him. He is shown in the resulting painting wearing a white robe and turban, with a bright red leather pouch around his neck that would have contained writings from the Koran. According to curators at England's National Portrait Gallery, the painting depicts "Diallo as a man of intelligence, character and compassion—providing rare insight into the emergence of more tolerant values in Britain during the Enlightenment."[6]

Although he was treated with respect and kindness by his British hosts, Diallo never lost sight of the fact that he was not a free man. Oglethorpe, his original benefactor, had promised to purchase Diallo from his enslaver, but Oglethorpe was now in North America, working to establish the Georgia colony. Oglethorpe's former business partners in the RAC devised a scheme to purchase the enslaved young man and send him back to Africa, where he could possibly assist the corporation in securing gold, ivory, and other commodities. The development alarmed Diallo, who told Bluett that he feared the slave traders intended to sell him to the highest bidder—or that, even if they sent him home, they would force him to pay an unreasonable ransom in exchange for his freedom. Bluett was also concerned that even if the corporation paid Oglethorpe's bond, the transaction would not change Diallo's enslaved status. He proposed instead that a public subscription be initiated to raise funds for purchasing Diallo's freedom. Before this could be accomplished, however, the RAC purchased Diallo from Captain Henry Hunt, who was senior officer on the slave ship *Arabella* and bearer of Oglethorpe's bond, for forty-five pounds plus interest.[7]

Bluett did not trust the motives of Diallo's new enslavers, so he quickly moved to raise the money needed to manumit him. After contributions were received from several influential Britons, a "handsomely engrossed" certificate of manumission was presented to Diallo on December 27, 1733, attesting that "Job [Diallo] is a free Man and is at Liberty to take his Passage to Africa . . .

in order to return to his Native Country." Historian Henry Louis Gates quips that Diallo successfully carried out the "oddest" recorded escape from bondage by literally writing "his way out of slavery." But while Diallo regained his freedom, he did not forget that Loumein Yoas, his loyal interpreter, was still enslaved in Maryland and appealed to RAC officials for help. In 1737 they directed Bluett to purchase Yoas's freedom and paid for his passage back to Africa the following year.[8]

In July 1734 Diallo sailed from London to his homeland on the *Dolphin Snow*, with a letter from RAC officials directing its employees to treat him "with the greatest respect and all civility you possibly can." Having by now lost their slave-trading monopoly, company officials were hopeful that Diallo would serve as a conduit to other lucrative trading opportunities. Following Diallo's directions, Bluett published the young man's memoirs shortly after he sailed for Africa. Printed in English and French, the book was titled *Some Memoirs of the Life of Job, the Son of Solomon, the High Priest of Boonda in Africa; Who was a Slave about Two Years in Maryland; and Afterwards Being Brought to England, Was Set Free, and Sent to His Native Land in the Year 1734*. Historians consider Diallo's book to be, like Equiano's, among the first and most influential slave narratives.[9]

Diallo arrived on the Gambian coast on August 8, 1734, completing his miraculous journey back to Africa. Although he had experienced many trials and tribulations, much like Job in the Old Testament, Diallo's sufferings had seemingly been rewarded tenfold. He returned to his native land a free man, laden with over five hundred pounds of gifts and treasures. However, as RAC agent Thomas Moore records in *Travels into the Inland Parts of Africa*, Diallo's triumphant return was bittersweet. On his arrival, Diallo was informed of his father's recent death and that war had decimated his beloved homeland. Presuming Diallo to be dead, one of his two wives had also remarried. Although he was distressed by the news, Diallo characteristically forgave his former wife and the man she wed, saying, "She could not help thinking I was dead; for I had gone to a land from whence no Pholey ever yet returned."[10]

Prior to Moore's own departure from Africa in April 1735, Diallo gave him several letters addressed to Oglethorpe, Bluett, the Duke of Montague, numerous RAC officials, and other supporters in which the formerly enslaved African expressed his appreciation for their benevolence and reaffirmed his commitment to promote British economic interests. According to Moore, Diallo promised to "spend his days endeavoring to do good to the English,

by whom he had been redeemed from slavery, and from whom he had received innumerable favors." Despite all that had befallen him, Diallo lived
for another forty years and died peacefully in 1773 at the age of seventy-two
or seventy-three. His death was noted with great sadness in England and
recorded in the minute book of the Spalding Gentlemen's Society.[11]

Although their lives were inextricably linked, Oglethorpe and Diallo may
never have met in person. Diallo arrived in London in April 1733, six months
after Oglethorpe had departed for North America to establish the Georgia
colony. A little over a year later, on June 16, 1734, Oglethorpe, Tomochichi,
and a delegation of Yamacraw Indians arrived in England, and the following month Diallo sailed for Africa. Details surrounding a possible meeting between the two men have thus far escaped documentation; however,
nineteenth-century American historian Robert Wright notes that Diallo had
been living in England for twelve months "before the return of Oglethorpe,
who immediately made arrangements for his restoration to his native land."
British historian Eveline Cruickshanks observes that Oglethorpe "sent him
[Diallo] home at his own expense." Nonetheless, Oglethorpe and Diallo's
unique "relationship" would help galvanize British antislavery sentiment.[12]

11

A Prohibition against Slavery

"O God, Where Are Thy Tender Mercies?"

OGLETHORPE WAS WELCOMED HOME AS a hero, and his Native Indian guests were showered with great fanfare and British curiosity. Following a four-month visit that included treaty signings and an audience with the king and queen, Tomochichi's delegation set sail from England on October 30, 1734. Oglethorpe disappointed his Native Indian friends by deciding to remain behind to lobby Parliament for financial support to construct additional military fortifications on Georgia's exposed southern borders.

During Oglethorpe's eighteen-month stay in England, arguments pro and con regarding slavery legalization were bandied about the Georgia colony fervently and tirelessly. However, antislavery forces won an important political battle in June 1735 when the Trustees enacted a law titled "An Act for ren'ring the Colony of Georgia more defensible by prohibiting the Importation and Use of Black Slaves or Negroes into the same." The first statute to expressly prohibit slavery in a British American colony, the law contained a detailed military rationale for the prohibition. According to its preamble, enslaved Black laborers would deter the immigration of English and Protestant settlers to Georgia, thereby reducing the number of white men who could be relied on to help defend the colony. Slavery would also expose white colonists to the dangers of slave "insurrections, tumults and rebellions," which would undermine internal security, especially during periods of military conflict with foreign enemies.[1]

The antislavery statute established a maximum fine of fifty pounds for any person convicted of importing, buying, selling, bartering, or utilizing slave labor in Georgia, and it granted local officials the power to seize any Black person found in the colony. The statute also contained a "fugitive slave" provision that allowed slaveholders from other colonies to reclaim Blacks fleeing enslavement after the payment of costs and damages associated with the apprehension. Unclaimed captives would become the property of the Trustees, who, with the consent of local officials, could export, sell, or dispose of captives in any manner considered in the best interest of the colony. Clearly, the intent was to keep slavery out of the colony, not to dismantle the institution itself.[2]

Passage of the slavery prohibition only served to intensify the debate between Georgia's antislavery minority and the growing proslavery lobby. A series of harshly worded petitions, counterpetitions, and letters were delivered to the Trustees in London, extolling or decrying the prohibition against slave labor. Oglethorpe lashed out at proslavery colonists and swore that he would completely dissociate himself from his beloved colony if slavery was legalized.[3]

Despite mounting criticism from his fellow Trustees and waning political support for Georgia's slavery prohibition, Parliament granted Oglethorpe's request for increased funding. In December 1735 he led a small flotilla of four ships carrying 490 new settlers across the Atlantic. Among the second wave of colonists were John and Charles Wesley, two Anglican missionaries associated with the Society for the Propagation of the Gospel in Foreign Parts (SPG). Also onboard were 150 rugged Highlanders from Scotland, noted throughout Europe for their skilled use of the broad sword, and recruited by Oglethorpe to defend Georgia's southern frontier. The Wesley brothers, the Scots, and the German Salzburgers, an industrious group of religious refugees who migrated to Georgia in March 1735, would form the core of Oglethorpe's antislavery contingent in the colony.[4]

In January 1736 the Scottish Highlanders established the seaside town of New Inverness, later renamed Darien. Located about fifty-three miles south of the Savannah settlement on the Atlantic seaboard, the Scottish settlement was the first line of defense against a potential Spanish invasion. Thus, the men of Darien primarily objected to slavery for military reasons, although they would later condemn the institution as an affront to humanity and a violation of God's will. The Scots initially maintained that enslaved Blacks would escape to Florida and fight with the Spanish, or worse, remain in Georgia, where Spanish instigators would incite them to rise up in rebellion. In either scenario, they argued, the importation of enslaved Africans gave British enemies a strategic military advantage. In letters and petitions addressed to the Trustees in England, Oglethorpe, the Darien Scots, and the German Salzburgers expressed agreement on this issue. The presence of enslaved Black laborers would render the colony vulnerable to slave retaliation, rebellions, and foreign invasion.[5]

Oglethorpe and others, including John Martin Bolzius, the Salzburger spiritual leader, contended that slavery would take employment away from poor white Georgia colonists who fled England in search of economic opportunity. At the time, there was a severe labor shortage throughout the British American colonies, which the Georgia Trustees attempted to resolve by employing white indentured servants, only to find them unreliable and expensive. Bolzius insisted that the immigration of additional Salzburgers would help the colony's lagging economy more than the legalization of slave labor. But proslavery advocates, who were called "Malcontents," argued that the admission of enslaved Blacks was necessary for Georgia to compete on equal footing with the South Carolina colony, where enslaved laborers provided cheaper, more productive labor.[6]

The Malcontents were primarily composed of settlers who were known as "adventurers" because they were able to pay for their passage to Georgia. They took up residence in and around the Savannah settlement and were led by Patrick Tailfer, a merchant; Captain Robert Williams, one of the colony's wealthiest inhabitants; and Thomas Stephens, the son of William Stephens, who would later serve as secretary to the Georgia Trustees. The younger Stephens migrated to Georgia in 1737 to help manage his father's business investments in the colony. He quickly became an outspoken critic of Oglethorpe's leadership and the slavery prohibition.[7]

In addition to the German Salzburgers and the Scots, a series of evangelical missionaries would join Oglethorpe's small but vocal antislavery chorus. Bolzius and the Reverend George Whitefield, a popular evangelist who came to Georgia in 1738, would engage in a heated debate over the religious justification for legalizing slavery in the colony. Whitefield was a slavery critic, but he argued that the importation of enslaved Africans would provide slaveholders with the opportunity to fulfill a divine purpose by Christianizing heathens. He professed too that God had created certain hot, inhospitable climates, like Georgia's, exclusively for Blacks because white men lacked the physical stamina to perform rigorous work under semitropical conditions. Not incidentally, he felt that his Bethesda Orphanage in Savannah could not survive without the use of enslaved laborers.[8]

Many proslavery advocates would adopt this theory, known as "climatic necessity." Writing from Charles Town, slave merchant Samuel Eveleigh argued that "without Negroes Georgia can never be a Colony of any great Consequence." He added: "I observed, whilst at Georgia great Quantity's of Choice good Land for Rice, And am positive that that Commodity can't (in any great quantity's) be produced by white people."[9]

Bolzius rejected outright the validity of climate-based proslavery reasoning but took exception to Whitefield's assertions regarding a divine justification for legalizing slavery in Georgia. Bolzius facetiously directed the reverend and others wishing to spread the Gospel among enslaved Blacks to work the "Large Field" available in South Carolina. Although there were a growing number of neglected and orphaned white children in the colony, he concluded it would be better to abandon Whitefield's "Orphan House" than allow its existence to justify the importation of enslaved Blacks into Georgia.[10]

John Wesley was born on June 17, 1703, the fifteenth child of Samuel and Susanna Wesley. Wesley's father was the rector at Epworth, North Lincolnshire, England, and both parents taught their children to read and write at an early age. John graduated from Christ Church, Oxford in 1724 where he subsequently earned a master's degree. He was ordained as a priest by the Church of England on September 22, 1728. His younger brother Charles also enrolled at Christ Church, and they along with a small group of fellow students that included George Whitefield, became derisively known as the Holy Club because they engaged in continuous fasting, prayer, and religious worship. The Wesley brothers also disdained materialism in religious worship and leapt at an invitation from Oglethorpe to go to the New World to evangelize British colonists, enslaved Blacks, and Native Indians.[11]

Although slavery was prohibited in the colony, Dr. John Burton, a Bray Associate and Georgia Trustee, had informed Wesley that "a door is opened" to evangelize enslaved Blacks not far from Georgia. According to Burton, slaveholding Swiss Protestant refugees in the village of Purrysburg in South Carolina were under the influence of the Trustees, and "Mr. Oglethorpe will think it advisable to begin there. You see the harvest is truly great."[12]

Shortly before embarking from England for the new colony with his brother Charles on October 14, 1735, Wesley penned a lengthy rationale for his decision to migrate to the New World. "My chief motive, to which all the rest are subordinate," he wrote, "is the hope of saving my own soul. I hope to learn the true sense of the gospel of Christ by preaching it to the heathens. —From these, therefore, I hope to learn the purity of that faith which was

Rev. John Wesley, widely acknowledged as being the "Father of Methodism," migrated to the Georgia colony in 1734. He was a member of the vocal minority of Georgia colonists who supported General James Oglethorpe's antislavery philosophy. James Oglethorpe invited Rev. John Wesley to the New World to convert enslaved Blacks, Native Indians, and white colonists to Christianity.

(Josiah Wood Whymper, *John Wesley*, lithograph, from Edward Ellis, *The Youth's History of the United States* [New York: Cassell & Company, 1886])

once delivered to the saints, the genuine sense and full extent of those laws which none can understand who mind earthly things."[13]

In July 1736 the Wesley brothers traveled from the Savannah settlement to Charles Town, South Carolina. The Reverend Alexander Garden, bishop of London's Commissary for South Carolina, had invited John to deliver the Sunday sermon on August 1. Wesley recalled, "About three hundred were present at the morning service . . . about fifty at the Holy Communion." He continued, "I was glad to see several Negroes at church, one of whom told me she was there constantly, and that her old mistress (now dead) had many times instructed her in Christian religion."[14]

The young missionary eagerly proceeded to explore the depths of the enslaved woman's Christian faith. "I asked her what religion was. She said she could not tell me. I asked if she knew what a soul was. She answered, 'No.' I said, 'Do you not know there is something in you different from your body? Something you cannot see or feel? She replied, 'I never heard so much before.' I added, 'Do you think, then, a man dies altogether as a horse dies?' She said,

'Yes, to be sure.'" Wesley was dismayed by her reluctance or inability to answer basic questions or comprehend rudimentary tenets of Christianity. He observed, "O God, where are Thy tender mercies? Are they not over all Thy works? When shall the Sun of Righteousness arise on these outcasts of men, with healing in His wings!"[15]

The Wesley brothers hurried back to Georgia the following day. Despite a very busy schedule, Charles Wesley found time to record his thoughts and impressions regarding the inhumanity of chattel slavery. In his account, Charles detailed the "horrid cruelties" meted out by South Carolina slaveholders. One proudly boasted that he directed an enslaved person to be nailed "by the ears" and whipped in the "severest manner." The macabre incident concluded with the pouring of scalding water over the Black man's body. He described another frequently utilized and "much-applauded punishment" that involved the "drawing" of teeth from the mouths of enslaved Blacks. And in yet another gruesome example, Wesley recounted that a Charleston dancing master "whipped a she-slave so long, that she fell down at his feet." After a physician revived the bloodied woman, the slaveholder "repeated the whipping with equal rigor, and concluded with dropping hot sealing-wax upon her flesh." He ended the harrowing notation by revealing that the woman's only crime was "over filling a tea-cup." The younger Wesley brother added that he was unable to "recount all the shocking instances of diabolical cruelty which these men (as they call themselves) daily practice upon their fellow creatures."[16]

On August 20, 1736, John Wesley spent two hours reading *The Negro's and Indian's Advocate*. Published in 1680, Morgan Godwyn's book advanced a controversial theological supposition: every human being has "an equal right to religion"; enslaved Blacks are human beings and are "invested with that same right"; therefore, any attempt "to deprive" them of the right to eternal salvation is "the highest injustice."[17]

Although Godwyn did not openly oppose slavery, his belief that enslaved Blacks were human beings deserving of salvation infuriated white Christians in the Virginia colony where he had served as a parish rector. He dolefully surmised that all but a few white Christians believed "that the Negros, though in their Figure they carry some resemblances of Manhood, yet are indeed *no Men*. They are Creatures destitute of souls, to be ranked among Brute Beasts, and treated accordingly." Proslavery white Christians ridiculed

Godwyn's writings and threatened his life, but his book inspired Dr. Thomas Bray to establish the SPG in 1701.[18]

In April 1737 Wesley traveled back to Charles Town where he attended a meeting of Anglican clergymen. Subsequently, he was invited to the home of Rev. Thompson, minister of St. Bartholomew's Church, who lived about forty miles outside the city near Pon Pon village, where, according to one Methodist historian, he engaged in perhaps the most important conversation he would have during his entire American ministry. In what was likely the "first lengthy, in-depth conversation" he had ever had with a Black person, Wesley conversed with an enslaved woman named Nanny, who was born into slavery in Barbados and forced to serve the minister's family her entire life.[19]

Finding her "more sensible" than the other Blacks he encountered at the Thompson residence, he put to her a series of probing questions. "I asked her whether she went to church there. She said, 'Yes, every Sunday, to carry my mistress's children.' I asked her what she had learned at church. She said, 'Nothing; I heard a great deal, but did not understand it.' But what did your master teach you at home?' 'Nothing.' I asked, 'But don't you know that your hands and feet, and this you call your body, will turn to dust in a little time?' She answered, 'Yes.' 'But there is something in you that will not turn to dust, and this is what they call your soul.—What do you think will become of your soul when your body turns to dust?' She replied, 'I don't know.'"[20]

Wesley eagerly shared with Nanny the Christian concept of spiritual immortality through heavenly salvation. "He made you to live with Himself above the sky," he explained, "and so you will, in a little time, if you are good. If you are good, when your body dies your soul will go up, and want nothing, and have whatever you desire." "No one will beat you or hurt you there," he must have stated pointedly. "The attention with which this poor creature listened to instruction was inexpressible," he observed. "The next day she remembered all, readily answering every question; and said she would ask Him that made her to show her how to be good."[21]

The young minister was encouraged, if not overjoyed, by Nanny's apparent receptivity to his Christian ministry. And while Wesley's professed interest in the woman was limited to saving her immortal soul, rather than any discussion or hope for mollifying her earthly condition of perpetual bondage, his acknowledgment that Nanny and her fellow bondmen possessed redeemable souls presented an existential threat to the institution of slavery. The divergence of antislavery Christian evangelism from the theological dehumanization of dark-skinned Africans was an important precedent to the rise of abolitionism.[22]

John Wesley's evangelism among enslaved Blacks did not go unnoticed by proslavery Georgia colonists and may have precipitated one of the most embarrassing episodes in the young evangelist's life. In an affidavit sworn before the mayor of Bristol, England, in March 1740, Captain Robert Williams, one of the leaders of the proslavery Malcontents, asserted that during his Georgia ministry Wesley had committed a series of damnable sins and transgressions with a young woman named Sophia Hopkey, the niece of Savannah chief magistrate Thomas Causton. According to Williams, the young minister "used too great familiarities with Miss Hopkey and continued to do so till she was married" and that Wesley sent "several letters and other messages after her marriage, desiring her to meet him at . . . unseasonable hours and places, many of which were at . . . Wesley's own closet." Williams also claimed that William Williamson, Hopkey's new husband, had filed a civil complaint against Wesley alleging that in a fit of jealousy, he had refused to give the sacrament of communion to his wife in a public place. Wesley categorically denied the sensational accusations and denounced Williams for spreading salacious, unsubstantiated rumors.[23]

Wesley also refuted claims that he "quitted the colony in . . . the middle of the night," failed to appear in court, and sought refuge in the South Carolina colony. Incensed by the slanderous attack, the young minister directly rebuked Williams: "Now, sir, as you know in your own soul that every word of this is pure invention, without one grain of truth from beginning to end . . . you must openly retract an open slander, or you must wade through thick and thin to support it; till that God, to whom I appeal, shall . . . sweep you away from the earth."[24]

After less than two years of ministry, a much-chastened Wesley "shook off the dust" of the New World and returned to England. That Williams "resented Wesley's attitude as to slavery" and was an outspoken proslavery advocate, who signed the 1738 petition that called for repeal of the slavery ban, which he personally "transmitted" to the Trustees in London, should not be overlooked in assessing the veracity of the alleged affair. Nevertheless, the prevailing scholarly view concludes that Wesley's American ministry, due in large part to the Sophia Hopkey scandal, was an embarrassing failure.[25]

Still, Wesley's exposure to the brutalities of chattel slavery and his inter-actions with enslavers and enslaved Blacks fostered a deepening abhorrence of slavery, and his ministry and writings ultimately played a key role in advancing the abolitionist cause in England and the Americas. In 1774, decades after his departure from Georgia, Wesley, who is celebrated as the father of Methodism, recalled: "Mr. Oglethorpe . . . went so far as to begin settling a colony without Negroes, but at length the voice of those villains prevailed who sell their country and their God for gold, who laugh at human nature and compassion, and defy all religion, but that of getting money."[26]

The Prophecy

THE GEORGIA SLAVERY DEBATE REACHED a crescendo on December 9, 1738, when 121 Savannah residents, including two magistrates, signed a petition that blamed the colony's economic deterioration on the absence of cheap slave labor. Robert Williams and other proslavery petitioners assured the Trustees that the "use of Negroes with proper limitations" would avert ruin and guarantee the struggling colony's success. The petition ignited a political firestorm.[1]

On January 16 and 17, 1739, Oglethorpe wrote his fellow Trustees two scathing letters in which he ridiculed the petitioners as men consumed by "idleness" whose self-serving ambitions could jeopardize the colony's future. In his letters, Oglethorpe argued against the importation of enslaved Blacks because he was convinced the colony would "immediately be destroyed, for it would be impossible to prevent them deserting to the Spaniards, our near neighbors who give freedom, land, and protection to all Negroes." He also anticipated the sentiments of nineteenth-century abolitionists by proclaiming that legalized slavery in Georgia would "occasion the misery of thousands in Africa, by setting men using arts to buy and bring into perpetual slavery the poor people who now live free there." This expression of concern for African people is the first documented statement by Oglethorpe that focused on the suffering of Black men, women, and children rather than the moral well-being, economic interests, or security of white colonists, and represents a significant progression on his journey to abolitionism.[2]

For their part, on January 3, 1739, eighteen Darien Scots issued an ominous, apocalyptic petition addressed to "Governor-General Oglethorpe," urging him not to repeal the 1735 antislavery statute. The document lays out specific military and economic objections to slavery. However, the petitioners' most compelling arguments were infused with moral and religious outrage. The petition brands slavery a sin and foretells a day of providential retribution for Georgia slaveholders. "It's shocking to human Nature that any Race of Mankind and their Posterity, should be sentenced to perpetual Slavery," the petition declares, "nor in Justice can we think otherwise of it, than they are thrown among us to be our Scourge one Day or another, for our Sins; and as Freedom to them must be as dear to us, What a Scene of Horror it must bring about! And the longer it is unexecuted, the bloody Scene must be the greater." According to one historian, with their petition, these early Georgians "wrote, signed and published ... the first protest against the use of Africans as slaves, issued in the history of the New World."[3]

The looming fear of divine retribution for the sin of slavery was the focal point of a school of thought known as providentialist theology with several distinct strands of reasoning. Judicial providentialism was the belief that "God rewarded or punished nations according to their moral character and actions." Historical providentialism held that God assigned specific missions and roles to certain nations, while apocalyptic providentialism asserted that God manipulated the actions of nations to fulfill the prophecies of revelation. Judicial providentialism became the rhetorical weapon of choice for early antislavery advocates. They identified the transatlantic slave trade as a contravention of God's will and provocation for divine wrath. These Christian evangelicals were among the first British American colonists to meld judicial providentialist thought with antislavery rhetoric. They argued that England's propagation of the transatlantic slave trade was a cardinal sin that would inevitably result in "national punishments." Early eighteenth-century antislavery Christians also believed that God's anger could be manifested in natural disasters such as hurricanes, floods, and earthquakes or in the man-made calamities of war and revolution. Oglethorpe was among the earliest and most prominent white Christian adherents of judicial providentialist thought and theology.[4]

Two months after the Darien petition was issued, on March 13, 1739, the Salzburgers at Ebenezer endorsed the document, adding the practical concern that the presence of enslaved laborers would undermine Georgia's economy. The Germans rejected the assertion that enslaved Blacks were essential for the production of rice: "We were told by several people after our arrival, that it proves quite impossible and dangerous, for white people to plant and manufacture rice, being a work for Negroes, not for European people; we laugh at such a tale." The petitioners implored the Trustees not to legalize the importation of enslaved Blacks into the colony because experience had shown, they claimed, that houses and gardens would be robbed and the safety of white settlers jeopardized. They urged instead the immigration of additional members of their German clan.[5]

On June 20, 1739, the Trustees in London responded to Savannah's proslavery petitioners by expressing indignation toward the local magistrates and colonists who had signed the controversial document. Their proslavery appeals were rejected, the Trustees explained, because petitions from Darien and Ebenezer more convincingly warned of the inherent dangers that accompanied slavery. The presence of enslaved laborers would also encourage idleness among white Georgians and lead the colony to become like South Carolina, where Blacks greatly outnumbered the white population. In that event, the Trustees maintained, the colonists would almost certainly become the victims of servile insurrections and slave-assisted invasions by foreign enemies.[6]

In their analysis, the Trustees proved correct. A few months after the Savannah petition was rejected, enslaved Blacks in South Carolina mounted the bloodiest insurrection to erupt on the North American continent during the entire colonial period.

The Stono Rebellion

SEPTEMBER 9, 1739, DAWNED PEACEFULLY in bucolic Stono, a village located twenty miles west of Charles Town. The colonists casually went about their routines. Most, as was their custom, put on their Sunday best and went to church. Among the village residents, the Godfrey family broke from routine and stayed home.

On that deceptively quiet South Carolina morning roughly twenty enslaved Kongolese Africans broke into a public storehouse, beheaded Mr. Robert Bathurst and Mr. Gibbs, "took a pretty many Small arms and Power," and set out on a defiant and bloody march toward freedom. Following behind two of their leaders named Jemmy and Cato, the insurrectionists hoisted banners in the wind and marched to the rhythmic beat of African drums. They planned on cutting a 150-mile path of destruction through South Carolina and Georgia on their way to the sanctuary for freedom seekers in Spanish Florida. Their cries of "Liberty!" rang out in a jubilant symphony of rage and exhilaration.[1]

Gathering supporters along the way, their numbers swelled to nearly a hundred armed Black men, engulfing the countryside in flames and bloodshed. When the rebels came upon the Godfrey homestead, they killed Godfrey and his son and daughter, plundered and burned their house, and continued their frantic march. They made their way southward along Pons Pons Road, reaching Wallace's Tavern before daybreak, but the innkeeper's life was spared because "he was a good man and kind to his slaves." As South Carolina lieutenant governor John Bull was returning home from Charles Town, he encountered the heavily armed Blacks. He escaped with "much difficulty" and alerted the congregation at the Wiltown Presbyterian Church and local militiamen. The men armed themselves, left their women and children behind, and rushed off to suppress the insurrection. Meanwhile the rebellious, now self-emancipated Blacks continued their march, burning several homes and killing "all the white People they found."[2]

Late in the afternoon, the insurrectionists, tired or drunk with stolen rum and a premature taste of freedom, halted their ten-mile march in an open field near the Edisto River and celebrated by singing, dancing, and yelling. Meanwhile, militiamen and colonists quietly encircled the celebrants and opened fire. Though some of the rebels "behaved boldly," fourteen died in a deadly barrage of hot musket balls. The others ran for their lives into the nearby woods—except for "One Negro fellow" who recognized his former enslaver and advanced on him, brandishing a pistol. The slaveholder asked the man if he wanted to kill him. The emboldened Black man answered by pulling the trigger, but the pistol misfired and his former enslaver promptly "shot him thro' the Head."[3]

A few Blacks ran back to their places of enslavement, mistakenly believing their absences had not been detected. As with most of the details surrounding the insurrection, accounts provided by white sources vary on what happened next. Oglethorpe claims in an after-action report that despite ample provocation, the colonists did not torture the captured rebels but "put them to an easy death." However, several contemporary accounts sharply contradict Oglethorpe's assessment. According to one source, forty Black men were briefly interrogated and summarily shot, hanged, or "Gibbetted alive." Gibbetting was a gruesome form of capital punishment utilized by British officials during the early eighteenth century. The deliberate process involved the encasement of a doomed prisoner in a wooden contraption shaped in the outlined form of the human body, suspension on a gallows, and ultimate death by exposure to natural elements. A final postmortem indignity included the public viewing of the rotting, stinking gibbetted corpse. Yet another eyewitness reports that approximately fifty rebels "were taken by the planters who cut off their heads and set them up at every Mile Post" along the road to Stono. By another account, twenty-one whites and forty-four Blacks were killed during the uprising. The fate of an undetermined number of insurrectionists who avoided capture is not known. They may have joined settlements of freedom seekers along the Georgia-Florida border or made good on their escape to Saint Augustine.[4]

Robert Cato, the believed-to-be great-great-grandson of "Commander Cato," speaking nearly two hundred years after the Stono Rebellion was suppressed, provided a 1930s Works Progress Administration Federal Writers' Project interviewer with the only known African American version of the rebellion. According to Cato family oral history, forty-three of the surviving

Blacks surrendered their arms and were summarily executed by the militiamen. Although the uprising ultimately failed, Commander Cato's descendant spoke proudly of his ancestor: "As it comes down to me, I thinks de first Cato take a darin' chance on losin' his life, not so much for his own benefit as it was to help others. Dat is pow'ful fine for de Catoes who has come after him."[5]

In the immediate aftermath of the revolt, Georgia and South Carolina officials blamed the carnage on Spanish instigators, contending that outside agitators had incited the deadly uprising. The Georgia militia captured two Spaniards and imprisoned them for allegedly encouraging enslaved Blacks to escape. Fearing some Stono insurrectionists might have avoided capture in South Carolina, Oglethorpe issued a proclamation requiring the imprisonment of all Black people found in Georgia. He also established a reward for the capture of freedom seekers and dispatched a company of rangers to patrol Georgia's southern frontier with orders to seal off all escape routes to Florida.[6]

On November 29, 1739, a special committee of the South Carolina Common House of Assembly charged with investigating the circumstances surrounding the rebellion published a surprisingly frank assessment of the conflict: "an Engagement ensued . . . wherein one [side] fought for Liberty and Life, the other for their Country and every Thing that was dear to them." The legislators proudly detailed the actions of July, an enslaved Black man "belonging to Mr. Thomas Elliot [who] was clearly and chiefly instrumental in saving his Master and his Family from being destroyed by the Rebellious Negroes." According to the report, July "bravely fought against the Rebels and killed one of them." The committee members recommended that as "a reward for his faithful Services" and "Encouragement to other Slaves to follow his Example," the enslaved man should be granted his freedom and "a Suit of Cloths, Shirt, Hat, a pair of stockings and a pair of Shoes."[7]

Several other enslaved Blacks and Native Indians were said to have "behaved themselves very well and been a great source in opposing the Rebellious Negroes." It was further recommended that each enslaved man who fought to protect slaveholders be rewarded with "a Suit of Cloths, hat, shirt, pair of Shoes, and a pair of Stockings," while the women would receive "a Jacket, and Petticoat, a Shift, a pair of Stockings, and a pair of Shoes." It was also suggested that all enslaved Blacks cited in the report be paid "the sum of 20 [pounds] in Cash." The committee proposed that "Neighboring Indians" who assisted "in hunting for, taking and destroying the [said] Rebellious Negroes" be rewarded with "a Coat, a Flap, a Hat, a pair of Stockings," and "a Gun, 2 pounds of powder and 8 Pounds of Bullets." Whether or not Stono slaveholders followed through on the legislative recommendations is not known.[8]

Predictably, antislavery Georgia colonists used the insurrection to bolster their arguments. But proslavery advocates in Georgia were apparently unfazed by the bloodshed. In December 1740 eighty-four proslavery Savannah residents issued a counterpetition that contradicted the arguments raised by the men of Darien and Ebenezer. They rationalized that "the late insurrection in Carolina was not immediately [caused] from their having Negroes to do the laborious work—but it proceeded from their having too great a number of Negroes."[9]

The petitioners specifically lashed out at the Darienites, claiming that Oglethorpe had authored their petition and bribed the Scots into signing the document by promising additional livestock and provisions. Oglethorpe certainly exerted a major influence over the Darien Scots, since he had encouraged their migration to the colony, and the general also possessed a lifelong affinity for the Highland Scots and their culture. Nearly four decades later, in 1775, the legitimacy of their antislavery advocacy was buttressed by a later generation of Darienites who once again raised their voices in protest of the peculiar institution. They petitioned the leaders of the American Revolution to abolish slavery because it was "an unnatural practice . . . founded in injustice and cruelty."[10]

Despite the violent uprising in neighboring South Carolina—and with cavalier disregard for the slavery prohibition—Georgians persisted in exploiting illegal slave labor throughout the colony. William Stephens, secretary to the Georgia Trustees from 1737 to 1750, recorded numerous instances of violations of the prohibition in his official journal.[11]

Violations of the slavery ban were especially prevalent in and around the bustling frontier settlement of Augusta. Established by Oglethorpe in 1736, Augusta quickly became the principal warehousing center for the overland fur trade with the Muscogee and Cherokee Indians. One contemporary observer noted that white Augustans all but ignored the Trustees' slavery prohibition, extensively utilizing enslaved Blacks in the planting and harvesting of their crops. By 1740 the use of enslaved laborers was so widespread that a complaint filed with Savannah officials alleged it was almost impossible for white men to find work in the settlement. In 1741 Georgia Trustee John Viscount Percival, the Earl of Egmont, reported that at least eight Blacks were permanently living in the settlement and many others were serving as guides and laborers in the Indian trade.[12]

That same year, the Malcontents published a scathing petition titled "A True and Historical Narrative of the Colony of Georgia in America, 1741," which ridiculed Oglethorpe and the slavery prohibition. The petitioners, now residing in Charles Town, claimed a considerable quantity of corn had been harvested in and around Augusta, in large part with enslaved laborers. They contended that Augusta slaveholders profited from the labor of more than eighty enslaved Blacks who performed all of the more laborious agriculture tasks. Several Georgia planters who owned plantations on the South Carolina side of the Savannah River easily circumvented the slavery ban by transporting enslaved Blacks back and forth across the river. The use of illegal slave labor was so pervasive in the area that Augusta was considered by many to be a de facto South Carolina town. The proslavery pamphleteers also blamed the Trustees for the colony's deteriorating economic condition because they expected colonists to cultivate "lands without Negroes" and, even worse, to work "without titles to their lands."[13]

The following year, in 1742, Thomas Stephens published "The Hard Case of the Distressed People of Georgia," in which he argued that "after *Nine Years* Experiments" the Georgia colonization "*Scheme*" had proven to be "utterly impracticable" and a complete failure. Relying on the "climatic necessity" rationale, he asserted that "the extraordinary Heats" made it impossible for white men to clear lands and cultivate fields. Stephens lamented that South Carolina slaveholders enjoyed a distinct economic advantage over Georgia colonists, writing, "Besides, our Neighbours having such an advantage, as the Privilege of Negroes, can always under-sell us in any manufacture or produce." Stephens also leveled an accusation that would forever stain Oglethorpe's reputation. "General Oglethorpe," he wrote, "Gentleman of the Trust, (and one, who to all Appearances was as obstinately prejudiced against Negroes as any Man could be) . . . 'tis plain, is now become reconciled to their usefulness, as he keeps a number of them on his Plantation, bordering on Georgia."[14]

On April 26, 1742, William Stephens responded to his son's broadside by labeling the Malcontents as rabble-rousing "Breeders of Sedition" who cavalierly dismissed the Trustees' antislavery arguments as "Idle" insinuations. He also recorded in his journal Thomas Stephens's bombshell allegation that Oglethorpe owned a South Carolina plantation that exploited slave labor.[15]

Encouraged by the stridency of Georgia's proslavery lobby, violations of the colony's slavery ban proliferated during the 1740s. Enslaved Blacks constituted most of the boatmen and deckhands involved in the coastal sea trade on the Georgia–South Carolina coast, and they were heavily engaged as drovers and herders on the cattle trails between the Edisto and Altamaha Rivers. Plantation owner Paul Amatis avoided the statute by moving from Georgia to Purrysburg, in the South Carolina colony, and then transporting his enslaved laborers down the Savannah River to work on his plantation near Savannah. Another slaveholder by the name of Dyson also transported enslaved Blacks "to and fro betwixt" South Carolina and Georgia.[16]

The most sensational case recorded in William Stephens's journal involved a Captain Davis and an enslaved woman who cared for the physically disabled man and managed his lucrative trading business. According to Stephens, the unnamed "Damsel" not only had "an exceedingly fine Shape" but also possessed "good knowledge" of the business and demonstrated expertise in the maintenance of the accounts and ledgers. She enjoyed Davis's full confidence, exercising complete control over all cash receipts and disbursements. All the businessman's employees and customers were expected to treat her with respect. When a white male employee named Pope and the woman became embroiled in a heated argument that ended with the "naturally surly" Pope striking her across the face with a handheld fan, Davis subsequently fired Pope, who promptly filed a lawsuit against his former employer, claiming, among other things, that he had been unjustly terminated. Although Stephens's journal is silent on how the case was resolved, the presence of the enslaved woman was a clear violation of Georgia's antislavery statute.[17]

A Fortress of Freedom

THE TACIT APPROVAL OF SLAVERY in Georgia came with an exceed-ingly high price because Black people who bore the yoke of bondage did not submit meekly to perpetual slavery. Enslaved Blacks in and around the colony regularly ran off from their places of enslavement, hiding themselves deep in the swamps of South Georgia and northern Florida. From camps and iso-lated settlements, freedom seekers known as maroons—a word with Spanish origins meaning wild and unruly—conducted sporadic raids against nearby villages and farms. During these sometimes-deadly forays, they would steal provisions and liberate willing Blacks. As early as 1734 John Bolzius reported the existence of several such settlements along the Georgia-Florida border. From time to time, South Carolina and Georgia militia carried out retaliatory search-and-destroy missions against these self-emancipated Blacks.[1]

Most of the freedom seekers headed for Saint Augustine, the sanctuary for freedom seekers in Spanish Florida. A handful of Blacks from South Carolina, enslaved by Captain James McPherson, successfully negotiated the tortuous route to Saint Augustine in 1738. After wounding McPherson's son and killing another man in their escape, the Blacks slipped through the dense Georgia swamps. They passed near the Salzburger village of Ebenezer, where they narrowly avoided capture by local rangers. As they neared the Florida border, one Black man was wounded, and another killed in a skirmish with hostile Native Indians. The survivors eventually reached their destination, where Spaniards showered them with "great honors," and their leader was granted a financial commission and a "Coat faced with Velvet."[2]

Shortly after his arrival in the New World, Oglethorpe realized that Saint Augustine was an important military target, the key to preserving security and peace on Georgia's southern frontier. The slave insurrection at Stono, believed by the British to have been instigated by Spanish agents, forced re-lations between the two colonial powers to a breaking point. But Oglethorpe, aware that additional military support would be needed to launch a successful attack on heavily fortified Saint Augustine, awaited a more advantageous opportunity.[3]

In 1739 that opportunity came when war erupted between England and Spain, the culmination of years of bitter international trade and boundary disputes. The so-called War of Jenkins' Ear got its name from an incident in 1731 when Spanish sailors boarded a ship commanded by Captain Robert Jenkins, confiscated his cargo, and cut off one of his ears. Although the incident received little attention at the time, subsequent outrages against British merchant ships stoked anti-Spanish sentiment throughout the British Empire. Following the official declaration of war several years later, Oglethorpe rushed to invade Florida, but in his haste the newly appointed commander of the Georgia and South Carolina militia badly underestimated the strategic significance of Spain's long-standing policy of offering sanctuary to Blacks who escaped British enslavement.[4]

Oglethorpe was probably unaware of the existence of Fort Mose, a fortified enclave established in 1738 by Florida governor Manuel de Montiano on the St. Johns River two miles north of Saint Augustine. Now heavily defended by a hundred self-emancipated Blacks, the encampment would stand for a quarter century as a "Fortress of Freedom" and the destination of choice for freedom-seeking Blacks from South Carolina and Georgia. According to British reports, the fort was constructed of wood, banked with dirt, and surrounded by a shallow moat. The walls were lined with prickly foliage and the fortification consisted of a church, a well house, approximately twenty homes, and a lookout tower. The Fort Mose settlers farmed the fertile land surrounding the fort and fished in the saltwater river that ran through the settlement. The men were organized into a militia unit commanded by Francisco Menendez, a formerly enslaved Black man from South Carolina. On June 10, 1738, the unit had pledged allegiance to Montiano and promised to "always be the most cruel enemies of the English." The men vowed to spill their "last drop of blood" in defense of Spain and the Catholic faith.[5]

Oglethorpe began his Florida campaign in January 1740 by capturing two Spanish forts northwest of Saint Augustine, buttressing his plans to capture the city. Then, in February, he requested assistance from the South Carolina Assembly, which promised to provide money, five hundred militiamen, and seven hundred enslaved laborers. The assault on Saint Augustine commenced with an invasion force of seven warships from the Royal Navy and fifteen hundred ground troops composed of regular British soldiers reinforced by

Located in Spanish-controlled Florida, Fort Mose provided sanctuary for Black freedom seekers willing to join the Catholic Church and pledge military allegiance to the king of Spain.

(Courtesy of Florida Museum of Natural History—Historical Archaeology Collections)

Francisco Menendez

Francisco Menendez, captain of the Fort Mose militia, fought bravely during the British invasion of Spanish Florida in February 1739. His soldiers included self-emancipated Blacks and Seminole allies.

(Courtesy of Florida Museum of Natural History—Historical Archaeology Collections)

Isavel de Los Rios

A sketch of Isavel de Los Rios, a Fort Mose settler.

(Courtesy of Florida Museum of Natural History—Historical Archaeology Collections)

Georgia and South Carolina militiamen, as well as a large war party of Muscogee, Chickasaw, and Uchee Indians.[6]

As the British invaders approached Saint Augustine, a detail of Spaniards and Blacks feverishly worked to improve fortifications near Fort Mose, while Montiano ordered the Fort Mose militia and their families to retreat to safety behind the walls of Saint Augustine. Following the withdrawal, Oglethorpe directed 140 battle-hardened Scots from Darien to occupy the abandoned fort as a base of operations for the campaign. For several days the British hammered the town with cannon fire, but the continuous bombardment failed to dislodge the Spanish and Black defenders from their fortress. Thwarted in his frontal assault, Oglethorpe prepared a land and sea blockade, hoping to starve the enemy into submission.[7]

At dawn on June 26, 1740, a detachment of three hundred regular Spanish soldiers, the Fort Mose militia, and allied Seminole warriors launched a surprise strike that literally caught the British sleeping. Acting on Montiano's orders, the Spanish force slipped into the fort and overwhelmed Captain John McIntosh Mohr and his 170 men. Startled out of their sleep, the Scots "fought like lions" but were "cut . . . almost entirely to pieces," according to historian Hugh McCall. Sixty-three British soldiers were killed and twenty-six captured during the attack, including Mohr. Ironically, it was the Darien Scots, vocal supporters of Oglethorpe's slavery prohibition in Georgia, who suffered the most casualties in what would become known to the Spanish as the Battle of Bloody Mose.[8]

Survivors of the battle limped back to Darien, where they were greeted by the mournful skirl of Scottish bagpipes. A somber Georgia colonist there observed: "I am sorry that I have no better intelligence from these parts, than that the number of widows are much increased at Darien by their husbands being killed or taken at the late expedition to Saint Augustine." The Darien Scots had warned fellow colonists that enslaved Blacks would escape to Florida and help the Spanish wage war against their former enslavers. However, it was the antislavery Scots, not their proslavery neighbors, who were forced to drink the bitter brew of slave retribution. For their part, the South Carolinians, "enfeebled by heat, dispirited by sickness, and fatigued by fruitless efforts," simply abandoned the expedition.[9]

The ill-fated invasion came to its ignominious end when Spanish reinforcements arrived from Cuba, and the British fleet promptly withdrew from the Florida coast. The humbling defeat completely demoralized Oglethorpe and his men. The crestfallen militia commander was "reduced to an extraordinary Weakness by continual Fever . . . the Disappointment of Success . . . and too great Anxiety of the Mind." In a petition to King George II in July 1740, the South Carolina Assembly blamed their "ill success" at Saint Augustine on "danger from our own Negroes." In a letter to the British prime minister the following year, Oglethorpe further explained that his invasion force was repulsed by a much larger Spanish force—which, according to him, included 1,515 Spanish troops, 400 Black Havana militiamen, and a battalion of 300 mulatto troops.[10]

Meanwhile in Florida, a triumphant Governor Montiano congratulated his soldiers and wrote a special commendation for Francisco Menendez, captain of the Fort Mose militia. He praised Menendez for his loyal service, specifically noting his courage and valor during the Battle of Bloody Mose. He also recognized Menendez for having distinguished himself in the establishment of Fort Mose and encouraging his "subjects" to work hard and develop good customs.[11]

This would not be the end of the hostilities. Two years after their stunning victory, the Spanish launched a major counterattack against the British colonies to the north. In late June 1742, an armada composed of Spanish troops, the Fort Mose militia, and a regiment of Black soldiers from Cuba appeared off the Georgia coast, eventually landing and occupying an abandoned British fort on Saint Simons Island. The Black soldiers, according to British sources, enjoyed the respect and camaraderie of their Spanish allies. Black commanders were "clothed in lace, bore the same rank as the white officers, and with equal freedom and familiarity walked and conversed with their comrades and chief." The invaders went about the countryside proclaiming liberty to all enslaved Blacks and offering them freedom and sanctuary in eastern Florida.[12]

After sending a message to the South Carolinians warning them to guard against possible slave revolts, Oglethorpe set off to intercept the Spanish and redeem his reputation, by defeating the invaders who were marching up the Georgia coast. Without help from South Carolina, the Georgia militia defeated the Spanish in two decisive engagements on July 7, 1742. The first, the Battle of Gully Hole Creek, took place on Saint Simons Island near Fort Frederica. Later that day the British victory at the Battle of Bloody Marsh marked the turning point in the protracted struggle between England and Spain for control of the southeastern region of North America. The Trustees' prohibition against slavery in Georgia may have influenced the outcome of these important battles. If the Spanish had landed in South Carolina, with its large, enslaved population, instead of Georgia, where relatively few enslaved Blacks lived, their attempts to incite widespread insurrections would likely have been more successful.[13]

Montiano's failed invasion was Spain's last full-scale attempt to dislodge the British from the southeastern section of North America and heralded their eventual demise as a major military power on the North American continent. Ironically, Oglethorpe's victory at Bloody Marsh also eliminated what had been his most persuasive argument against the importation of enslaved Blacks into Georgia. With the erosion of the Spanish military threat, Georgia colonists no longer concerned themselves with the possibility of freedom seekers escaping to Florida and allying themselves with the Spaniards.[14]

Following a second failed invasion of Florida the following year, on July 22, 1743, Georgia's most ardent antislavery advocate, James Oglethorpe, departed his beloved colony. Despite his crucial victory at Bloody Marsh, he sailed to England, toward a future clouded by a pending court-martial and the possibility of personal financial ruin. The military proceedings that called him home had been initiated by a disgruntled militia officer who filed nineteen formal charges against Oglethorpe ranging from treason to "defrauding his regiment by making them pay for the provisions the Government sent them gratis." Meanwhile, acting on numerous complaints from proslavery Georgia colonists, British officials refused to reimburse him for substantial expenses he had incurred on behalf of the colony, pending a full accounting. Although he was subsequently vindicated on all charges and fully reimbursed, Oglethorpe never returned to Georgia.[15]

Ten Times Worse than Pagans

OGLETHORPE'S FORCED EXIT FROM THE colony was the opportunity that Georgia's proslavery contingent had long awaited. After nearly a decade of intense lobbying in Georgia and Parliament, repeal of the slavery prohibition was in sight. Oglethorpe's departure and the growing influence of proslavery activists fueled a proliferation of infractions and evasions of the slavery prohibition. On July 18, 1743, colonist John Dobell informed the Trustees by letter that "Negroes, nothing but Negroes" was the constant "cry" of his fellow colonists. By 1748 slave traffickers were disembarking chained Africans at the port of Savannah and openly auctioning them to the highest bidders. In May of that year, Lieutenant Colonel Alexander Heron, commander-in-chief of the Province of Georgia, claimed that legalized slavery was "the one needful thing," and everyone in the colony was aware that "Negroes have been in & about Savannah for these several years." According to him, local magistrates "knew & wink'd" at blatant violations of the antislavery statute.[1]

"Negro Fever" had even taken hold in Darien, where many of the Scots now supported repealing the slavery ban. All but forgotten was the 1739 antislavery petition and the prophecy of a day of retribution for slaveholders. At Ebenezer, staunch slavery critic Reverend Bolzius concluded that religious arguments alone could not stave off the institution, and reluctantly gave his support to the legalization of slavery.

Oglethorpe remained active with the Georgia Trustees and continued to advocate against repeal of the colony's founding principles. However, the death of John Percival, Oglethorpe's strongest ally among the Trustees, in May 1748 signaled the eminent demise of Georgia's slavery prohibition. He began attending Trustee meetings in London less often and, after his fellow social reformers voted to abandon the antislavery principles that had led to the establishment of the colony, Oglethorpe attended his last meeting on March 16, 1749.[2]

Although Oglethorpe was no longer actively involved in the Georgia trust, his strident antislavery advocacy may have influenced the drafting of the statute that would eventually legalize slavery in the colony. Following the conclusion of the "Grand Assembly" that convened in mid-1748, Bolzius proclaimed that in the event of a repeal, the enslavement of Blacks in Georgia "would be regulated by the most humane and sensible laws that could be formulated." Georgia's political leaders eagerly drafted and presented to the Trustees proposed legislation to repeal the slavery prohibition and regulate the importation of enslaved Blacks into the colony. Although several Trustees were skeptical that proslavery colonists would follow the provisions drafted to mitigate the brutality of enslavement, slavery was legalized in Georgia on January 1, 1751.[3]

The provisions of the new statute required slaveholders to (1) maintain one white male servant for every four enslaved males; (2) treat enslaved Blacks humanely; (3) register all Blacks born, sold, or imported into Georgia; (4) establish quarantines to prevent the transmission of contagious diseases; (5) support the production of silk by maintaining one enslaved woman, skilled in the art of winding silk, for every four enslaved men; (6) pay an import duty and a yearly per capita tax on all enslaved persons imported into the colony; (7) agree not to hire an enslaved person as an apprentice, and, most significantly, (8) require religious instruction be provided to all enslaved Blacks and observance of the Sabbath as a day of rest. Despite some nagging reservations, Georgia leaders aggressively, even recklessly, instituted the enabling mechanisms for legalized slavery. Within sixteen years of legalization, the number of enslaved Blacks in Georgia grew by nearly 800 percent, from about five hundred in 1750 to more than thirty-five hundred by 1766.

The most controversial provision of the new statute was the requirement of mandatory Christian instruction for enslaved Blacks. Since conversion required learning religious tenets and catechisms, a bitter debate raged throughout the colony regarding slave literacy and the existential threat it posed to the institution of slavery. Many Georgia slaveholders vehemently opposed teaching enslaved Black people to read and write, contending that such learned chattel would entertain dangerous thoughts and aspirations that produced a threat "ten times worse . . . than in his state of paganism." William Knox supported the effort to Christianize enslaved Blacks, but he argued that a Black man taught "to read one book will of himself read another, and such has been the imprudence of some ill-informed writers, that books are not wanting to exhort the Negroes to rebel against their masters." Knox claimed to have developed an alternative catechism that could be learned by memory and was better suited to the "capacities and conditions" of enslaved Blacks.[4]

Henry Melchior Muhlenberg, a German missionary who would later be recognized as the patriarch of the Lutheran Church in North America, recalled a revealing encounter with an enslaved young man at Ebenezer. According to Muhlenberg, the young Black Christian would spend half the day in the shade studying the Bible. Eventually, he informed the devout unnamed young man that, according to his interpretation of the Scriptures, "One must work if one would eat." With a "wry mouth," the enslaved young man informed his enslaver that this brand of Christianity "was not becoming or suitable to him." Muhlenberg summarized the incident: "The knowledge of letters even in the lowest degree, is too often supposed to carry with it a sort of qualification for an easy life, and an exemption from a laborious one and the latter being the Negroes lot, they might perhaps bear it with more unwillingness, or seek some desperate means of ridding themselves of it."[5]

In March 1751—less than three months after slavery was legalized—the Society for the Propagation of the Gospel (SPG), along with the Bray missionaries, appropriated funds to hire an itinerant teacher or schoolmaster to provide religious instruction to Blacks enslaved in Georgia. A year later the Trustees passed a resolution instructing the Common Council in the colony to appropriate an additional twenty pounds sterling to supplement the salary.[6]

Despite such official support, the first ministers to proselytize enslaved Blacks in the colony regularly clashed with slaveholders who preferred their bondsmen to remain illiterate and unsaved. In 1761 Joseph Ottolenghe, who had been born in Casale in Italy's Piedmont region and was a Jewish convert to Christianity, won election to the Georgia General Assembly. Following his appointment as catechist, Ottolenghe promised "to use his best endeavors, with Divine assistance," to bring about "the conversion of these ignorant people" to the kingdom of God.[7]

However, his efforts to provide a rudimentary Christian education to enslaved children were plagued by chronic pupil absenteeism, primarily the result of lukewarm support from slaveholders. In a letter dated December 20, 1750, Ottolenghe wrote: "Our school in Savannah at present consists of 41 children and might increase to many more if masters of slaves would shew a greater concern to have their young Negroes instructed and brought up in the knowledge and fear of God." He later complained that the number of pupils in his school fluctuated wildly between as many as fifty and as few as ten; some would attend for six months and then disappear for a year or longer. The painstaking educational process prompted the young missionary to conclude that "slavery is certainly a great Depressor of the Mind."[8]

Since many of Ottolenghe's enslaved pupils were from different African tribes and cultures, the language barrier posed a daunting challenge as well. "Our Negroes are so ignorant of ye English language, and none can be found to talk in their own," the teacher wrote. "It is a great while before you can get them to understand what ye learning of words is." Obviously frustrated, the instructor posed a rhetorical question: "How can a proposition be believed, without first being understood?" Hoping to solve this problem, William Knox suggested that missionaries limit their instruction to Blacks who had been born in British colonial America or those familiar with the English language. Following a year of instruction, Ottolenghe filed an encouraging report regarding the progress of these select pupils; they were learning quickly, several were reading "tolerably well," and the entire class had memorized the catechism.[9]

Ottolenghe was especially pleased by the efforts of an unnamed enslaved lay preacher who also provided Christian instruction to Black children. On June 4, 1752, he filed a glowing report: "After talks to them upon some of the moral duties . . . through God's blessing, he hath brought most of them through the Catechism, and some of their masters have acknowledged, that their slaves have grown better than heretofore." Although the mandatory Christianization provision was repealed in 1755, Ottolenghe continued to serve as schoolmaster to the Blacks of Georgia until 1759, when he was relieved of his duties by the SPG.[10]

During his tenure as rector of Christ Church in Savannah from 1745 to 1766, another cleric, Bartholomew Zouberbuhler, encouraged white members to allow enslaved adults to attend Sunday worship services. On July 7, 1750, Zouberbuhler and his congregation celebrated the opening of Christ Church, as well as the baptism of an enslaved woman—the first recorded baptism of a Black person in Georgia. Zouberbuhler originally proposed the establishment of a "Public School" for enslaved children, but slaveholder opposition forced him to employ itinerant catechists who visited the various plantations. When Zouberbuhler died in 1766, he directed through his will that income from one of his plantations, Beth Abrams, be held in trust and used to hire a qualified person to instruct the fifty-two enslaved Blacks living there in the principles of Christianity. The Beth Abrams trustees were also directed to manumit and ordain all enslaved adult males who excelled in their Christian studies.[11]

His trustees selected Cornelius Winter, a Methodist minister, to succeed Zouberbuhler as the religious instructor on the plantation. Shortly after Winter's arrival in 1769, Reverend George Whitefield warned him that he would be "whipped off" Beth Abrams by angry Georgia colonists if he tried to teach and Christianize enslaved Blacks. Whitefield was proven correct: Winter, who was derisively labeled the "Negro parson," suffered a barrage of threats and other forms of intimidation from Georgia colonists. An attempt was made in the local council to have him officially branded a public nuisance, but the measure failed to receive a majority vote. Winter abruptly left the colony after just twelve months and never returned.[12]

Early in 1770 Reverend John Rennie succeeded Winter as schoolmaster to Blacks enslaved at Beth Abrams and pastor of Christ Church in Savannah. But the gathering storm of the American Revolution put an end to his missionary work in Georgia. In September 1777 Rennie was forced to leave the American colonies because of his alleged loyalty to the British. Although the war ended the work of Anglican missionaries among Georgia's enslaved population, the occupation of Savannah by British troops in 1779 would later open a new pathway to religious freedom for enslaved Blacks. In war-torn Savannah three Black preachers—George Liele, David George, and Jesse Peter—would convert hundreds of freedom seekers. These pioneer evangelists established the Black preacher as principal community spokesperson and their churches as the cornerstone of institutional life in free and enslaved Black communities.[13]

Decades later, a delegation of Black ministers, the majority of whom received their ministerial and leadership training at Savannah-area Black churches, would meet with triumphant Union general William T. Sherman in Savannah. The Black clergymen advised Sherman that newly freed Blacks should be allowed to pursue a path of self-determination through landownership. Sherman's revolutionary plan to temporarily redistribute Confederate lands to freedmen would become known as "Forty Acres and a Mule."[14]

Arming Enslaved Soldiers

THE DEBATE OVER THE EDUCATION and Christianization of enslaved Black Georgians—though certainly contentious—paled in comparison to the virulent controversy that swirled around another pressing question that arose after the slavery prohibition repeal: Should enslaved Black men be armed in defense of the colony?

Although Oglethorpe's victory at Bloody Marsh had severely weakened Spain as a colonial power in the Southeast, the British were still engaged in long-running hostilities with France and their Native Indian allies. The fierce backcountry fighting during the French and Indian War, from 1756 to 1763, also known as the Seven Years' War, grew out of conflicting claims between England and France over territory in the Ohio River valley. During the early 1750s the threat of full-scale war with France intensified and Georgia leaders desperately sought to improve the colony's meager defenses. The colonial militia was severely undermanned, primarily because of inadequate funding and a shortage of white adult males available for service.

Many slaveholders and overseers dared not leave their farms and plantations unguarded, a predicament Oglethorpe had foreseen some twenty years earlier. Now the only immediate solution to the colony's problem appeared to be conscription of enslaved Black men in the militia. In *The Sailor's Advocate*, published in 1729, Oglethorpe had argued against the practice of impressment or forcing British subjects to serve on Royal Navy ships. "How can it be expected," he wrote, "that a Man should fight for the Liberty of others, whilst he himself feels the pangs of Slavery, or expose his Life to defend the property of a Nation, where his dearest pledges, his Wife and Children, are pining away with want." Nevertheless, the General Assembly soon enacted the Militia Act of 1755, which noted in its preamble that "several Negroes and other slaves have in Time of War behaved themselves with great faithfulness and courage in repelling attacks of his Majesty's Enemies."[1]

The new law required slaveholders to maintain a census of all Black males between the ages of sixteen and sixty, and it promised freedom to enslaved soldiers who "shall courageously behave . . . in battle so as to kill any one of the enemy or take a prisoner alive," the caveat being that the act of heroism must have been witnessed by a white soldier. Less heroic service by an enslaved soldier would receive "public notice," and on each anniversary of the Black man's act of valor, he was to be exempted from all personal labor and service by his enslaver. According to the statute, each enslaved soldier would be issued, at the expense of the public treasury, a livery coat, breeches made of "red Negro Cloth turned up with Blue," a black hat, and a pair of black shoes.[2]

To overcome opposition by slaveholders who were fearful of potential economic losses, the authors of the act provided that slaveholders would be paid one shilling per diem during each enslaved soldier's tour of duty. Slaveholders were also entitled to the "full value" of any enslaved Black soldier killed in the line of duty, as well as reasonable compensation for those who may be injured or disabled. On June 17, 1760, the Council of Safety, fearful of slave insurrections, amended the Militia Act by requiring an examination of the histories of all enslaved soldiers to determine their trustworthiness. Only one-third of such qualified enslaved Black men could be conscripted into the militia at one time, apparently to guard against the unwelcome possibility of enlisting a majority Black militia.[3]

These provisions were drafted to allay the fears of colonists who worried that armed Black militiamen would rebel against their enslavers. Much of this apprehension was fomented by the *Georgia Gazette*, the colony's only newspaper, which published detailed and gruesome accounts of slave rebellions throughout the British Empire. An April 1763 report, for example, told of Black insurrectionists in what is now Guyana who, "in the most cruel manner, murdered all the white people they could come at." In that same issue, another article detailed the events surrounding a Jamaican uprising in which several enslaved men "butchered" a slaveholder by cutting off his hands, arms, feet, and legs.[4]

When the French and Indian War ended in victory for the British in 1763, Georgia colonists looked forward to greater safety and prosperity. Only a few skirmishes had been fought in the colony, rendering a full-scale mobilization of enslaved soldiers unnecessary. The two most powerful British colonial adversaries, Spain and France, had now been vanquished, setting the stage for a postwar population boom, fueled by a highly profitable slavery-driven economy. But there were troubling side effects: white Georgians were being forced to confront complex and disturbing issues associated with the growing number of enslaved Blacks living in their midst.

In the three decades that followed Oglethorpe's departure from Georgia, chattel slavery became firmly entrenched in the colony, and the dire consequences he predicted would accompany legalized slavery were beginning to materialize. A series of violent events had already shown that white Georgians lived under the threat of slave retaliation, organized rebellion, and alliance with foreign invaders. The concentration of wealth in the hands of a small number of slave traders and plantation owners had also spawned a growing underclass of poor, landless white Georgians. Oglethorpe must have ruminated over Georgia's plight: his utopian dream of an "American Zion" was being trampled on by those who profited and benefited from the enslavement of Black people.[5]

III

"Give Me Liberty or Give Me Death!"

A Sincere Lover of Justice

ONE YEAR AFTER OGLETHORPE RETURNED to England, on September 15, 1744, the forty-seven-year-old general married thirty-five-year-old Elizabeth Wright, a wealthy heiress. The couple lived primarily at Cranham Hall, her sprawling estate located nineteen miles on the northeastern outskirts of London, and maintained a townhome in London. As noted previously, Oglethorpe remained active with the Georgia Trustees and continued to advocate against repeal of the prohibition against slavery. Following the death of his ally John Percival, Earl of Egmont, in May 1748, Oglethorpe began attending Trustee meetings less often, and after his fellow Trustees voted to abandon the antislavery principles that had led to the colony of Georgia's establishment, he attended his last meeting on March 16, 1749. Without Oglethorpe's strident voice of opposition, the Trustees quickly transmitted legislation to Parliament to repeal Georgia's slavery ban. The adopted statute legalized slavery in Georgia on January 1, 1751.[1]

This abandonment of the Georgia plan's philosophical cornerstone would be followed by Oglethorpe's stinging defeat in a bid for reelection to Parliament in 1754. He then returned to service in the British military, fought in the Seven Years' War, lived for a brief period with his sister in Paris, and in 1768 waged another unsuccessful campaign to regain a seat in the House of Commons. Thereafter, Oglethorpe managed to reinvent himself as a celebrated senior statesman and member of London's literati.[2] But although he was no longer engaged in military or public service, Oglethorpe maintained a keen interest in Georgia, as well as developing a deepening aversion to the transatlantic slave trade. Despite the proliferation of slavery in his beloved colony, the elderly but still spry Oglethorpe was the center of gravity for an eclectic circle of antislavery friends and acquaintances.

Oglethorpe's cadre of like-minded Britons included Beilby Porteus, the Anglican bishop of Chester and of London who was the first Anglican leader to criticize the church's position on the transatlantic slave trade; attorney

GEN. JAMES OGLETHORPE.

This sketch was taken in February preceeding his decease when he
was reading without spectacles at the sale of the library of Dr S. Johnson.

W. & J. O. Sharp's Lith. Boston.

History remembers James Oglethorpe as the founder of Georgia, but later in life he advocated for the abolition of slavery.

(*Elderly James Oglethorpe*, lithograph, from Thaddeus Mason Harris, *Biographical
Memorials of James Oglethorpe Founder of the Colony of Georgia, North America*
[Boston: Freeman & Bolles, 1841])

Capel Lofft, an antislavery activist; and, most notably, Dr. Samuel Johnson, the preeminent and prolific British literary talent of the eighteenth century who had, among other works, compiled his *Dictionary of the English Language*, which predated the *Oxford English Dictionary* by 150 years.[3]

Johnson was a frequent dinner guest at the Oglethorpe home, and according to his biographer James Boswell, who espoused an opposing position, the loquacious Johnson was "very zealous against slavery." During one dinner party at Oxford University in 1769, the boisterous wine-drenched conversation had turned to several bloody slave insurrections that had occurred in British colonies throughout the Atlantic world when Johnson interrupted the drunken banter by offering a shocking toast: "Here's to the next insurrection of the Negroes in the West Indies." Writing in 1776, Johnson pinned an essay titled *Taxation No Tyranny: An Answer to the Resolutions and Address of the American Congress*, in which he mocked slaveholding American patriots by proclaiming, "How is it that we hear the loudest yelps for liberty among the drivers of Negroes?" Following his death in 1784, Johnson bequeathed his entire estate to Frank Barber, a formerly enslaved Jamaican he had educated and adopted as a surrogate son.[4]

Most significantly, Oglethorpe befriended and mentored three emerging British abolitionists who would shape the course of events throughout the Americas and the British Empire: Granville Sharp, Hannah More, and Olaudah Equiano. The general encouraged and inspired Sharp, a tireless slavery critic, to lobby Parliament to adopt legislation abolishing slavery. He awakened the moral outrage of Hannah More, an early feminist writer, who used her pen to ignite a national backlash against the British transatlantic slave trade. And he served as an advisor to Equiano, a self-emancipated man who would become eighteenth-century England's most influential Black abolitionist.

History is silent regarding how, when, or where James Oglethorpe and Olaudah Equiano first became acquainted. Whatever the circumstance, in addition to their disdain for slavery, the two men shared a detailed knowledge of the Georgia colony. As a master seafarer and world traveler, Equiano had visited Georgia on several occasions, as both an enslaved and free man.

In his autobiography, *The Interesting Narrative of the Life of Olaudah Equi-*

ano, or Gustavus Vassa, the African, Equiano recounts that during his adolescence he was kidnapped by indigenous slave raiders, sold to several different African slaveholders, and eventually taken to the Atlantic coast, where he was purchased by British slavers and shipped to the Virginia colony. Michael Pascal, a British naval lieutenant, purchased Equiano and renamed him Gustavus Vassa, after the king of Sweden.[5]

Initially, Equiano refused to acknowledge his new name, but after several beatings he relented. He traveled with Pascal to England on multiple occasions and was sent to a school for Black children by his enslaver's relatives. The enslaved young man was subsequently trained to be a sailor and saw action in several naval battles in Canadian waters and in the Mediterranean during the Seven Years' War between England and France. After the war ended, Pascal reneged on his promise to free Equiano and instead sold him to Captain James Doran of the Royal Navy. Heartbroken and despondent, Equiano "called upon God's thunder, and his avenging power, to direct the stroke of death to me, rather than permit me to . . . be sold from lord to lord." Despite his fervent prayers for deliverance from bondage, he was sold again in May 1763 to Robert King, a Quaker merchant and slave trader stationed in Montserrat.[6]

According to Equiano, King was "very charitable and humane" to him, compared to other British slaveholders. He was surprised when his enslaver encouraged him to earn income for himself by selling small goods and fruit during their numerous trading missions to Georgia and other British colonies. However, chief among the "commodities" King traded and sold were enslaved Black men, women, and children. Equiano recalled that he was "often a witness to cruelties of every kind, which were exercised on my unhappy fellow slaves." He grimly confirmed what former slave ship captain John Newton noted was a frequent practice on British slave ships: the serial rape of enslaved Black girls and women. "I used . . . to have different cargoes of new Negroes in my care for sale," Equiano recorded, "and it was almost a constant practice with our clerks, and other whites, to commit violent depredations on the chastity of the female slaves—I have known our mates to commit these acts most shamefully, to the disgrace, not of Christians only, but of men. I have even known them to gratify their brutal passion with females not ten years old; and these abominations some of them practiced to such scandalous excess, that one of our captains discharged the mate and others on that account."[7]

Equiano also documented harrowing eyewitness accounts of the violence and indignities perpetrated against enslaved Blacks. He recalled an incident involving an enslaved man who was "staked to the ground, and cut most shockingly, and then his ears cut off bit by bit, because he was connected to a white woman who was a common prostitute." Another enslaved Black man was "half hanged, and then burnt, for attempting to poison a cruel overseer." Equiano pointed out that "many humane gentlemen, by not residing on their estates, are obliged to leave the management of them in the hands of the human butchers (overseers), who cut and mangle the slaves in a shocking manner on the most trifling occasions."[8]

On July 11, 1766, due to "God's grace," hard work, and thrift, the industrious twenty-one-year-old Equiano paid forty pounds to King in exchange for his freedom. Equiano recalled the overwhelming emotion that accompanied his self-manumission: "Heavens! who could do justice to my feelings at this moment! ... My feet scarcely touched the ground, for they were winged with joy.... I who had been a slave in the morning, trembling at the will of another, was become my own master, and completely free. I thought this was the happiest day I had ever experienced; and my joy was still heightened by the blessings and prayers of the sable race, particularly the aged, to whom my heart had ever been attached with reverence." Equiano initially wanted to relocate to England but subsequently decided to remain in Montserrat and work for his former enslaver. Though he had managed to achieve his cherished goal of emancipation, Equiano was constantly reminded of dangers that shadowed the life of a free Black man living in a racialized society, now tormented daily by racial discrimination, hatred, violence, and the fearful prospect of being sold back into bondage.[9]

Two decades after Oglethorpe's departure from Georgia, Equiano would experience how fully the colony had embraced the racist practices of its neighboring slaveholding societies. On numerous trading missions to Georgia before and after his manumission, Equiano was viciously beaten by two white men and jailed for burning a candle after nine o'clock in the evening; he barely escaped being kidnapped and re-enslaved. Although he was befriended by enslaved Blacks, given lifesaving treatment by a benevolent white doctor, and, after hearing a sermon preached by evangelist George Whitefield, converted to Christianity, Equiano's experience had been brutal. Following his final trading mission to the colony in the spring of 1767, Equiano wrote: "I thus took a final leave of Georgia; for the treatment I had received in it disgusted me very much against the place."[10]

By the spring of 1774 Equiano was living in London and sought General Oglethorpe's counsel and assistance. His close friend John Annis, a former enslaved person, had been arrested in England and re-enslaved on the Caribbean island of Saint Kitts, a British colony. Equiano and Annis had become acquainted the previous year when they both served on Captain John Hughes's ship, the *Anglicania*, during a voyage to Smyrna in Turkey. Hearing Equiano recount the details of the case, Oglethorpe "advised" him to "call on" Granville Sharp, a young attorney who had gained notoriety by representing several formerly enslaved Blacks threatened with re-enslavement. In a landmark legal ruling in the fight against British chattel slavery, Sharp had recently represented James Somerset, a freedom seeker who was emancipated on June 22, 1772, by Lord Chief Justice Mansfield, who ruled that chattel slavery was not supported by British law. The judge based his decision on the rationale that Parliament had not officially adopted a statute legalizing slavery in the mainland of England.[11]

According to the report of King's Bench cases published by Capel Lofft, a respected legal writer and attorney, Mansfield had ruled that "the state of slavery is of such a nature, that it is incapable of being introduced on any reasons, moral or political: but only positive law, which preserves its force long after the reasons, occasion, and time itself from whence it was created, is erased from memory: it's so odious, that nothing can be suffered to support it but positive law." Thus, the legendary jurist concludes, any enslaved person who "breathes British air . . . is forever free." Lofft's expansive interpretation of Mansfield's ruling was widely disseminated and celebrated by free and enslaved Blacks and antislavery whites throughout the British Empire. This, in the words of G. M. Ditchfield, "allowed the nascent anti-slavery movement to derive a considerable political advantage," but it also led to confusion surrounding the legal implications of the decision and inconsistent enforcement, limiting its legal impact on the lives of the fourteen thousand enslaved Blacks living in England. More importantly, the decision did not apply to British colonies in the Caribbean and North America, where slavery continued to flourish.[12]

Nonetheless, Sharp was a hero to those who fought against British chattel slavery. As Equiano wrote, "I proceeded immediately to that philanthropist, Granville Sharp, Esq. who received me with the utmost kindness, and gave me every instruction that was needful on the occasion. I left him in full hope that I should obtain the unhappy man his liberty." Though the meeting between Equiano, a former enslaved person, and Sharp, the emerging abolition-

Olaudah Equiano visited Georgia as an enslaved and free man. Equiano was mercilessly beaten by a white colonist in Georgia. As an abolitionist in Britain, he was befriended by James Oglethorpe.

Attorney Granville Sharp was General James Oglethorpe's friend and
mentee who advocated against British chattel slavery. Sharp and Olaudah
Equiano formed an influential interracial partnership that spurred the
birth of the formal abolitionist movement in England.

ist, would develop into an influential interracial partnership, their relationship did not begin smoothly. After Sharp failed to secure the release of his friend, Equiano lashed out, writing that "my attorney proved unfaithful; he took my money, lost me many months of employ, and did not the least good in the cause." Notwithstanding his initial frustrations, within a decade the two men would join forces again.[13]

On September 26, 1776, two and a half years after he directed Equiano to retain Sharp, Oglethorpe himself wrote a letter of introduction to the young attorney he had admired from afar. Writing at the dawn of the American Revolution, Oglethorpe praised Sharp's recently published volume, *The Law of Retribution: A Serious Warning to Great Britain and Her Colonies, Founded on Unquestionable Examples of God's Temporal Vengeance against Tyrants, Slaveholders and Oppressors*. In the book Sharp argued that an angry God would exact divine vengeance on anyone who profited from the enslavement of Black people and that England's propagation of the transatlantic slave trade was a national sin that would result in cataclysmic consequences for the British people.[14]

Oglethorpe himself was a longtime adherent of such a view. Almost four decades earlier, he may have authored or at least influenced the first antislavery petition issued by the Darien Scots in Georgia, which incorporated providentialist themes in their arguments. Now, Oglethorpe praised Sharp in his letter: "I was greatly rejoiced to find that so laborious and learned a man had appeared as champion for the rights of mankind, against avarice, extortion, and inhumanity," he wrote, "that you had, with heroic courage, dared to press home, on an infidel, luxurious world, the dreadful threats of the Prophets. The ruins of Babylon, Memphis, and Tyre, are strong mementos to a Paris, a London, and a Lisbon, of the retribution paid to those who fat their luxuries on the labour of wretched slaves." Oglethorpe was convinced the "unnatural war" that had broken out between England and the British colonists in America was a divinely ordained national punishment for England's exploitation of enslaved Black laborers.[15]

On September 27 Sharp wrote a gracious response thanking Oglethorpe for his words of encouragement and support. Sharp candidly acknowledged being deeply troubled by the prospect that his "poor attempts to warn the public of approaching evils" were weak and ineffective. Nevertheless, Sharp was delighted that his efforts had earned the approval of "sincere lover(s) of justice" like General Oglethorpe.[16]

On October 13 Oglethorpe penned another extraordinary letter to Sharp, recalling with great enthusiasm the fight he had waged to prohibit the importation of enslaved Blacks into Georgia. Although they faced vehement proslavery opposition, Oglethorpe asserted that he and his fellow Trustees resolved not "to make a law permitting such a horrid crime." His antipathy toward the men who worked to legalize slavery in Georgia had intensified over the years, and Oglethorpe lambasted those colonists who had lobbied British officials to repeal the ban on slavery.[17]

Relying on his extensive knowledge of ancient civilizations, Oglethorpe laid out a sweeping historical analysis that depicted slavery as inhumane and ungodly. He castigated ancient Romans for originating the "cruel custom" of chattel slavery that was subsequently adopted throughout the Western Hemisphere. According to Oglethorpe, the Romans created an absurd "solecism": the Roman state granted to the slaveholder greater power over the enslaved than the state could exercise over the enslaver himself. He also claimed that the "horrid cruelty" of slavery incited Spartacus to inspire a slave rebellion that almost felled the mighty Roman Empire.[18]

Oglethorpe buttressed this last accusation by enumerating a damning bill of particulars detailing atrocities committed by Roman slaveholders against their enslaved. Decius Brutus, a wealthy Roman general and politician who kept enslaved gladiators, was maligned for defending the conspirators who plotted to murder Julius Caesar. He noted one especially gruesome occurrence when four hundred "innocent slaves" were executed because "two fellow slaves" allegedly murdered their Roman enslaver. In another incident "useless" enslaved elderly people were thrown into a pond so that their enslaver's fish could consume "an excellent taste."[19]

Continuing his critique, Oglethorpe referenced historical research conducted by the explorer Sir Walter Raleigh, which led Oglethorpe to conclude that slavery had precipitated the collapse of several once-dominant empires. The Greeks and Persians, he argued, were conquered because "vast numbers of slaves" heeded the call of Islamic invaders, who offered freedom to those who would profess the Muslim faith and take up arms against their former enslavers. Oglethorpe's opinions no doubt were informed by the military prowess of self-emancipated Blacks who had helped defeat his own forces during the Battle of Bloody Mose in February 1740.[20]

With little supporting evidence, Oglethorpe then surmised that Rome's "*Christian* Emperors" would have adopted more humane laws regulating the treatment of the enslaved if pagan senators had not circumvented their ef-forts. He referenced Saint Augustine, who argued that idolatry, not Chris-tianity, had led to the decline and fall of the Roman Empire. Oglethorpe claimed that heathenism was the root cause of Roman capitulation because slavery was "sunk into the marrow" of pre-Christian Romans. He concluded his searing attack by arguing that the sacking of Rome by Germanic Visigoths in 410 CE was "necessary dispensation of Providence to root out idolatry."[21]

Oglethorpe then brought his argument forward and redirected his ire to-ward David Hume, the eighteenth-century Scottish Enlightenment philoso-pher whom Sharp had criticized for asserting that Black people were geneti-cally inferior to white Europeans. An early proponent of what became known as scientific racism, Hume had argued that dark-skinned people were incapa-ble of civilized behavior. In *Of National Characters, Essays Moral, Political and Literary* he wrote, "I am apt to suspect the Negroes and in general all other species of men—(for there are four or five different kinds) to be naturally infe-rior to the whites. There never was a civilized nation of any other complexion than white, nor even any individual eminent either in action or speculation. No ingenious manufactures amongst them, no arts, no sciences."[22]

Oglethorpe then concurred with Sharp in angrily challenging Hume's racist theories. "You mention an argument by Hume, that the Africans were incapable of liberty, and that no man capable of government was ever pro-duced by Africa. What a historian!" he exclaimed. Oglethorpe continued, "He must never have heard of Shishak, the great Sesostris, of Hannibal, or of Tir-haka [also spelled Taharqa or Tirhakah], king of Ethiopia, whose very name frightened the mighty Assyrian monarch."

In a single flourish, Oglethorpe had referenced Shishak, a Black Egyptian pharaoh whose defeat of the kingdom of Judah and sacking of Jerusalem is chronicled in 1 Kings 14:25; Sesostris I, a twelfth-dynasty Black Egyptian pharaoh who conquered much of present-day Turkey, Georgia, and Romania, along with ancient Greece; Hannibal, the legendary military leader from the North African city-state of Carthage, who famously crossed the Alps and waged war against the Romans in 218 BCE; and Tirhaka the warrior king of Ethiopia, who challenged the powerful Assyrian Empire, conquered Egypt, and served as pharaoh over the consolidated kingdoms during the fifteenth Ethiopian dynasty.[23]

Oglethorpe followed with a condescending rhetorical question: Was it possible Hume had never read Herodotus, where the mighty works of the

Egyptians who built the ancient pyramids are chronicled? Or the celebrated *Description of Africa*, published by the explorer and diplomat Leo Africanus in 1550 and now considered by antiquarians to be the most accurate and detailed treatise on the African continent prior to its modern exploration? Oglethorpe reasoned that if Hume had studied the matter, he would have discovered "that Africa had produced races of heroes."[24]

Oglethorpe concluded his lengthy text by congratulating Sharp for his advocacy: "You have with great judgement, showed the threats of the Prophets against the slave-owners and slave-sellers." He was "exceedingly glad" the attorney had "entered the lists in opposition to these horrors." Oglethorpe then implored Sharp to lobby Parliament to enact legislation that would abolish slavery throughout the British Empire. He contended that it was "proper time to bring these abominable abuses under consideration" by imploring the members of Parliament who possessed the "power of legislation" to "correct" the inhumane practice.[25]

The language and tenor of his revealing jeremiad provides compelling evidence that Oglethorpe's antislavery activism had evolved into the uncompromising moral outrage that would define radical abolitionism. The implications of Oglethorpe's directive to Sharp would have been revolutionary. Almost 250 years ago, when Oglethorpe wrote those provocative words, millions of human beings bore the weight of perpetual bondage. In a world dominated by forced uncompensated labor, most white Europeans were convinced that Blacks were subhuman and genetically preconditioned to endure backbreaking labor. Millions of devout white Christians believed that Blacks were also preordained to be enslaved and incapable of spiritual redemption. More importantly, the lucrative transatlantic slave trade was the cornerstone of England's booming late eighteenth-century economy. The almost universal acceptance of chattel slavery throughout the British Empire rendered the adoption or even the consideration of legislation by Parliament that would regulate or abolish slavery all but inconceivable.

For his part, Sharp returned Oglethorpe's admiration. After reading an early history of Georgia that chronicled Oglethorpe's efforts to prohibit slavery in the colony, Sharp informed the colony's founder by letter that he had gained "much greater esteem" for him. He praised Oglethorpe for supporting and defending the "noble principles" that led to the enactment of Georgia's slavery prohibition. Sharp noted that Oglethorpe's exemplary behavior was a "most instructive and exemplary piece of history" and correctly predicted that his pioneering antislavery strategies would be adopted by "present and future ages." He counseled Oglethorpe to "enjoy the heartfelt satisfaction" derived from having practiced the "disinterested principles and duties" that Sharp himself had "only been able to recommend in theory."[26]

Sharp graciously accepted Oglethorpe's subsequent invitation to visit with him at his London residence on Lower Grosvenor Street, and the two men developed a close "friendship" that was sustained with the most "cordial sincerity." Sharp agreed to write a new introduction to Oglethorpe's influential (and still anonymously written) book, *The Sailor's Advocate*. He would later incorporate elements of Oglethorpe's Savannah settlement design into his plans for the establishment of a colony for formerly enslaved Blacks on the west coast of Africa.[27]

During this period, General Oglethorpe also maintained an endearing relationship with Hannah More, a pioneering feminist and one of eighteenth-century England's most prolific and influential authors. Born in 1745, she abandoned a career as a teacher and successful playwright to devote her literary talents to promoting the Christian faith. More and Oglethorpe became acquainted in 1784, when he voiced support for and defended the "Bluestockings," a small society of "women writers and intellectuals, who were ridiculed and attacked on every side." Judging from available historical accounts, the two were completely infatuated with each other. The beautiful thirty-nine-year-old author wrote whimsically to her sister about their relationship: "I have got a new admirer, and we flirt together prodigiously; it is the famous General Oglethorpe, perhaps the most remarkable man of his time . . . the finest figure you ever saw. He perfectly realizes all my ideas of Nestor. His literature is great, his knowledge of the world extensive, and his faculties as bright as ever; —He is perhaps the oldest man of a gentlemen living. I went to see him the other day, and he would have entertained me by repeating passages from Sir Eldred. He is quite a preux chevalier, heroic, romantic, and full of old gallantry." The following year More wrote another note to her sister: "I am just going to flirt a couple of hours with my beau, General Oglethorpe."[28]

More and Oglethorpe's mutual infatuation was fueled by a shared desire to promote social justice and economic progress throughout the British Empire. Very likely, it was Oglethorpe who nurtured More's interest in the abolition of the transatlantic slave trade and "prepared her for a commitment to the emerging abolitionist movement." In 1785 More was awestruck by a

Hannah More, a pioneer British feminist author, and General James Oglethorpe were infatuated with each other. More was also one of the founders of the formal abolitionist movement.

powerful sermon preached by Sir John Newton, the former slave ship captain turned abolitionist. Shortly afterward William Wilberforce, the outspoken abolitionist leader in Parliament, convinced More to use her literary skills to advance the abolitionist cause. Her best-known work, *Slavery: A Poem*, was published in 1788 to coincide with the first debate about slavery to be conducted in Parliament:

> Shall Britain, where the soul of Freedom reigns,
> Forge chains for others she herself disdains
> Forbid it, Heaven! O let the nations know
> The liberty she loves she will bestow;
> Not to herself the glorious gift confined,
> She spreads the blessing wide as humankind;
> And, scorning narrow views of time and place,
> Bids all be free in earth's extended space.
> What page of human annals can record
> A deed so bright as human rights restored?
> O may that godlike deed, that shining page,
> Redeem OUR fame and consecrate OUR age![29]

Because only a relatively small number of enslaved Blacks lived in England, most Britons had never witnessed the brutality of the slave trade firsthand. More's poem asserted the humanity of Africans and exposed the hypocrisy of freedom-loving Britons who profited or benefited from the enslavement of Black people and helped stoke a growing British abolitionist fervor.

"A Very Uncommon Case"

ON MARCH 19, 1783, OLAUDAH EQUIANO hurried through the streets of London on his way to a meeting with attorney Granville Sharp, a now celebrated antislavery activist. All but forgotten was his frustration with Sharp after the lawyer had failed earlier to rescue his friend John Annis from re-enslavement. During the ten years that followed Oglethorpe's recommendation that he retain the young attorney to represent Annis, Sharp had earned the admiration of antislavery activists throughout England by representing scores of formerly enslaved Blacks threatened with re-enslavement. Equiano was confident Sharp would be appalled by the news he was carrying about the horrific events that had transpired on the slave ship *Zong*.[1]

The saga of the *Zong* began on September 6, 1781, when the British slaver set sail from the Atlantic coast of Africa with 442 chained men, women, and children packed below deck. During the three-month Middle Passage to Jamaica, the overcrowded, filthy conditions on the 110-ton vessel led to a deadly outbreak of dysentery and scurvy. Six weeks into the trip more than sixty captured Africans and seven crew members had died. James Collingwood, a former slave ship's surgeon serving on his first voyage as captain, also became stricken with a debilitating illness that left him weakened and bedridden.[2]

The *Zong*'s precarious state spiraled into crisis when Collingwood steered the ship three hundred miles off course from its intended destination. As the ship wandered in the open seas, some crew members alleged that a large quantity of fresh water had leaked from the *Zong*'s rotting casks. One eyewitness later claimed the captain informed his crew that there was not enough fresh water to sustain both the ship's crew and the captured Africans. While "in a delirium, or fit of lunacy," Collingwood made a fateful decision. He ordered that all captives that showed signs of illness be thrown into the ocean to preserve the lives of the crew and as many healthy Africans as possible.[3]

The ship finally arrived at Black River, Jamaica, on December 22, 1781, with 208 captured Africans *and* 430 gallons of fresh water on board. The surviving captives were auctioned to Jamaica slaveholders for an average price of thirty-six pounds apiece. Collingwood's health continued to deteriorate; he died three days after the *Zong* made landfall. The ship then proceeded to Liverpool, England, where James Gregson, the *Zong's* owner, subsequently submitted a claim against his insurers for 4,000 pounds to cover the value of 132 of the 143 Africans who lost their lives during the massacre. Following two years of contentious and fruitless negotiations, Gregson and his business partners filed suit against their insurance underwriters in civil court. On March 6, 1783, a jury was empaneled to hear the case of *Gregson v. Gilbert*, with Lord Chief Justice Mansfield presiding.[4]

The testimony of two surviving witnesses revealed the shocking details of how the massacre unfolded. Just before nightfall on November 29, 1781, the *Zong's* crew began shoving fifty-four women and children "singly through Cabin windows" into the Atlantic Ocean. Two days later forty-two Black males were thrown or forced into the shark-infested waters. All the men were condemned to the depths "fettered with Irons." What was more, the executions were conducted randomly with no regard to the physical condition of the doomed Africans. The "Shrieks" of terrified men, women, and children begging and fighting for their lives alerted fellow captives imprisoned below deck that desperate measures had to be taken.[5]

Speaking in broken English, one captured Black man pleaded with the sailors to accept a gut-wrenching compromise: in exchange for their lives, the remaining captives would endeavor to survive without food or water. This desperate last-ditch attempt to halt the killings was rejected, however. According to Sharp, ten African men then "sprang disdainfully from the grasp of their tyrants" and leapt into the sea, achieving "a momentary triumph in the embrace of death." One of the men experienced an apparent change of heart and managed to climb undetected back onboard the ship. On the third and final day of the massacre, thirty-eight more enslaved Africans were thrown overboard, raising the grim tally to 143.[6]

In his deposition, James Kelsey, the ship's first mate, stated that he initially objected to his captain's orders. Kelsey also proffered sensational testimony that suggested the financial calculus that went into the captain's command. According to Kelsey, prior to ordering the killings, Collingswood explained to his crew that under established British maritime law, African captives were "cargo," and the ship's owners would therefore be entitled to compensation if their "property" was destroyed at sea. Conversely, if sickened Africans died

Slave ship crewmen throwing enslaved Africans into the Atlantic Ocean during the Zong massacre. Olaudah Equiano sought justice for enslaved Africans murdered during the Zong massacre, but a judge ruled that enslaved Blacks were property.

(Courtesy of the Library of Congress Prints and Photographs Division)

after the *Zong* arrived in Jamaica, there would be no basis for a legal claim for damages from their insurers. In short, Collingwood and his crew, whose compensation was partly based on commissions generated by profits from the sale of African captives, chose to mitigate their mounting economic losses. Though the murderous acts Kelsey described had clearly been perpetrated for the purpose of fraud, the jury ignored the allegations and quickly ruled in Gregson's favor. The insurance company lawyers moved to have the verdict set aside and requested a new trial.[7]

Despite the calculated brutality, the *Zong* massacre might well have passed into history had not an anonymous letter recounting the legal proceedings, published in the *Morning Chronicle and London Advertiser*, caught the attention of Equiano, who immediately resolved to seek justice for the murdered Africans. He realized that any possibility of success in the matter hinged on whether he could convince Granville Sharp to get involved in the case.[8]

In a letter written to his niece Ann Jemima, Sharp recalled their meeting. "Gustavus Vassa [Equiano], a Negro called on me, with an account of 130 Negroes being thrown alive into the sea." He reacted as Equiano had anticipated, later recalling: "Having been earnestly solicited and called upon by a poor Negro, for my assistance to avenge the blood of his murdered Countrymen, I thought it my duty to spare neither labour nor expense in collecting all the information concerning this horrible transaction that I could possibly procure."[9]

Sharp immediately began inciting public outrage over the incident. He lobbied British officials to prosecute the surviving *Zong* crewmen for murder. The incensed attorney also arranged several meetings to solicit the support of influential Britons, including Oglethorpe, legal experts, admiralty court commissioners, and Anglican and Unitarian Church leaders. He volunteered as well to advise the insurer's legal team, who incorporated into their arguments his call for the *Zong* crewmen to be prosecuted for murder.

The hearing on the motion for a new trial was heard by a three-judge panel, with Lord Mansfield again presiding, on May 21–22, 1783, at the Court of King's Bench in Westminster Hall. Despite their concerted efforts to expand the trial's scope, Mansfield ruled that the *Gregson* case involved damages due to loss of property, not potential guilt for mass murder. The presiding judge matter-of-factly rejected numerous requests by the defense to include the question of premediated murder into the proceedings.[10]

The panel ultimately reaffirmed long-standing British legal precedent by ruling that Black men, women, and children were property, not human beings. "What is this claim that human people have been thrown overboard?" they opined with chilling detachment. "This is a case of chattels and goods. Blacks are goods and property; it is madness to accuse these well-serving honorable men of murder. They acted out of necessity and in the most appropriate manner for the cause. The late Captain Collingwood acted in the interest of his ship to protect the safety of his crew." The famed jurist concluded, "To question the judgement of an experienced well-travelled captain held in high regard is one of folly, especially when talking of slaves. The case is the same as if wood had been thrown overboard."[11]

Although Mansfield refused to consider charges of murder, he did allow the introduction of new evidence not presented during the first trial. A heavy rainstorm may explain why the *Zong*, allegedly running short on water during the voyage, arrived in Jamaica with 430 gallons of fresh water onboard. According to first mate Kelsey, "no person in the ship had been put on short allowance of water"; more significantly, the second group of Africans "were thrown overboard a Day after the rain." Kelsey's testimony contradicted claims by Gregson's attorneys that the executions were justified under the law of "maritime necessity" because drinkable water was in short supply.[12]

This shocking revelation was a pivotal factor in Mansfield's decision to grant the insurer's request for a new trial. Writing on behalf of the three-judge panel, Mansfield declared, "It is a very uncommon Case and I think very well deserves a re-examination." However, there is no record of subsequent legal proceedings. Whether compensation was paid for the captured Africans who were thrown or forced overboard is unknown. Only one fact is certain: the surviving *Zong* crewmen were not prosecuted for murder.[13]

Undeterred by the inconclusive *Zong* trial verdicts, Sharp and Equiano used the gruesome murders to further arouse the consciousness of the British public. On May 22, 1787, Sharp, Hannah More, and Thomas Clarkson, an early slavery opponent, along with several Quakers and other pioneer abolitionists, founded the Society for the Abolition of the Slave Trade with Sharp elected to serve as the first president. Equiano and Ottabah Cugoano, likewise an educated formerly enslaved Black man, formed their own organization called the Sons of Africa. The "corresponding society" was composed of educated formerly enslaved Blacks living in London, who used their literary skills to write letters to newspapers, petition Parliament, and engage in speaking tours. The two advocacy groups forged an influential alliance and successfully lobbied Parliament to adopt the Slave Act of 1788, the first statute passed to regulate the transatlantic slave trade. These trailblazing abolitionists also developed other innovative tactics that would become staples of modern lobbying campaigns, including the printing and distribution of logos, flyers, and posters; the publication of poems, essays, newsletters, and books; establishing local chapters of like-minded individuals; hosting lectures; writing members of Parliament; distributing reports detailing the voting records of legislators; marketing abolitionist memorabilia; and encouraging consumer boycotts of crops and materials produced by enslaved Black laborers.[14]

In the twilight of his eventful life, Oglethorpe had successfully handed off his decades-long fight against slavery to Equiano, Sharp, More, and other first-generation British abolitionists. This interracial coalition of men and women embraced the nascent antislavery struggle that emerged from the Georgia wilderness and transformed it into a powerful abolitionist crusade.

"We Hold These Truths to Be Self-Evident"

THE COMING OF THE AMERICAN Revolutionary War raised hopes among free and enslaved Blacks and white antislavery activists that freedom might be in the offing for approximately seven hundred thousand men, women, and children held captive throughout the British American colonies. The enslavement of Black people made a mockery of Lockean revolutionary ideology based on principles of "personal freedom" and the "liberty of man." Despite the glaring moral and political contradictions, Patrick Henry's iconic rallying cry "Give me liberty or give me death!" also resonated with those who bore the yoke of perpetual bondage. Benjamin Quarles provides an enlightening observation: "The Negro's role in the Revolution can best be understood by realizing that his major loyalty was not to a place nor to a people, but to a principle." The fundamental principle was that all human beings, regardless of color, were endowed with the "inalienable" right to life, liberty, and the pursuit of happiness. Whoever offered freedom in exchange for military allegiance, British or American, could count on an enthusiastic response from enslaved Blacks.[1]

On April 19, 1775, the "shot heard round the world" heralded the beginning of America's fight for independence from England; however, General George Washington, commander of the Continental military, and Congress initially refused to authorize the enlistment of free or enslaved Black men in the patriot military. They were concerned that allowing Blacks to enlist would shatter their alliance with South Carolina, Georgia, and the other colonies whose agriculture-based economies were totally dependent on the use of enslaved laborers.[2]

On June 30, 1776, Sir Henry Clinton, commander of British troops in North America, sought to exploit Washington's decision to prohibit Black enlistment by issuing the Philipsburg Proclamation, which offered freedom to all Blacks enslaved by American patriots who pledged allegiance to the king of England. Just as Oglethorpe predicted, the promise of freedom prompted approximately sixty-five thousand enslaved Blacks to seek refuge behind British lines.[3]

In an early draft of the Declaration of Independence, presented to the Continental Congress that convened in Philadelphia during the summer of 1776, Thomas Jefferson, a Virginia slaveholder himself, acknowledged the serious threat posed by Clinton's proclamation. Jefferson included language in the document that accused King George II of "violating the most sacred rights of life and liberty in the persons of a distant people who never offended him, capturing and carrying them into slavery in another hemisphere, to incur miserable death in their transportation hither." The future third president of the United States also asserted that the British, who pioneered the transatlantic slave trade, were now encouraging enslaved Blacks to take up arms against patriot slaveholders. The controversial antislavery language was struck out to appease proslavery Georgia and South Carolina convention delegates.[4]

In January 1777 manpower shortages and military setbacks forced patriot leaders in the northern colonies, with the support of General Washington, to execute an about-face and authorize the enlistment of free Black men in the Continental army. In May of that year Congress adopted a resolution encouraging the enlistment of enslaved Black men with a promise of manumission, monetary compensation, and land bounties. The northern colonies also permitted enslaved Black men to be designated as substitutes for wealthy slaveholders in their militia units. More than five thousand free *and* enslaved Black men would eventually shoulder arms on behalf of the American rebels during their seven-year struggle for independence from England. Georgia and South Carolina military leaders allowed a few Black men to join their ranks, but the great majority of enslaved Blacks in the southern colonies pinned their hopes for liberation on the British, not proslavery Americans.[5]

In Georgia thousands of formerly enslaved Blacks earned the boon of freedom by serving the British as soldiers, spies, orderlies, and laborers. A Black man named Sampson guided British ships through the maze of waterways and tributaries along the Atlantic coast during their invasion of the colony in December 1778. Quamino or Quash Dolly, who was enslaved by loyalist Georgia governor James Wright, led thirty-five hundred British soldiers through secret pathways in the swamps to stage a surprise attack on Savannah, catching the local militia off guard and allowing the invaders to take

Quamino Dolly, an enslaved Black Georgian, leading British troops, on horse and foot, through swamps near Savannah during the attack on Savannah, Georgia, in December 1778.

(Courtesy of Georgia Historical Society, Edwin Jackson Collection)

the city with relative ease. Historians estimate that 75 percent of Georgia's prewar enslaved Black population of fifteen thousand escaped to Savannah and freedom during the British occupancy of 1778–1783.[6]

Of the approximately twelve hundred Black men who worked for the British in Savannah, more than two hundred served as armed soldiers. In addition, in April 1779 British navy captain Hyde Parker employed twenty-four formerly enslaved men to man two boats assigned to patrol the Savannah River, directing that they be treated as "Ordinary Seamen being part of the Galley's Crews." In 1781 the British garrison at Fort Cornwallis, near Augusta, consisted of four hundred regular soldiers and two hundred Black recruits. The Black soldiers later distinguished themselves at the Battle of Briar Creek on March 3, 1779, where they helped rout a regiment of Georgia militiamen commanded by General Samuel Elbert.[7]

Among the thousands of freedom seekers who took refuge in war-torn Savannah, three were pioneer Black preachers: George Liele, David George, and Jesse Peter (sometimes called Jesse Galphin after his enslaver, George Galphin). Prior to their reunion in Savannah, Liele, George, and Peter had worshipped together at the Silver Bluff Baptist Church, a congregation composed of about thirty enslaved Black Christians that had been established

Rev. George Liele was an enslaved and later free pioneer Black Baptist preacher during the American Revolutionary War era. Liele converted hundreds of freedom seekers.

around 1773 on the Galphin plantation at Silver Bluff, South Carolina, located directly across the Savannah River from Augusta. The congregation had been ministered to by Reverend Waith Palmer, a white evangelist who came south during the First Great Awakening, and his assistant, George Liele.[8]

Born into slavery around 1750 in Virginia, Liele moved with his enslaver, Henry Sharp, to Burke County, Georgia, just prior to the beginning of the American Revolution. As was the custom, he was allowed to attend worship services at the local white Baptist church. After six months of Bible study, prayer, and worship, Liele was baptized and accepted as a member of Sharp's church and soon called to preach the Gospel. According to Liele's personal testimony, "Desiring to prove the sense I had of my obligation to God, I endeavored to instruct . . . my own color in the Word of God." Moved by the sincerity of his sermon, church leaders granted Liele a probationary license to preach, and he became the first Black man to be officially ordained as a minister in the Baptist church.[9]

The enslaved minister developed an extensive circuit which included plantations along a seventy-five-mile strip of the Georgia–South Carolina border on both sides of the Savannah River, including frequent stops at the Silver Bluff Baptist Church, where he first became acquainted with David George and Jesse Peter. Though little is known about the early life of Peter, his fellow Silver Bluff worshipper, George, was born on a plantation in Essex County, Virginia, around 1742. George and his family were enslaved by a "brutal" man who regularly whipped and tortured them. He eventually escaped in the wilderness, was captured by Muscogee Indians, and later sold to George Galphin, the owner of a plantation and trading post at Silver Bluff, South Carolina. During his enslavement, George came under the powerful influences of the Christian faith and Reverend Liele.[10]

Liele subsequently purchased his freedom and the freedom of his wife, Hannah Hunt Liele, and their four children from Sharp and moved to Tybee Island near Savannah. Shortly thereafter his former enslaver, who had sided with the British, was killed in battle. After Sharp's death, his relatives claimed that Liele's manumission was invalid and attempted to re-enslave the Black preacher and his family. They had him arrested and jailed in Savannah. During his incarceration, Liele was befriended by a British officer who authenticated Liele's "free papers" and arranged for his release from prison.[11]

About the same time, approximately ninety enslaved Blacks, including George and Peter, fled the Galphin plantation and joined the Blacks crowding into Savannah. The two men were soon reunited with Liele, their spiritual mentor. Realizing that their newfound freedom and that of all Blacks formerly enslaved by American patriots was dependent on a British victory, they encouraged fellow Blacks to support the British war effort. Such a deepening alliance between the British and formerly enslaved Blacks alarmed patriot leaders and fundamentally altered their political and military calculus.[12]

Early in 1779, desperate Georgia and South Carolina patriot leaders sent General Isaac Huger to lobby the Continental Congress for additional military support. Huger informed the delegates that the two colonies were weakened militarily because the "great proportion of the citizens" were forced to "remain at home to prevent insurrection among the Negroes, and to prevent the desertion of them to the enemy."[13]

On March 25, 1779, a special congressional committee, which included delegates from Georgia and South Carolina, issued a report confirming that the "exposed condition" of the two colonies made them vulnerable to attack, and their militia was ill prepared for deployment against loyalist and British troops. The committee recommended conscription of enslaved Black men to strengthen their militias. The delegates were also convinced that mandatory Black enlistment would reduce the possibility of slave insurrections because the most "vigorous and enterprising" Black men would be occupied with military service.[14]

Four days later the Continental Congress passed a resolution, reminiscent of Georgia's 1755 Militia Act, proposing that the two southern colonies conscript three thousand able-bodied enslaved Black soldiers. The resolution stipulated that white officers would command a single battalion in each colony and that slaveholders would receive not more than $1,000 compensation for each Black conscript. Most significantly, enslaved soldiers who faithfully performed their duties and surrendered their weapons after the war would receive fifty dollars and their freedom, according to the legislation. Acknowledging that the measure might create "inconveniences" for slaveholders, congressional delegates granted Georgia and South Carolina leaders the option of accepting or rejecting the proposal.[15]

To lobby for the measure, General Washington dispatched South Carolinian John Laurens, son of Henry Laurens, a South Carolina slaveholder, who had served as president of the Congress and was a strong supporter of the plan. The elder Laurens cautioned his son that it would be difficult, if not impossible, to persuade slaveholders to part with the basis of their wealth, enslaved Blacks, and what they also believed was the source of their happiness. Most of the delegates, however, were optimistic that Laurens would succeed, because several southern congressmen, including William Houston and Archibald Bulloch of Georgia, had initially supported the idea of mobilizing enslaved soldiers as had General Nathaniel Greene, the patriot commander of the Southern Army.[16]

On March 20, 1778, Washington had penned his "first crude thoughts" regarding the conscription of enslaved Blacks, expressing "not the smallest doubt" that given the opportunity Black men would fight for their freedom alongside white patriots. Alexander Hamilton, a senior aide to General Washington, offered his unqualified support for the conscription and manumission plan in a letter to his friend John Jay. He began by acknowledging that "prejudice and self-interest" existed throughout the colonies, particularly in the South: "The contempt we have . . . for the blacks makes us fancy many things that are founded neither in reason nor experience; and an unwillingness to part with property so valuable . . . will furnish a thousand arguments to show the impracticability or pernicious tendency of a scheme which requires such a sacrifice." Nonetheless, he advised that "Col. Laurens . . . is on his way to South Carolina, on a project which I think . . . is a very good one, and deserves every kind of support and encouragement."[17]

In May 1780 members of the South Carolina legislature angrily rebuffed the controversial conscription and manumission strategy. Washington correctly predicted that certain failure awaited the congressional proposal in Georgia. Although Georgia governor Richard Howley voiced support for the conscription of enslaved Black men, the legislature refused to adopt the plan. Disappointed and disillusioned, Laurens was consoled by Washington, who wrote: "That spirit of freedom, which at the commencement of this contest would have gladly sacrificed everything to the attainment of its object, has long since subsided and every selfish passion has taken its place. It is not the public, but private interest, which influences the generality of mankind, nor can the Americans any longer boast an exception. Under these circumstances it would rather have been surprising if you had succeeded."[18]

Despite the legislature's rejection of the conscription and manumission proposal, Black people made significant voluntary and involuntary contributions to the patriot war effort in Georgia. In October 1779 a French force of thirty-five hundred men joined American forces at Savannah in an unsuccessful attempt to liberate the city from British control. Fighting with

Savannah monument dedicated to free and enslaved Black Haitian soldiers who fought with Franco-American soldiers during the American Revolutionary War.

(Courtesy of the Library of Congress Prints and Photographs Division)

the French was a battalion of six hundred free and enslaved Black Haitian soldiers known as Frontages Legion, named after their commander, Viscount François de Frontages. The Haitians charged into the breach after the French and American soldiers were overwhelmed by the British, and they saved the Franco-American army from annihilation by heroically covering its retreat.[19]

In addition, enslaved Black laborers also made other important noncombat contributions to the patriot cause. During the fall of 1775, the Georgia Council of Safety impressed scores of enslaved Blacks in Savannah to help General Charles Lee enclose a military storehouse. Much to the chagrin of Georgia slaveholders, the council repeatedly used enslaved laborers to build military fortifications and other duties. Colonial leaders tried to address their concerns by assuring slaveholders that sick or injured enslaved laborers would be provided "sustenance, medicines, and attendance" and by agreeing to compensate slaveholders for enslaved Blacks who were killed or permanently injured.[20]

Captured Blacks who had been enslaved by British loyalists were also used as bounty to compensate American militiamen and officials. Following the recapture of Savannah, the Safety Council ordered those Black captives who had been enslaved by loyalists be sold at public auction, and the proceeds divided among American soldiers. In 1782 Georgia governor John Martin received ten enslaved Blacks in lieu of salary, and the entire Executive Council was subsequently compensated with captured Blacks. In fact, the latter stages of the Revolutionary War in Georgia and the other southern colonies were largely financed by revenue generated from the sale or confiscation of enslaved Blacks formerly owned by British loyalists.[21]

In April 1781 Georgia and South Carolina patriots began a critical offensive that ultimately ended hostilities in Georgia. The British surrendered Savannah to the Continental Army in July 1782. On July 10 and 11 British soldiers, white loyalists and their enslaved Blacks, and self-emancipated Black loyalists began the British emancipation of Georgia's largest city. Among the evacuees was Reverend Liele, who prior to his departure preached a final sermon and baptized Andrew Bryan, his wife Hannah, and two other Black converts. Bryan became the second pastor of the First Colored Baptist Church (later renamed the First African Baptist Church), America's first independent Black church.[22]

According to an embarkation record dated August 10, 1782, six ships transported Liele and about fifteen hundred Blacks to British-controlled Jamaica during the first month of the evacuation. The Black preacher worked as an indentured servant for two years and was subsequently granted his certificate of freedom. Liele proselytized the island's free and enslaved Black populations, but he and several worshippers were persecuted by local British officials. They were imprisoned and charged with sedition, a capital offense. He barely escaped the hangman's noose, while one of his colleagues was found guilty and executed. Undeterred by his close call with death, he established on January 12, 1793, the Windward Road Baptist Church in Kingston, Jamaica's first Baptist church. Liele is also celebrated as being the first Baptist missionary and "Negro slavery's prophet of deliverance."[23]

During the next twelve months an additional 1,956 Blacks, including 107 women and 452 children, left Georgia for British-controlled eastern Florida. All told, it is estimated that more than thirty-five hundred Black war refugees were eventually evacuated by British vessels from Savannah to eastern Florida. By the end of 1783, most of the formerly enslaved Blacks were relocated from Florida to Nova Scotia, the Bahamas, Jamaica, and various European ports. David George sailed from Charleston, South Carolina, to Nova Scotia, where he devoted the next ten years of his life to preaching to Black settlers in the Canadian cities of Shelbourne, Brichtown, Ragged Island, and Saint John, New Brunswick. After establishing a church in Shelbourne, he led the migration of some disgruntled Black settlers to British-controlled Freetown, Sierra Leone, where he established another church in 1792.[24]

A handful of enslaved Black men managed to earn their freedom by serving in the "all-white" Georgia militia. The most celebrated Black Georgia militiaman was Austin Dabney, who was brought to Georgia by his enslaver, Richard Aycock, shortly after the beginning of the Revolutionary War. Aycock avoided military service by claiming that the mixed-race Dabney was a free person of color whom he offered as his substitute—a practice that Georgia and other colonies permitted. The young recruit served under Colonel Elijah Clark and distinguished himself as a brave and loyal patriot. Following the American victory, the Georgia General Assembly purchased Dabney's freedom and accorded the war hero "all the liberties, privileges and immunities of a free citizen . . . so far as free negroes and mulattos are allowed."[25]

Still, Dabney's heroic military service and free status could not shield him from the pervasive racism that permeated every aspect of Georgia culture. Although patriot veterans were eligible to receive land pensions, Dabney was denied the opportunity to participate in the 1819 Georgia land lottery because of his race. Two years later, the legislature passed a special resolution granting Dabney 112 acres of land for his "bravery and fortitude." Angry white Madison County residents complained that it was an insult to white men for a formerly enslaved Black man to be placed on equal terms with them in the land distribution lottery. But Dabney had the support of Georgia governor George Gilmer and state representative Stephen Upson of Oglethorpe County, who introduced the legislation. Governor Gilmer reminded the Madison County residents that Dabney had rendered "courageous service" during the Revolutionary War, and he chastised them for displaying what he described as "unpatriotic" attitudes.[26]

Dabney's contributions to the patriot war effort were singular; however, several other enslaved Black men also served with distinction as combat troops in the Georgia militia and subsequently earned their freedom. Nathan Fry joined Colonel Samuel Elbert's regiment at Savannah in 1775 and was later freed. Monday Floyd secured his freedom in 1782 by an act of the Georgia General Assembly, which cited his heroic military service and directed the public treasury to pay Floyd's enslaver for his manumission.[27]

Hundreds of formerly enslaved Blacks failed to secure passage on British evacuation ships, while others were recaptured or voluntarily returned to enslavement. Included among those who returned to a life of bondage was Jesse Peter. Peter's new enslaver granted him "uncommon liberties" and encouraged him to expand his ministry to three or four enslaved congregations, including the remnants of the Silver Bluff Church. He subsequently relocated the Silver Bluff congregation across the Savannah River to Augusta, Georgia, where he founded the First African Baptist Church, later renamed Springfield Baptist Church.[28]

The signing of the Treaty of Paris on November 30, 1782, officially ended the American Revolutionary War. The British evacuation of formerly enslaved Blacks, and its refusal to compensate American slaveholders for their financial losses, set off a long and bitter diplomatic dispute between England and her former colonies. American diplomats in Europe officially protested the evacuation and repeatedly denounced the British as "slave stealer(s)." However, England's diplomats refused patriot demands to return the freedom seekers or purchase their freedom, and the majority of formerly enslaved Black Georgians retained their hard-won freedom.

———————

The fifty-five Founding Fathers who gathered in Philadelphia in May 1787 to draft a constitution and officially give birth to the United States of America were faced with many difficult challenges. The constitutional delegates were painfully aware that the ultimate success of the convention was dependent, in large part, on their ability to resolve differences of opinion between the southern and northern colonies. Delegate James Madison astutely observed that "the institution of slavery and its consequences formed the line of discrimination" between the contending delegations at the Constitutional Convention.[29]

The principal question before the convention was not whether slavery should be abolished. "It was rather, who shall have the power to control it—the states or the national government?" Although the delegates carefully avoided using the word "slavery" while drafting the historic document, bitter sectional disputes regarding continuance of the transatlantic slave trade threatened to disrupt the deliberations. South Carolina and Georgia delegates bluntly declared that they would not support the effort to forge a stronger, more centralized government unless the individual states were afforded the exclusive power to control the slave trade within their borders. Georgia delegate Abraham Baldwin, the founding president of the University of Georgia, insisted that the convention restrict its deliberations to "national objects alone," and the scholarly Georgian argued that slavery was strictly a "local" issue that should be regulated by the individual states. Baldwin added that the people of Georgia fully supported the enslavement of Blacks, but he claimed that, if left alone, the state would "put a stop to the evil."[30]

The southern delegates' intransigence and willingness of their northern colleagues to seek compromise resulted in the adoption of key provisions that affirmed the constitutionality of American slavery. The northern delegates secured the coveted elimination of a clause that required a two-thirds majority vote in the House of Representatives to pass trade legislation. The southerners walked away with several proslavery concessions, including a fugitive slave clause that gave slaveholders the right to recapture Black freedom seekers who escaped to slave-free states, and a "compromise" between northern and southern delegates that for the purposes of levying taxes and apportionment of seats in the House of Representatives, enslaved Blacks would be counted as three-fifths of a person. Most significantly, Article I, Section 9, of the Constitution prohibited the federal government from banning the "importation" of enslaved Africans into the United States for twenty years, until 1808.[31]

By 1800 several northern colonies, and later states, had already taken steps to either prohibit the importation of African captives or abolish slavery outright. In 1777 Vermont became the first colony to abolish slavery, followed by Massachusetts in 1780. During the next two decades Pennsylvania, Rhode Island, Connecticut, and New York adopted statutes that gradually emancipated enslaved Blacks living within their borders. On January 1, 1808, immediately following the expiration of the slave trade protection provision, Congress outlawed American participation in the transatlantic slave trade. Although this statute did not affect the domestic slave trade, antislavery activists believed or at least hoped that the prohibition would eventually result in the demise of chattel slavery throughout the United States. They were wrong.[32]

The agricultural economies of the southern states had become totally dependent on the labor of enslaved Blacks. The planting, harvesting, and manufacturing of lucrative cash crops such as rice, sugar, indigo, and cotton required the brains and brawn of a vast enslaved workforce. However, the institutionalization of American chattel slavery under the new nation's

Constitution did not dampen the resolve of Blacks enslaved in America who were yearning to be free.

———————

Both during and after the American Revolutionary War, the inspiring story of southern freedom seekers risking their lives by following the North Star is the cornerstone of African American history. However, a steady stream of Blacks chose a lesser-known, more direct route to freedom, into the dense woods and swamps of southern Georgia and northern Florida. Several thousand self-emancipated Blacks sought refuge and found sanctuary in the land where the Seminole held sway. Formerly enslaved Black Georgians and their descendants intermarried and assimilated with the Seminole, eventually developing a unique Negro-Seminole culture. These Blacks or Estelusti, as they were called in the Muskogee Seminole language, later played a pivotal role in helping defend Seminole territory against multiple invasions by Georgia militia and the U.S. military.[33]

Enslaved Black Georgians also found freedom, albeit temporarily, by establishing secret camps in the swamps along the Savannah River. From these isolated settlements, the maroons conducted sporadic raids against nearby villages, farms, and plantations. Prior to the British surrender of Fort Cornwallis on June 4, 1781, more than two hundred Black men who had helped defend the fortification escaped into the swamps along the Savannah River between Augusta and Savannah. These loyalist Blacks formed the nucleus of a Maroon band that became known as the "King of England's Soldiers."[34]

Timothy Lockley provides a detailed and fascinating account of loyalist Blacks who struggled to maintain their freedom long after the final shots were fired in the Revolutionary War. Described as the "best disciplined band of marauders that ever infested [Georgia] borders," these guerrilla fighters used skills learned from the British to plunder at will on both sides of the Savannah River. White Georgians feared these "freebooters" would instigate widespread insurrections among Georgia's enslaved population, and on several occasions local militia tried unsuccessfully to end the depredations. On May 6, 1786, Georgia and Carolina militia, guided by Catawba Indians, attacked and burned their makeshift fortress, which consisted of a rectangular breastwork of logs and cane. Several of the King of England's Soldiers were killed or captured in the battle, although an unknown number escaped into nearby swamps and forest.[35]

The October 1786 edition of the *Massachusetts Gazette* carried a report of approximately one hundred Blacks who lived in a secret community on Bel-lisle Island, about twenty miles north of Savannah. The band, which may have included surviving members of the King of England's Soldiers, conducted numerous raids against white settlements along the Savannah River until the Georgia militia was ordered to locate and destroy the settlement. On October 11, 1786, Black fighters repulsed the Savannah Light Infantry's initial attack, but two days later General James Jackson's troops stormed the camp, burned their houses and huts, and destroyed four acres of green rice. Most of the Blacks were killed, wounded, or captured, although a few escaped.[36]

The remaining freedom fighters and possibly some new recruits resumed their raids of farms and plantations, carrying off rice and other provisions. This prompted South Carolina's governor to issue a proclamation like one issued earlier by the governor of Georgia, establishing a bounty of ten pounds for every Black maroon that was captured or killed. A force of a hundred "minutemen" and twenty Catawba Indians was hurriedly assembled to hunt down the remaining fighters.[37]

In April 1787, the militiamen launched a surprise attack against a newly constructed maroon camp, killing six Blacks, capturing nine, and forcing several others to flee. A week later "Captain Lewis," one of the Black leaders, was captured, incarcerated in Savannah, put on trial, and convicted of having committed numerous capital offenses. He was executed by hanging on June 9, 1787, and pursuant to his death sentence, Lewis's head was "Cutt off and Stuck upon a pole" facing in the direction of "the Island of Marsh opposite the Glebe land in [the] Savannah River."[38]

Thirty years after the Revolutionary War guns fell silent, Americans found themselves embroiled in another bloody conflict with England. This second war between England and America grew out of long-standing conflicts over western North American territorial boundaries, international trade disputes, and impressment of American citizens on British naval vessels. During the War of 1812, Georgia slaveholders were once again tormented by British military strategy envisioned decades earlier by James Oglethorpe: the emancipation and arming of enslaved Blacks by foreign adversaries to wage war against those who had enslaved them.

On January 10, 1815, approximately fifteen hundred Black and white British marines landed without opposition on the northern end of Cumberland Island on Georgia's Atlantic coast. The Black marines were formerly enslaved Blacks who had joined the elite Third West Indian Regiment of the British

Admiral Sir George Cockburn led white and Black British marines to invade Cumberland Island off the Georgia coast. Cockburn enlisted hundreds of formerly enslaved Black men into the British Royal Marines.

(Courtesy of the National Maritime Museum, Greenwich, London)

A formerly enslaved Black Georgian who answered the British call to arms during the War of 1812. The new recruit is dressed in the colorful dress uniform of the Third West Indian Regiment of the British Colonial Marines.

(Courtesy of Don Troiani)

Colonial Marines during the invasion of the Chesapeake Bay area the previous winter. The man responsible for masterminding the amphibious invasion of Georgia was Admiral Sir George Cockburn. Born into British aristocracy, Cockburn's prior military action included escorting deposed French emperor Napoleon Bonaparte into exile in August 1815 and the attack and burning of "Washington City" (later Washington, D.C.) on August 24, 1814.[39]

By the end of January, the British had gained control of Cumberland, Jekyll, and Saint Simons Islands. Cockburn's next objective was to enlist formerly enslaved Black Georgians in the British military. Vice Admiral Alexander Cochrane had issued an official British proclamation of emancipation nine months earlier on April 2, 1814, promising all persons desirous of emigrating from the United States sanctuary on His Majesty's ships or on military posts. According to the document, enlistees and their families would be taken as "Free Settlers" to British colonies in North America or the West Indies.[40]

Details regarding the British offer of freedom spread quickly along the coastal slave grapevine. Hundreds of enslaved Black Georgians escaped from mainland and island plantations, and all but a few arrived at the British encampment on Cumberland Island in small boats and dug-out canoes. Among the first to reach Cumberland was Ben, who arrived at the British camp with his wife and young child, having escaped from the Thomas Ellis plantation on the Little Satilla River in Camden County. He immediately volunteered to serve in the West Indian Regiment of the Royal Marines. Seventeen other enslaved Camden County Blacks fled from slaveholder William McNish and landed on Cumberland during the second week of February 1815. Three other enslaved Black men from the McNish plantation, Polydore, Alick, and Jerry, also came to the island and joined the British marines. On Saint Simons 183 Blacks enslaved on the James Hamilton plantation escaped under the protection of British soldiers; Samuel Parker, a Camden County slaveholder, reported the escape of thirty enslaved Blacks, and Peter Dibignon, a Jekyll Island plantation owner, complained that twenty-two of his bondmen had "absconded" to the British.[41]

By the first week of February, more than 450 Blacks had crowded onto the island, forcing Cockburn to request additional military uniforms. The admiral wrote a letter to his superiors that the number of Black men volunteering to serve in the British military was much greater than the number who stepped forward in the Chesapeake Bay area. Cockburn assured his superiors that he would transport all freed Blacks to Bermuda at every available opportunity. A second outpost manned by a contingent of Black marines was subsequently established in Spanish-controlled western Florida at Prospect Bluff on the Apalachicola River, about sixty miles below the Georgia-Florida border. Known as the "Negro Fort," the British stronghold quickly became a sanctuary for more than three hundred freedom seekers from Georgia, Alabama, and South Carolina.[42]

The War of 1812 came to an abrupt and inconclusive end when the Treaty of Ghent was ratified by Great Britain on December 31, 1814, and by the United States on February 17, 1815. Terms of the treaty essentially restored the nations to their prewar status and provided for various commissions to deal with unsettled questions. Article 1 of the treaty, which required the return of all formerly enslaved Black Americans evacuated by the British, became the focus of another contentious, long-running dispute between England and the United States.[43]

The exact number of enslaved Blacks who gained their freedom during the British evacuation of Georgia's Sea Islands is unknown. Historian Mary Bullard, in a detailed study based on the registers of British evacuation ships, puts the figure at 1,483 Black "super-numeraries." Other estimates range from two to three thousand evacuees. What is certain, though, is that the newly freed Blacks constituted an international diaspora that swept over such diverse cities, nations, and British colonies as Canada, Bermuda, Ireland, Jamaica, and Havana, Cuba.[44]

Even before the last British evacuation ship sailed from American waters, a political storm began to rage in the Georgia legislature. In November 1815 angry legislators passed legislation that exempted Georgia slaveholders from "paying taxes for property [a euphemism for enslaved Blacks] plundered and taken away by the British." Georgia governor David B. Mitchell quickly signed the tax relief measure into law.[45]

Georgia lawmakers also passed a resolution, along with several other southeastern legislatures, requesting that the federal government seek indemnification in the International Court of Law for the costs of the formerly enslaved persons and other "property" lost during America's second war with England. In 1818 the emperor of Russia was asked to arbitrate the bitter diplomatic dispute and determine whether American slaveholders were entitled to restitution under the provisions of the Treaty of Ghent.[46]

In 1822 the Russian arbitrator ruled in America's favor. American representatives presented evidence documenting the evacuation of 3,601 Black people;

however, they offered to settle the dispute for an amount equal to the value of 1,650 enslaved Blacks. British officials initially rejected the compromise, but in 1827 they ended the twelve-year dispute by agreeing to pay 250,000 pounds, or $1.2 million, to American slaveholders from the Royal Treasury for the official emancipation of the formerly enslaved Black Americans.[47]

Although collective and individual flight from bondage was the primary strategy utilized by enslaved Blacks seeking freedom, a small population of free born and formerly enslaved Black people chose to live in jurisdictions dominated by legalized slavery. "Free persons of color" lived in a precarious world that hovered between slavery and citizenship. They were victimized by harsh legal proscriptions that denied them full citizenship rights, including the right to vote, hold public office, serve on a jury, or testify against whites in court proceedings. A series of state and local registration statutes limited their mobility, and they were required to carry on their person, at all times, a certificate documenting their free status. Free Blacks also lived under the threat of being kidnapped and sold into slavery by slave hunters and unscrupulous whites.

In June 1740, five years after slavery was officially prohibited in the Georgia colony, the Trustees had briefly debated a proposal that would have encouraged the immigration of free Black people into the colony. Trustee James Vernon, "one of the original Associates of Dr. Bray and an architect of the charter," argued that the slavery ban did not preclude the admission of free Blacks, who could be employed "in the same manner as . . . White Servants." Following robust internal debate, the Trustees requested a legal opinion by Dudley Ryder, the British attorney general, regarding the legality of admitting free Blacks into Georgia. Ryder quashed the proposal by ruling that the 1735 ban against the importation of enslaved Black laborers prohibited "the using of Negroes in any manner or way whatsoever in the province." The legal opinion ended any further consideration of the proposal; nevertheless, by 1760 the colony's free Black population totaled approximately a hundred persons.[48]

Georgia's colonial leaders revisited the idea of encouraging free Black immigration in 1765. According to an act adopted by the General Assembly, free Blacks would be welcomed in the colony if they proffered "good Testimony of their humble duty and loyalty to his Majesty and their obedience to the Laws and their Affection to the Inhabitants." Once they were officially admitted, free Black Georgians would enjoy "all the Rights, Privileges, Powers and Immunities" of any "person born of British parents within this Province" except the right to vote or serve as a member of the General Assembly. In 1767 the free Black immigration provision, as well as the entire 1765 slave code, was disallowed by British authorities.[49]

Due to Georgia's 1735 antislavery statute, prior to the American Revolution the colony's free Black population was primarily composed of light-skinned mixed-race persons born out of sexual intercourse between white men and enslaved Black females. White biological fathers, stricken by conscience or moved by affection, sometimes freed "mulatto" children by "deathbed" manumission. On other occasions slaveholders voluntarily manumitted the enslaved mothers of their children. In 1770 the Georgia legislature enacted a statute that clarified the uncertain legal status of mixed-race children by declaring that they inherited the status of their enslaved Black mothers, not their free white fathers.[50]

Despite these formidable obstacles, free Blacks in Savannah, Augusta, and Milledgeville helped establish several "independent" churches during the antebellum period where free and enslaved worshippers were exposed to Christian teachings. As mentioned earlier, the First African Baptist Church of Savannah was officially constituted in December 1777, just one year after the American patriots issued the Declaration of Independence. Free Blacks also owned and operated small businesses that produced income used to purchase the freedom of other family members, loved ones, and friends.[51]

Decades before hostilities commenced in the Civil War, free Black Savannahians established at least five clandestine "schools" that gave free and enslaved children access to rudimentary education. Although local white officials were most certainly aware of these illegal educational activities, they apparently did not interfere. The most famous "graduate" of at least two of these schools was Susie King Taylor, who later became a teacher, nurse, and laundress for the First South Carolina Volunteers, America's first all-Black army regiment, and the author of the only Civil War memoir written by a Black woman. More importantly, by their mere existence free persons of color offered enslaved Black Georgians a striking contrast to the degradation of perpetual bondage. To the chagrin of many whites, free Blacks were living proof that people of color could rise above the condition of perpetual enslavement.[52]

Another narrow pathway to freedom traveled by enslaved Blacks was the "purchase of self," or buying one's own freedom from a slaveholder. The legal right of an enslaved person to purchase his or her freedom was recognized and protected by the Georgia courts. The first recorded instance of an enslaved Black Georgian purchasing his own freedom occurred in 1772 when Peter Fleming paid his enslaver the relatively small sum of five shillings. In 1782 an enslaved Black woman named Celia paid David Brydie ten pounds sterling for her freedom. In that same year, John Galphin's will manumitted Sapho, a "Negro wench," and her five children in exchange for her faithful service to him and a small amount of money.[53]

Although the struggle for American independence had minimal impact on the legal status of the vast majority of enslaved Georgians, the spread of revolutionary ideas based on the "rights of men" indirectly led to a significant increase in the number of free Blacks living in the state. The first federal census of 1790 revealed that 82,548 people lived in Georgia's eleven counties; of that number, 52,886 were white, 29,264 were enslaved Blacks, and 398 were free Blacks.[54]

In 1791 Henri Christophe, an enslaved Haitian who according to some historians served as drummer boy in the Franco-American force that attempted to dislodge the British during the Battle of Savannah in 1779, helped lead the revolt that ended decades of French colonial rule on the island of Santo Domingo on January 1, 1804 (Haiti was called Santo Domingo prior to the revolution). The violent insurrection forced thousands of frightened French war refugees to flee to the United States. Most of the migrants were white, although hundreds of mixed-race free Black French loyalists also arrived on American shores. The Americans welcomed the white refugees, but the mixed-race immigrants were met with suspicion and contempt. Although their legislative efforts had little effect, Georgia political leaders barred the migration of formerly enslaved Haitians into the state, and Savannah officials prohibited any ship that had weighed anchor in Haiti from docking at its port.[55]

By 1800, due primarily to the arrival of these light-skinned Haitians, Georgia's free Black population had grown to approximately sixteen hundred—an increase of nearly 300 percent in twenty years. According to 1810 U.S. census data, Georgia's population of 254,148 residents was composed of 147,217 whites or 58 percent of the total population; 105,218 enslaved Blacks or 41 percent of the total; and 1,713 free Blacks or 0.7 percent of the total. On the national front the free U.S. Black population had grown from a few thousand in 1760 to more than 250,000 by 1810.[56]

Widespread concern over the growing number of free Blacks living in America led to the founding of the Society for the Colonization of Free

Robert Finley was the principal founder of the American Colonization Society, whose primary mission was to remove all free Black people from the United States. Finley also served briefly as the president of the University of Georgia. Most free Blacks and white abolitionists, as well as proslavery white people, rejected Robert Finley's plan to relocate all free Blacks to Liberia.

(Sketch by G. Pischner, Wikimedia)

People of Color of America, later renamed the American Colonization Society (ACS) in Washington, D.C., on December 21, 1816. The society was the brainchild of Reverend Robert Finley, a graduate of Princeton College and a Presbyterian minister who also served briefly as president of the University of Georgia. Finley was a critic of slavery, but his support for emancipation was contingent on the forced emigration of all free Blacks from American soil. The influential minister argued that the removal of all freeborn and manumitted Blacks would reduce the specter of slave rebellions and provide America with the final solution to its "Negro Problem."[57]

On February 15, 1815, Finley wrote a lengthy letter explaining why he supported the colonization movement: "Our fathers brought them [enslaved Blacks] here, and we are bound if possible, to repair the injuries inflicted by our fathers. Could they be sent to Africa, a three-fold benefit would arise. We should be cleared of them; we should send to Africa a population particularly civilized and Christianized for its benefits; our blacks themselves would be put in a better condition."[58]

Some three decades earlier, Oglethorpe friend and mentee Granville Sharp had promoted a similar colonization strategy designed to relocate impoverished formerly enslaved Blacks living in England to a colony on Africa's Atlantic seaboard. Sharp utilized Oglethorpe's Savannah plan to design

Freetown, the first settlement established in the Sierra Leone colony, in 1787. Olaudah Equiano, another Oglethorpe acquaintance, was briefly involved in the effort, but he became disenchanted and disassociated himself from the Black colonization scheme.[59]

Finley recruited some of the most influential white men in America to lead the ACS: Thomas Jefferson, James Madison, James Monroe, John Marshall, Francis Scott Key, Bushrod Washington, and U.S. congressmen Daniel Webster of Massachusetts and Henry Clay of Kentucky were among the first to join the organization. William H. Crawford of Oglethorpe County, an influential Georgia politician and slaveholder, served as one of the vice presidents. Congressman Clay would become the political mentor of a young Illinois politician and future U.S. president named Abraham Lincoln. Before Lincoln became known as the "Great Emancipator," he was a vocal colonization advocate who supported the removal of all Black people from America.[60]

A small contingent of free Blacks supported colonization because they were convinced free and enslaved Blacks would never receive full citizenship rights and equal justice in America. The earliest Black proponent of colonization was Paul Cuffe (or Cuffee), a Quaker ship captain who helped thirty-eight free Blacks from Massachusetts immigrate to Sierra Leone in 1815.

On December 5, 1816, Finley wrote Cuffe inquiring if there might be a more favorable location for his proposed freed slave colony than along Africa's Atlantic seaboard. Finley explained, "The great desire of those whose minds are impressed with this subject is to give an opportunity to the free people of color to rise to their proper level and at the same time to provide a powerful means of putting an end to the slave trade and sending civilization and Christianity to Africa." Cuffe responded that he would recommend the Cape of Good Hope on the southern tip of Africa as a preferable resettlement location. Prominent free Black Americans who briefly supported then adamantly opposed colonization during the antebellum period were James Forten and Absalom Jones, two successful free businessmen in Philadelphia, and Richard Allen, the founder of the African Methodist Episcopal Church.[61]

In January 1817 Forten, Jones, and Allen convened approximately three thousand anticolonization Blacks from throughout the northeastern states in Philadelphia. These free Blacks adopted the following resolutions: "that we never will separate ourselves voluntarily from the slave population of this country" and "that we view with deep abhorrence the unmerited stigma attempted to be cast upon the reputation of the free people of color, by the promoters of this measure, that they are a dangerous and useless part of the community." Stunned by the intensity of Black opposition to the colonization movement, the ACS directed Finley to travel to Philadelphia and explain to the convention delegates that only free Blacks who volunteered would be returned to Africa. His appeal for support was rejected outright. The following year a second anticolonization meeting was held, and the delegates reaffirmed their opposition to the ACS colonization scheme, declaring that the removal of free Blacks from America was "not asked for by us nor will it be requested by any circumstances of our present or future condition."[62]

In 1816 Finley published a widely read pamphlet titled *Thoughts on the Colonization of Free Blacks*, in which he asserted, "Let no time be lost—let a colony or colonies be formed on the coast of Africa, and let laws be passed permitting the emancipation of slaves on the condition that they shall be colonized. By this means the evil of slavery will be diminished, and in a way so gradual as to prepare the whites for the happy and progressive change." The notoriety that Finley received from his advocacy for Black colonization played a key role in his selection as president of the University of Georgia in July 1817. Due to Finley's exhaustive travel schedule promoting colonization and a recruiting and fundraising tour on behalf of the university, the newly minted forty-five-year-old president contracted typhus and died on October 3, 1817.[63]

Undeterred by Finley's death and the vocal opposition of the great majority of free Blacks living in America, in 1821 the ACS, with the support of President James Monroe, acquired land on the western coast of Africa. The following year the organization began the voluntary "repatriation" of free Blacks living in the United States to the American colony of Liberia, located on the southern border of Sierra Leone, the British freed-slave colony. The first group of eighty-four Black emigrants, led by white ACS members, departed New York Harbor on the *Elizabeth* on January 31, 1822.[64]

By 1832 all-white auxiliary chapters of the ACS had been formed in counties and cities around the state of Georgia. The most active chapters were in Jackson, Burke, Putnam, and Baldwin Counties and in Augusta, where male and female chapters raised money to support African colonization. Between the ten-year period of 1846–1856, Georgia supporters contributed $12,669.90 to the ACS.[65]

In 1833, 180 Black colonists departed Savannah destined for Liberia on the ship *Hercules*. Traveling onboard were 156 passengers from South Carolina and 24 from Georgia and Florida. This expedition generated a great

Idealized depiction of Native Africans and Free Black American Liberian colonists. About twelve thousand free Blacks became colonists by migrating to Liberia as part of the failed African colonization movement.

(Public domain)

deal of optimism throughout the ACS because many of the migrants were well-educated missionaries. Late in November 1833 another ship set sail from Savannah with eighty-three free and formerly enslaved Black Savannahians and fourteen other freed Blacks.[66]

In 1836 the will of deceased slaveholder Richard Tubman of Augusta directed his wife and executrix, Emily Tubman, to manumit all his enslaved Blacks and relocate them to a section of "the United States best calculated to secure to them the rights and immunities of free persons of color." Tubman hoped to avoid a state statute that prohibited intrastate manumission by establishing a fund in the amount of $10,000, half of which would be donated to the University of Georgia if the legislature allowed the freed Black Georgians to remain in the state. It is interesting to note that $5,000 would have nearly equaled the total amount appropriated to the university by the Georgia General Assembly in 1836.[67]

Georgia's proslavery political leadership refused to amend or vacate the intrastate slave manumission prohibition statute. Emily Tubman, colonization officials, and the Blacks enslaved by Tubman decided that their best remaining option would be to migrate back to Africa. On May 17, 1837, forty-two Blacks manumitted by Tubman and four other free Black Augustans traveled to Baltimore, where they boarded the brig *Baltimore* and sailed for Liberia. Following their arrival on the African coast, the Black colonists helped transform "Fort Tubman" into a thriving agricultural community. Liberia became the first African republic to proclaim its political independence in 1847. In 1851 William Vaccanarat Tubman, a descendent of the Tubman colonists, was elected president of the Republic of Liberia.[68]

The twelve thousand Blacks who migrated to Liberia prior to 1860 represented only a fraction of the nearly four million free and enslaved Blacks living in America. The majority of free Blacks rejected colonization because they perceived African colonization to be a diabolical scheme conceived, promoted, and designed to protect the institution of slavery. White supporters of colonization failed to appreciate or simply ignored the fact that the great majority of Blacks living in America—free and enslaved—simply did not want to be exiled to a continent from which they were generations removed. Although Black people were fully aware that chattel slavery was imbedded in the U.S. Constitution, they would not accept expatriation as the final solution to the nation's racial problems.

Robert Finley's quixotic plan to save the union by removing all free Blacks from American soil proved to be politically naive, economically unfeasible, and practically impossible. Proslavery whites, primarily in the South, opposed any effort to moderate the institution of slavery; white colonization leaders also failed to comprehend the important cultural and political transformations that had occurred among America's free and enslaved Black populations. Black people were not "Africans" and for better or worse, America—not Liberia—was their home. After the African colonization movement failed to resolve the contradictions arising from America's embrace of chattel slavery, the only remaining options were southern secession and a cataclysmic Civil War.

"An Act of Justice"

FOLLOWING HIS ELECTION TO THE U.S. Congress in 1846, Abraham Lincoln, an up-and-coming thirty-seven-year-old lawyer from Illinois, went to great lengths to assure white Americans that he was not an abolitionist. Although he was certain that slavery was morally wrong, Lincoln acknowledged that the U.S. Constitution granted individual states the right to legalize the enslavement of Black people. While campaigning for the U.S. Senate in 1858, Lincoln supported an antislavery strategy that had been pioneered decades earlier by Oglethorpe and the Georgia Trustees: prohibiting the spread of slavery into slave-free jurisdictions. Lincoln hoped to appease southern slaveholders by promising not to abolish slavery where it existed, but he supported federal legislation that prohibited slavery in newly created western states and territories that were being established by the expansionist nation.[1]

During the 1860 presidential campaign, as the Republican candidate Lincoln reaffirmed this position, promising that if elected he would respect the rights of slaveholders in states where legalized slavery existed but prohibit its further expansion. Following his election as America's sixteenth president, angry southerners refused to accept any impediments to their perceived right to export slavery westward. On December 12, 1860, South Carolina became the first of seven slave states to secede and form a new nation, the Confederate States of America. The incoming Lincoln administration refused to recognize the legitimacy of secession, and rebel soldiers ignited the Civil War by opening fire on the federal garrison at Fort Sumter in the Charleston, South Carolina, harbor on April 12, 1861. Lincoln called out the federal militia to suppress the insurrection, prompting four other slave states to secede and join the Confederacy.[2]

Shortly after the first shots were fired in the Civil War, free Black men in the North began to form militia units and volunteer for service in the Union army.

Black volunteers realized that military service afforded them the opportunity to prove their loyalty to the United States and manhood in the war against southern slaveholders. More importantly, they were certain that Confederate defeat would ultimately lead to the end of American slavery. However, before Black men could march off to fight for the liberation of their enslaved brethren, they first had to fight for the opportunity to join America's military.

Despite their heroic service during the Revolutionary War fighting alongside American patriots, the U.S. Congress enacted a statute in 1792 that prohibited Black men from serving in state militias or the U.S. Army or Navy. At the war's outset President Lincoln adamantly opposed the enlistment of Black men because he feared their participation would change the meaning and purpose of the conflict. During the first eighteen months of the war, the ever-cautious president reassured whites in the North and South that the Civil War resulted from political differences concerning "state's rights" rather than a desire to abolish slavery. Despite a string of devastating military defeats, an ever-dwindling pool of white enlistees, and growing antiwar sentiment, as late as July 4, 1862, the president reassured Congress that he would not interfere with slavery where it existed.[3]

Rather than allowing Black men to fight in a war to destroy slavery, Lincoln argued that the best way to resolve the nation's "Negro Problem" was to emancipate and remove freed Blacks to colonies in Africa or South America. Lincoln first spoke in favor of colonization in 1852 by revealing that his first instinct was "to free all the slaves and send them to Liberia." Ten years later, in August 1862, while drafting the document that would become the Emancipation Proclamation, President Lincoln invited a delegation of five free Black ministers to the White House. He encouraged them to endorse his plan to gradually emancipate enslaved Black Americans, compensate former slaveholders, and remove most freed Blacks to colonies in South America. Lincoln argued that given the "differences" between the white and Black races, it would be "better for us both, therefore, to be separated."[4]

Lincoln's support for colonization evoked a firestorm of indignation among all but a few Black and white abolitionists who countered that free and formerly enslaved Black men should be allowed to join the military and be granted the same citizenship rights as white men. Frederick Douglass, the famed Black abolitionist, categorically opposed Lincoln's Negro colonization scheme. "[T]he destiny of the colored American," Douglass wrote, "is the destiny of America. . . . The allotments of Providence seem to make the black man of America the open book out of which the American people are to learn lessons of wisdom, power and goodness—more sublime and glorious than any yet attained by the nations of the old or the new world. To imagine that we should ever be eradicated is absurd and ridiculous. . . . We shall neither die out, nor be driven out; but shall go with this people, either as a testimony against them, or as evidence in their favor throughout their generations." The chastened president quickly removed the controversial language encouraging Black colonization from the preliminary Emancipation Proclamation.[5]

Douglass also chided Lincoln for refusing to transform the war into a struggle to liberate four million enslaved Blacks, arguing that a Union victory could not be achieved unless Black men were allowed to join the fight. "Once let the Black man get upon his person the brass letters, US," he wrote, "let him get an eagle on his button, and a musket on his shoulder and bullets in his pockets, and there is no power on this earth which can deny that he has earned the right to citizenship in the United States." After much deliberation and soul-searching, Lincoln subsequently included another provision to the final draft of the document that would transform the war over "state's rights" into a crusade to abolish American slavery.[6]

Like Oglethorpe, as a wartime commander Lincoln shouldered the burden of ordering men to fight and die on the fields of battle. Although he initially resisted calls by abolitionists to enlist free and formerly enslaved Blacks in the U.S. military, like Oglethorpe before him, he was able to grasp the strategic importance of enslaved populations during times of war. Both men understood that enslaved people, regardless of race or color, would exercise agency by fighting on behalf of anyone who offered freedom in exchange for military allegiance.

During a July 21, 1862, cabinet meeting, Lincoln announced that he was drafting a proclamation that would free all enslaved Blacks living in states and jurisdictions still in rebellion. Most importantly, after nearly two years of vacillation, Lincoln's Emancipation Proclamation would also authorize the enlistment of Black men in the U.S. Army and Navy. Secretary of State W. H. Seward bluntly observed that because of recent military setbacks, white northerners might view the issuance of the proclamation as an act of desperation, "the last measure of an exhausted Government, a cry for help; the Government stretching forth its hand to Ethiopia, instead of Ethiopia stretching forth her hand to the Government." Lincoln accepted his secre-

The First South Carolina Volunteers Regiment, the first all-Black U.S. military regiment, made up of the formerly enslaved, were tasked with maintaining law and order in Savannah.

(Artokoloro / Alamy Stock Photo)

tary's advice and withheld the proclamation until a northern victory could be claimed on the battlefield. On September 22, 1862, following a limited victory at the Battle of Antietam, Lincoln issued a preliminary Emancipation Proclamation decreeing that all enslaved persons living in states still at war with the United States on January 1, 1863, "shall be then, henceforward, and forever free."[7]

During the most critical stages of the Civil War, 137 years after Oglethorpe's humbling defeat at Fort Mose, President Lincoln belatedly realized what history and military experience had taught General Oglethorpe. The South's enslaved Black population was a valuable strategic asset that could be leveraged against the Confederate military. Prior to the issuance of his proclamation, only a few independent efforts to organize all-Black Union army regiments had been initiated, in South Carolina, Kansas, and Louisiana; this would be the first national recruitment campaign.[8]

During the last two years of the conflict, approximately two hundred thousand Black men, 80 percent of whom were formerly enslaved, joined the fight against the Confederacy. The president's proclamation placed the undermanned Confederate military in the untenable position of having to engage an enemy without (advancing northern forces) and defend against a newly aroused enemy within (enslaved Black southerners who could now fight for the freedom of their people).

Although only a few enslaved Black men bore arms on behalf of Confederate rebels, a vast army of enslaved laborers supported the Confederate war effort by serving as orderlies, teamsters, and military laborers. On the home front, enslaved Black southerners supplied the labor for plantations, factories, arsenals, and mines. President Lincoln, America's commander-in-chief, finally acknowledged what Black and white abolitionists had asserted from the beginning of the war: enslaved Blacks should be emancipated and transformed into a much-needed reservoir of manpower for America's military.[9]

Having made the monumental decision to proclaim the abolition of slavery in the rebellious states and enlist Black men in the war to save the Union, Lincoln humbly requested that his historic order be blessed with "the considerate judgement of mankind, and the gracious favor of Almighty God." Although in the concluding paragraph of the Proclamation, Lincoln explained that his decision to free enslaved Black southerners was "an act of justice, warranted by the Constitution upon military necessity," it would soon become apparent that it also coincided with the president's profound spiritual awakening.[10]

"Let My People Go!"

DURING THE SPRING OF 1864, General William Tecumseh Sherman and his army abandoned their encampments around Chattanooga, Tennessee, marched into northern Georgia, and engaged Confederate forces in a series of bloody battles. Constantly flanking and outmaneuvering the entrenched rebels, Sherman relentlessly pushed the desperate defenders back to the outskirts of Atlanta. The pivotal fighting of the campaign occurred on July 22, 1864, during the Battle of Atlanta, when thirty-five thousand Confederate and forty thousand Union soldiers clashed in a series of pitched battles, resulting in nearly ten thousand combined casualties. Following an ensuing five-week federal siege, Confederate general John Hood evacuated the Army of Tennessee from Atlanta. On September 3, 1864, Sherman occupied the city and dispatched a brief telegram to President Lincoln: "Atlanta is ours and fairly won."[1]

The capture of Atlanta was a major Union victory that also reenergized Lincoln's faltering 1864 reelection campaign and boosted northern morale. On November 8, the president won a landslide victory over the Democratic Party candidate, former Union general George B. McClellan, who had promised, if elected, to secure a negotiated peace with the Confederacy. Despite his stunning victory, General Sherman had no intention of permanently occupying or garrisoning Georgia's fourth-largest city. He informed Commanding General Ulysses S. Grant of his plan to forcibly evacuate all civilians from Atlanta and burn the South's most industrialized city to the ground. Following the destruction of Atlanta, he planned to lead his army on a daring march to the Atlantic Ocean. The primary purpose of the march was to undermine the morale of white southerners still supporting the rebellion, by destroying Confederate factories, farms, railroads, and telegraph lines. Northern troops would also be authorized to "forage liberally" by raiding farms and plantations, confiscating cows, chickens, hogs, cattle, and horses. Enslaved young Black men, the most productive plantation workers, would be employed to support the invading army by working as pioneers and laborers. Following weeks of intense lobbying, Sherman secured Grant's permission to implement his controversial "total war" strategy.[2]

Atlanta's mayor and council protested the pending evacuation, arguing that it would force thousands of innocent white civilians into homelessness in the midst of winter. Sherman responded that his order was not intended to "meet the humanities" but to end the war. "You cannot qualify war in harsher terms than I will," he wrote. "War is cruelty and you cannot refine it. . . . You might as well appeal against the thunder-storm as against these terrible hardships of war. . . . We don't want your Negroes, or your horses, or your land, or anything you have, but we do want and will have obedience to the laws of the United States."[3]

General Hood dispatched an angry letter to Sherman denouncing the "studied and ingenious cruelty" of his evacuation order. Hood asserted, "You came into our country with your army, avowedly for the purpose of subjugating free white men, women, and children, and not intending to rule over them, but you make Negroes your allies, and desire to place over us an inferior race, which we have raised from barbarism to its present position. . . . Better die a thousand deaths than submit to live under you or your Government and your Negro allies!"[4]

Beginning on the night of November 14, 1864, into the following day, Sherman's men methodically set fires throughout Atlanta. Historians still debate the extent of the damage inflicted on the city; however, there is little debate that the general was determined to make good on his promise to "make Georgia howl." As the fires blazed out of control, a dark cloud of smoke engulfed the deserted city. From a hill overlooking Atlanta, Sherman paused to observe the conflagration, but he soon turned his attention to the daunting task that lay ahead.[5]

To camouflage his true intentions, Sherman marched his army eastward over several parallel roads across a sixty-mile front. A "devil-may-care" attitude buoyed the officers and soldiers as they "struck up" the abolitionist hymn "John Brown's Soul Goes Marching On," and Sherman later recalled that he had not "heard the chorus 'Glory, glory, hallelujah!' done with more spirit, or in better harmony of time and place." His soldiers were ordered to step lively as they marched into DeKalb County, filing through Decatur, "a dilapidated village," and along the road to the battle-ravaged town of Stone Mountain. Joy-filled newly freed Blacks rushed to greet their liberators and later hon-

General William T. Sherman captured and burned Atlanta in November 1864. He then made good on his pledge to "make Georgia howl" by leading his sixty-thousand-man army on a devastating three-hundred-mile march from Atlanta to the sea.

(Courtesy of the Library of Congress Prints and Photographs Division) ored Sherman by naming their settlement of makeshift shanties Sherman-town. From Stone Mountain, the union columns headed toward Lithonia, where Sherman spent the night. From there the general could clearly see the hauntingly grayish hues of Stone Mountain, "a mass of granite" illuminated by the glow of "bonfires of rail-ties" and burning Confederate buildings. The following day a dusty blue stream of soldiers passed through "the handsome town of Covington." Several hundred jubilant and grateful Blacks crowded the roadsides and cheered their conquering heroes.[6]

It was here that northern soldiers first witnessed the unrestrained religious fervor that would accompany the liberation of Black Georgians throughout their march to Savannah. According to Sherman, the newly freed Blacks were "simply frantic with joy." Tens of thousands of jubilant Black Christians greeted the arrival of Sherman's army as an act of divine Providence and fulfillment of the millennial prophecies. The devoutly religious and mostly illiterate formerly enslaved Christians liberally interposed belief in the Exodus and Jubilee prophecies with other religious scriptures and parables. In the Old Testament God selects Moses to lead the Israelites out of Egyptian enslavement and directs him to tell Pharaoh to "let my people go" (Exodus 7:16).[7]

Disavowing the "Slave Religion" forced on them by Christian slaveholders, they now proclaimed Sherman's conquering army to be the Army of the Lord, sent to set his chosen people free. Black Christians were certain a living God had once again intervened in the affairs of men to rescue His children from perpetual bondage. To them, the arrival of their blue-coated liberators heralded the dawning of their long-prayed-for Day of Jubilee.[8]

"Whenever they heard my name," Sherman wrote, "they clustered about my horse, shouted and prayed in their peculiar style, which had a natural eloquence that would have moved a stone." In a letter to his wife, Sherman later observed, "They [Blacks] flock to me, old and young, they pray and shout and mix my name with that of Moses, Simon and other scriptural ones as well as 'Abram Linkom,' the Great Messiah of 'Dis Jubilee.'" An elderly, gray-headed Black man gazed reverently at Sherman and exclaimed, "I have seen the great Messiah and the army of the Lord!" Although most federal soldiers possessed a strong racial bias against Blacks, some found it difficult not to be affected by the outpouring of religious fervor. "The whole land seemed to be inhabited by Negroes," recalled an unidentified soldier, "and the appearance of the army . . . awakened in them the most extraordinary religious emotion."[9]

All but a few of the enslaved Black Georgians who lived in the path of the

CONTRABANDS ACCOMPANYING THE LINE OF SHERMAN'S MARCH THROUGH GEORGIA.—FROM A SKETCH BY OUR SPECIAL ARTIST.

Approximately eighteen thousand enslaved Black Georgians escaped from bondage and joined General William T. Sherman's army during their March to the Sea.

(From *Frank Leslie's Illustrated Newspaper,* March 18, 1865)

advancing army deserted their slave quarters as more than eighteen thousand Blacks exercised the agency of flight by following in the wake of Sherman's army. Men, women, and children of all ages and conditions joined the march at every mile along the way to Savannah. They did not know where they were going or how long it would take them to get there, but the newly emancipated Blacks demonstrated a collective willingness to risk everything to secure their freedom. One northern journalist addressed the broader implications of the mass escape from Georgia bondage: "The oft expressed fallacy that they preferred slavery to freedom . . . [has been] 'crushed to earth,' . . . never to rise again."[10]

Although some slaveholders stubbornly clung to the idealized notion of the loyal and devoted slave, they could not ignore the wholesale escape of their former bondsmen. Myrta Avary, wife of a Georgia slaveholder, wrote: "We went to sleep one night with a plantation full of Negroes, and woke to find not one on the place every servant gone to Sherman. . . . We had thought there was a strong bond of affection on their side as well as ours!" White Georgians were slow to realize or acknowledge they were witnessing the largest mass escape of enslaved Blacks in the history of North American slavery.[11]

Grateful Blacks provided Union soldiers with critical intelligence regarding local terrain, Confederate troop movements, and the locations of hidden food, jewelry, and other valuables. An unidentified soldier observed, "Let those who choose to curse the Negro curse him; but one thing is true. . . . They were the only friends on whom we could rely for the sacred truth in Dixie. What they said might be relied on, so far as they knew; and they knew more and could tell more than most of the poor white population."[12]

Writing seven decades after the Civil War ended, W. E. B. Du Bois spoke lyrically of the Black exodus from Georgia bondage: "Some see all significance in the grim front of the destroyer, and some in the bitter sufferers of the Lost Cause. But to me . . . neither speaks with so deep a meaning as that dark human cloud that clung like remorse on the rear of those swift columns, swelling at times to half their size, almost engulfing and chocking them. In vain they were ordered back, in vain were bridges hewn beneath their feet; on they trudged and withered and surged, until they rolled into Savannah, a starved and naked horde of tens of thousands."[13]

Death at Ebenezer Creek

SHERMAN WAS REVERED AND WORSHIPPED by his Black camp followers, but he was, at best, a reluctant liberator of enslaved Black southerners. He disliked the institution of slavery, but the enigmatic general also stated that if given a choice, he would not abolish or modify it. He was criticized by northern abolitionists for issuing orders in Atlanta that prohibited all Blacks, except those who could be of service to the army, from joining the march. (These orders were ignored by thousands of formerly enslaved Georgians, but Sherman's critics argued that others were unnecessarily left behind.) The general also angered white northerners by refusing to enlist Black men recruited by state agents who used trickery, fraud, and deceit to secure their agreement to join the Union military.

By mid-November 1864, as Sherman and his army were about halfway to Savannah, twenty miles or so from Milledgeville, the state capital, the Georgia legislature conducted a chaotic, emergency session and on November 19 passed a statute that immediately drafted all white men in Georgia—except legislators and judges—into the army. But it was too little, too late. On November 22, 1864, federal troops entered, without opposition, the mostly abandoned city.[1]

The regimental bands played "Yankee Doodle," columns of northern soldiers sang the national anthem, and the Stars and Stripes replaced the Confederate flag above Georgia's fallen state capitol. Thousands of Blacks joyfully gathered along the sidewalks to cheer their triumphant liberators. The white residents who chose not to flee stayed in their homes, although Sherman sarcastically noted that Governor Joseph Brown and members of the legislature had "ignominiously fled, in the utmost disorder and confusion . . . some by rail, some by carriages, and many on foot."[2]

With hundreds of drunk and rowdy soldiers cheering them on, some of the soldiers conducted a mock session of the Georgia legislature in the statehouse. A speaker and other officers were elected, and the men roared with laughter as the "legislators," many of whom were suffering from "bourbon fits," were laid out unconscious on the floor. The boisterous session was finally adjourned when several soldiers rushed into the chambers and shouted, "The Yankees are coming! The Yankees are coming!" The drunken men mocking the departed Georgia legislators pretended to cringe in terror and fled the building.[3]

Despair and desperation consumed the city's remaining white population as Sherman established his headquarters in the governor's mansion, where city leaders sought an audience with him to request protection for homes and businesses. "We were despondent," wrote Anna Marie Green, the daughter of the superintendent of the state insane asylum. "Our heads are bowed and our hearts crushed, the Yankees in possession of Milledgeville. The Yankee flag waved from the Capitol. Our degradation was bitter."[4]

Marauding soldiers laid waste to the government offices, and millions of dollars of unsigned (and worthless) Confederate currency was burned by the bundle or used to light pipes and cigars. Private homes were looted and gardens stripped clean. But, to the surprise of Milledgeville's white residents, only the penitentiary, arsenal, and weapons storehouses were set alight.[5]

On November 24 Sherman's army began to vacate Milledgeville. By nine o'clock the next morning, the last brigades crossed over to the east bank of the Oconee River, leaving behind a thoroughly disemboweled city. The editor of the local paper observed: "A full detail of all the enormities . . . would fill a volume, and some of them too bad to publish. In short, if an army of Devils just let loose from the bottomless pit were to invade the country, they could not be much worse than Sherman's army."[6]

Although Sherman's troops left the countryside in ruins, there had been very little loss of civilian life. That would change nine days later during one of the war's most tragic and controversial episodes. By early December, under the command of Union brigadier general Jefferson Davis (no relation to the Confederate president), the fourteen thousand men that composed the rear guard of Sherman's army had cut a northerly path from Atlanta through the heart of Georgia. In fact, the general's men had marched almost unimpeded across two hundred miles of enemy territory, until they were finally halted in Effingham County about twenty-five miles north of Savannah, where Ebenezer Creek flowed near the village of Springfield and meandered eastward past the historic Ebenezer settlement—ancestral home of German Salzburgers who migrated to Georgia in 1735. Several days of heavy rains had transformed the creek, a tributary of the Savannah River, into a raging stream a hundred feet wide and at least ten feet deep. Normally placid, the creek was now virtually impassable.[7]

Davis ordered his engineers to construct a pontoon bridge across Ebenezer Creek, and two days later, on December 3, the entire Fourteenth Corps crossed safely over the hastily built structure. An official messenger had misled the Blacks accompanying the troops into believing that fighting was occurring on the other side of the creek and that they should not proceed until all the soldiers and wagons had crossed over. After the Union columns, including the young Black men who were supporting the soldiers as pioneers, reached the opposite bank, the pontoon bridge was taken up, leaving mostly women with children and elderly Blacks stranded on the other side.[8]

Shortly thereafter Confederate soldiers rode up in a full gallop with swords slashing and firing indiscriminately into the terrified crowd. One eyewitness, John Hight, a chaplain from Indiana, recalled what happened next. Hight remembered that someone shouted, "The Rebels are coming!" and "There went up from that multitude . . . a cry of agony that should have melted the stoniest heart." Realizing their dire predicament, hundreds of formerly enslaved Blacks rushed to the water's edge, raising their hands and begging the Union soldiers for protection. The panic-stricken Blacks "made a wild rush. . . . Some of them at once plunged into the water and swam across. Others ran wildly up and down the bank, shrieking with terror and crying for help."[9]

The trapped freedom seekers made desperate attempts to save themselves. A muscular young Black man was among the first to dive into the treacherous waters; he swam until he reached the far bank. Women carrying small children in their arms rushed in behind him but were swept downstream and presumably drowned. Union soldiers acting without official orders, frantically tossed felled logs and pieces of wood into the floodwaters to aid those who were fighting for their lives.[10]

Several Black men fashioned a makeshift raft out of wood and blankets, and although it sank several times, it managed to ferry scores of women and children to safety. At one point a Black woman riding on the raft lost her balance and tumbled into the water. Her husband dragged her back onboard, and they reached the shore exhausted but thankful. "I'd rather drown myself than lose her," the man exclaimed. An elderly couple also made it across, and the grateful man cried out, "Praise the Lord, we got away from the Rebels. . . . We got troubles on our road but bless the Lord, it will be all right in the end."[11]

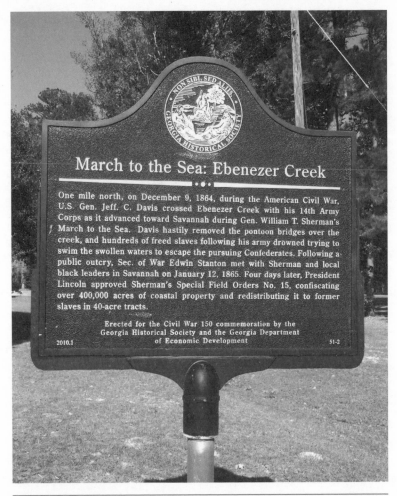

March to the Sea: Ebenezer Creek

One mile north, on December 9, 1864, during the American Civil War, U.S. Gen. Jeff. C. Davis crossed Ebenezer Creek with his 14th Army Corps as it advanced toward Savannah during Gen. William T. Sherman's March to the Sea. Davis hastily removed the pontoon bridges over the creek, and hundreds of freed slaves following his army drowned trying to swim the swollen waters to escape the pursuing Confederates. Following a public outcry, Sec. of War Edwin Stanton met with Sherman and local black leaders in Savannah on January 12, 1865. Four days later, President Lincoln approved Sherman's Special Field Orders No. 15, confiscating over 400,000 acres of coastal property and redistributing it to former slaves in 40-acre tracts.

Erected for the Civil War 150 commemoration by the
Georgia Historical Society and the Georgia Department
of Economic Development

2010.1   51-2

Georgia Historical Society marker at Ebenezer Creek in Effingham County, Georgia.

As the columns pressed onward toward Savannah, one officer of the Ninety-Second Indiana Regiment encountered a grief-stricken woman whose infant son had been lost during the chaotic crossing. The now childless mother "was crying as though her heart would break," as "if she and her child were white." Later that evening, the still shaken soldier solemnly recorded in his diary, "The sights I this morning witnessed I cannot get out of my head."[12]

Major James A. Connolly of the 123rd Illinois Infantry was seething with anger: "The idea of five or six hundred black women, children and old men being returned to slavery by such an infernal Copperhead as Jeff C. Davis was entirely too much." Connolly told his fellow staff officers that he considered Davis's abandonment of the formerly enslaved Blacks to be "inhumane" and "barbarous." He declared, "I am determined to expose this act of his publicly." Connolly made good on this threat by writing a letter of protest to the Military Committee of the U.S. Senate; he also delivered a copy of the letter to General Absalom Baird, who subsequently delivered it to the *New York Tribune*.[13]

Although his statements were contradicted by northern media accounts, Confederate general Joseph Wheeler later claimed that his soldiers did not kill any of the abandoned Blacks. However, he did admit that hundreds of the Blacks were captured and presumably returned to enslavement. A northern journalist provided a decidedly different and chilling narrative: "The waters of the Ogechee and Ebenezer Creek can account for hundreds who were blocking up . . . [the Union] columns, and then abandoned. Wheeler's cavalry charged on them, driving them, pell-mell, into the waters, and mothers and children, old and young, perished alike!" According to Colonel Charles Kerr of the Sixteenth Illinois Cavalry, "I . . . witnessed a scene the like of which I pray my eyes may never see again." Kerr lamented, "I speak of what I saw, and no writer who was not on the ground can gloss the matter over for me. It was claimed this was done because rations were becoming scarce; in short, that it was a military necessity. There was no necessity about it. It was unjustifiable and perfidious and my soul burns with indignation as I recall it."[14]

Most northern soldiers rarely sympathized with the plight of newly freed Blacks, but the heart-wrenching events at Ebenezer Creek infuriated even battle-hardened troops. Private Harrison Pendergast of the Second Minnesota Regiment lambasted Davis, whom he presumed to be a Christian, for the callous treatment of the Black freedom seekers. "Where can you find in all the annals of plantation cruelty anything more completely inhuman and fiendish than this? Legree [the villain of the novel *Uncle Tom's Cabin*] was an angel of mercy in comparison. . . . This barbarous act has created a deep feeling against Davis in this Division." Chaplain Hight concurred: "Davis is a military tyrant, without one spark of humanity in his makeup. He was an ardent pro-slavery man before he entered the army and has not changed his views since."[15]

The exact number of victims of the Ebenezer Creek massacre will never be known, but the abandonment of the freedom seekers and senseless loss of life had a profound effect on public opinion in the North. Jacob Cox of the Ninety-Second Illinois posed and then answered the critical question that millions of white northerners were undoubtedly pondering: "And what is it all for? It is freedom; They are periling their lives for freedom, and it seems to me that any people who run such risks are entitled to freedom." He continued, "I believe it is a burning shame and disgrace, and inhuman to leave them to struggle in thirty feet of water for their lives; for they prefer sinking to the water to returning to slavery." However, Cox was certain the newly freed Blacks who lost their lives at Ebenezer Creek had not died in vain. Their death-defying plunge into the dangerous currents had demonstrated beyond question that they literally preferred "to die freemen rather than live [as] slaves."[16]

General Sherman was not present at the deadly crossing, but no doubt he hoped that the tragic incident would be overlooked in the celebration of his triumphant march. This turned out to be a severe miscalculation. Angry northern abolitionists accused him of barbarity and mass murder. Following his arrival in Savannah three weeks later, Sherman confided in a close friend that additional mistakes or missteps regarding the "Negro Question" could "tumble my fame into infamy." Despite his best efforts, the ghosts of the unnumbered dead who perished at Ebenezer Creek would haunt the general as he basked in the glory of military conquest.[17]

"Glory Be to God, We Are Free!"

SHERMAN'S ARMY CULMINATED THEIR daring march with the surrender of Savannah on December 21, 1864. The city was taken without a major battle after its nine thousand Confederate defenders, commanded by General William Hardee, escaped under cover of darkness across the Savannah River over a pontoon bridge to Hutchinson Island. The bridge had been constructed primarily by enslaved Black laborers. The next day Sherman sent a telegram to President Lincoln in which he presented the city of Savannah as a "Christmas gift" to his commander-in-chief. More than 131 years after Oglethorpe and the Georgia Trustees established their slave-free colony, the protracted crusade to abolish chattel slavery had returned to the city of Savannah.[1]

Black Savannahians who were likely unaware of Oglethorpe's providentialist beliefs nonetheless celebrated the arrival of their Yankee liberators as an act of divine intervention. As he rode through the streets of the city, Sherman observed, "The Negroes are having their 'jubilee.'" Reverend James Simms, a minister who would become one of the first Blacks to serve in the Georgia legislature, recalled, "When the morning light of the 22d of December, 1864, broke in upon us, the streets of our city were thronged in every part with the victorious army of liberty; every tramp, look, command, and military movement told us that they had come for our deliverance ... and the cry went around the city from house to house among our race of people, 'Glory be to God, we are free!'"[2]

Sherman commander General Oliver O. Howard (later the principal founder and namesake of Howard University, one of America's most prestigious historically Black universities) noted that the day federal soldiers first appeared in Savannah was "a day of manifest joy" for local Blacks. Howard posed a rhetorical question: "Wasn't it a visible answer to their long-continued and importunate prayers?" A Black woman explained to one of her liberators, "I'd always thought about this, and wanted this day to come, and prayed for it and knew God meant it should be here sometime, but I didn't believe I should ever see it. I bless the Lord for it." Another Black woman exclaimed, "It's a dream, sir a dream!"[3]

The realization of Black Savannah's freedom dreams was viewed by all but a few white Savannahians as a horrible all-consuming nightmare. Fanny Cohen recorded in her diary that Christmas 1864 was "the saddest Christmas that I have ever spent." Local whites were disheartened by Savannah's occupation; however, they were especially perturbed by the hero's welcome extended to northern soldiers by freed Blacks. Savannah's former slaveholders were also surprised and angered by how quickly liberated Blacks deserted their former places of bondage.[4]

Sherman's bold military campaign earned him national and international acclaim. However, this admiration was not universal. Detractors in the North argued that Sherman had prolonged the war by allowing two large rebel armies to escape prior to capturing Atlanta and Savannah. Abolitionists and radical Republicans in Congress accused him of betraying the true cause of the war by discouraging enslaved Blacks from following and joining his army. The stinging criticism was, in large part, because several of his soldiers exposed the alleged "military decisions" that led to the massacre of Black people at Ebenezer Creek.[5]

On January 11, 1865, Lincoln's secretary of war, Edwin Stanton, arrived unexpectedly in Savannah. The outcry in the North had prompted Lincoln administration officials to dispatch Stanton to gather facts surrounding Sherman's treatment of formerly enslaved Blacks and to urge once again the general to enlist Black men in his army. Stanton questioned Sherman about the conduct of his commanders, prompting the general to summon General Davis into the room. Although Davis admitted that some Blacks had drowned trying to cross Ebenezer Creek, he contradicted the eyewitness accounts by claiming that rebel soldiers had not killed any of the Black people he had deserted there.[6]

Stanton then directed Sherman to assemble a delegation of Black leaders so that he could engage them in a discussion regarding the future of their emancipated race. Sherman subsequently assembled twenty ministers and lay leaders from Savannah's Black community to meet with the secretary on Thursday, January 12, 1865, at 8:00 p.m. in Sherman's headquarters, located in the home of Charles Green, a wealthy Savannah cotton broker. Known today as the Green-Meldrim House, the mansion is located a stone's throw south of the site at Yamacraw Bluff where Oglethorpe established the Savannah settlement in February 1733.[7]

Stanton later intimated to a friend that the meeting marked the first time that a representative of the U.S. government had ever reached out to the "poor debased people to ask them what they wanted for themselves." Exactly one month later, a verbatim report of the meeting was delivered to the prominent abolitionist Reverend Henry Ward Beecher, who distributed copies to his Plymouth Church congregation in Brooklyn, New York. On February 13, 1865, the *New York Tribune* printed the text of the historic discussion in its entirety.[8]

The designated spokesman for the delegation was sixty-seven-year-old Garrison Frazier, who formerly served as pastor of the Third African Baptist Church. Frazier had been enslaved until shortly before the Civil War, when he purchased freedom for himself and his wife for $1,000 in gold and silver. Other key members of the delegation were William J. Campbell, age fifty-one, the pastor of the First African Baptist Church, who had been manumitted by his enslaver's will in 1849; John Cox, fifty-eight, the pastor of the Second African Baptist Church, who had purchased his freedom for $1,100 in 1849; and Ulysses L. Houston, forty-one, the pastor of the Third African Baptist Church, who was freed by the U.S. military. Houston would be among the first of his race to serve as a state senator in the Georgia General Assembly. Also present were William Bentley, seventy-two, the pastor of Andrews Chapel Methodist Church, who had been emancipated by the will of his enslaver at the age of twenty-five; William Gaines, forty-one, who had served as a Methodist pastor for the last sixteen years and was enslaved by Confederate senator Robert Toombs and his brother Gabriel until freed by American soldiers; and James Porter, thirty-nine, who was born free in Charleston, South Carolina, and had served as president of the Board of Wardens and Vestry at St. Stephen's Protestant Episcopal Colored Church of Savannah. During the Reconstruction era Porter would represent Chatham County in the Georgia House of Representatives. The youngest member was James Lynch, twenty-six, who was born free in Baltimore and served as the presiding elder of the Methodist Episcopal Church and a missionary to the Department of the South.[9]

Stanton began what amounted to an interrogation by asking Frazier to elaborate on his understanding of the meaning of the Emancipation Proclamation. Frazier responded, "So far as I understand President Lincoln's proc-

Sherman meeting with Black preachers at the Green-Meldrim House in Savannah, Georgia, on January 12, 1865, to solicit their opinion on how the U.S. government could assist formerly enslaved Black Americans.

(Courtesy of the Ralph Mark Gilbert Museum)

lamation to the Rebellious States," Frazier stated, "it is, that if they would lay down their arms and submit to the laws of the United States before the first of January 1863, all would be well, but if they did not, then all the slaves of the Rebel States would be free henceforth and forever." Stanton followed with a question regarding the meaning of slavery and the freedom authorized by Lincoln's proclamation, to which Frazier replied, "Slavery is receiving by *irresistible power* the work of another man, and not by his *consent*. The freedom ... promised by the proclamation, is taking us from under the yoke of bondage, and placing us where we could reap the fruit of our own labor, take care of ourselves, and assist the Government in maintaining our freedom."[10]

Stanton then posed a question to Frazier regarding a last-ditch Confederate plan to conscript and possibly manumit enslaved Black men who had served in the rebel army: "If the rebel leaders were to arm the slaves, what would be its effect?" Frazier responded, "I think they would fight as long as they were before the bayonet, and just as soon as they could get away they would desert." However, the minister was certain that "thousands of young [Black] men" would prefer to enlist in the Union army because "they have suffered so long from the Rebels that they want to shoulder the musket."

Frazier added that he, like Sherman, opposed compulsory enlistment of formerly enslaved men by unscrupulous state recruiting agents because a Black man serving as "substitute" for a white man leaves one white man at home and ultimately does not strengthen the army.[11]

The next question focused on the most critical issue facing the Lincoln administration: Could newly free Blacks care for themselves? The venerable pastor must have sensed that, in his response, he was articulating the hopes, dreams, and aspirations of four million Blacks who were literally standing on the threshold of freedom: "The way we can best take care of ourselves, is to have land, and turn it and till it by our own labor—we can soon maintain ourselves and have something to spare." Frazier added that Black people wanted to take control of their post-slavery destinies by establishing small farms on confiscated Confederate land until they could save enough money to purchase it.[12]

Sherman and Stanton listened intently to the thoughtful answers spoken by the devout Savannah preacher. The secretary took copious notes and occasionally stared in amazement at Frazier, whose ideas impressed him as being "shrewd, wise and comprehensive." The next question concerned an issue that would be a continuing source of racial conflict and tension in America: "In what manner would you rather live—scattered among the whites or in colonies by yourselves?"[13]

"I would prefer to live by ourselves," stated Frazier. "There is a prejudice against us in the South that will take years to get over; but I do not know if I can answer for my brethren." Aware of some internal disagreement regarding this issue, he paused to allow the other men to speak. Only James Lynch, the freeborn minister from Baltimore, disagreed. Lynch, who could be described as more progressive than his Black colleagues, insisted that whites and Blacks should be allowed to live together in integrated communities.[14]

After more than an hour of questioning, Stanton asked Sherman, who later confessed that he was insulted by the request, to leave the room. The secretary posed a final question to the delegation regarding their opinion of the general. Despite the withering criticism being leveled at Sherman by northern abolitionists, Frazier lavished praise on the conquering hero: "We looked upon Gen. Sherman prior to his arrival as a man in the Providence of God specially set apart to accomplish this work, and we unanimously feel inexpressible gratitude to him. Some of us called upon him immediately upon his arrival, and . . . he met us . . . as a friend and a gentleman. We have con-

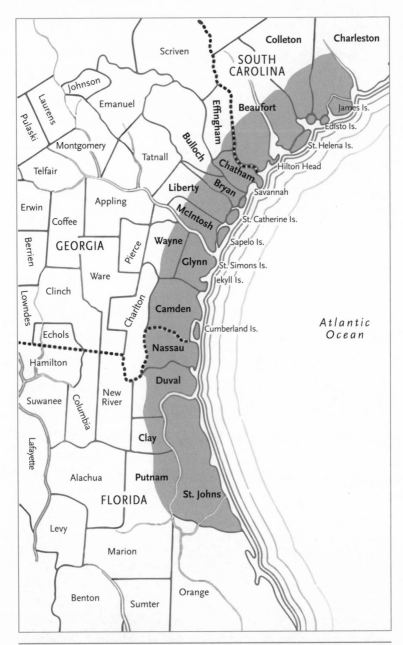

Map of the "Sherman Reservation" setting aside approximately four hundred thousand acres of land in South Carolina, Georgia, and Florida from Charleston, South Carolina, to Jacksonville, Florida, "30 miles in from the sea," for newly freed Blacks. Sherman's Field Order no. 15 became known as "forty acres and a mule."

(Julie Witmer Custom Map Design)

fidence in General Sherman and think that what concerns us could not be under better hands."[15]

Hoping to quell abolitionist outrage over the Ebenezer Creek massacre, Stanton instructed Sherman to devise a plan for the provision of food, shelter, and other support for newly freed Black southerners. On January 16, 1865, the general issued Special Order no. 15, based largely on Frazier's framework, which stated in part that "young and able-bodied Negroes must be encouraged to enlist as soldiers in the service of the United States, to contribute their share toward maintaining their own freedom, and securing their rights as citizens of the United States." Sherman's order also decreed: "The islands from Charleston south, the abandoned rice fields along the rivers for thirty miles back from the sea, and the country bordering the St. John's River, Fla., are reserved and set apart for the settlement of the Negroes now made free by the acts of war and the proclamation of the President of the United States." One aspect of Sherman's land redistribution order bore a striking resemblance to the colonization plan that was originally devised by Oglethorpe and the Georgia Trustees. Each Black family living in the "Sherman Reservation" would be given a "possessory license," rather than an outright fee simple title to forty acres of tillable land.[16]

The "Sherman Reservation" contained more than 435,000 acres, and by the spring of 1865 more than forty thousand Blacks had established themselves in "colonies" of subdivided farms along the southeastern seaboard. Sherman also provided Black colonists with hundreds of mules and horses confiscated during his march from Atlanta to Savannah, which resulted in Sherman's plan being popularized as "forty acres and a mule." In many ways, Sherman's field order was more revolutionary than Lincoln's Emancipation Proclamation as thousands of freedmen were granted "temporary" possession of a sizable portion of the land they and their ancestors had tilled without compensation. The newly freed Black Christians joyfully, albeit prematurely, proclaimed that the Exodus and Jubilee prophecies had been fulfilled.[17]

In mid-January 1865 Sherman and his army left Savannah and continued their march of devastation and revenge into South Carolina, the birthplace of the rebellion. Although Sherman officially renounced his opposition to the enlistment of Black men in the Union military, none were allowed to join his all-white army. During the following spring, the First South Carolina Volunteers, America's first all-Black military regiment, arrived in Savannah. The First South, now renamed the Thirty-Third United States Colored Troops, was composed of Black enlistees from South Carolina, Georgia, and Florida. Much to the dismay of most white Savannahians, they along with the famed Fifty-Fourth Massachusetts all-Black regiment were assigned the task of maintaining law and order in Georgia's first city.[18]

CHAPTER TWENTY-ONE

Lincoln's Second Inaugural Address

PRESIDENT ABRAHAM LINCOLN DELIVERED HIS second inaugural address on March 4, 1865, only a few weeks before he was assassinated by John Wilkes Booth. Lincoln's "greatest speech" contained rhetoric that was eerily reminiscent of the sentiments raised in a January 1739 antislavery petition that was endorsed and possibly authored by Oglethorpe. The Darien petition, Oglethorpe's October 1776 jeremiad to Granville Sharp, and Lincoln's second inaugural address were infused with the judicial providentialist concepts of "providential intervention" and "retributive justice." Judicial providentialism was the theological thread that connected Oglethorpe and other early antislavery activists to eighteenth-century British and American abolitionists.[1]

More than a century before Lincoln asserted that "American Slavery" was an "offence" to "a living God," the Darien petitioners wrote that sentencing "any race to perpetual Slavery was a sin shocking to human Nature." They prophesized that the "Scourge" of slavery would culminate in a divinely ordained conflagration of death and destruction. Were the men of Darien referencing the looming prospect of a cataclysmic American civil war? Their fateful premonition was both chilling and prescient. The petitioners were certain that enslaved Blacks valued freedom just as much as white people, and their continued enslavement would someday result in a "Scene of Horror."[2]

Echoing ominous words voiced by Oglethorpe and the Darien colonists, Lincoln informed the huge, racially diverse crowd that four million enslaved Black people, held captive primarily in the southern states, was "somehow" the cause of the Civil War. He asserted that the carnage wrought by the "terrible war" between the North and the South was "the woe due to those" who had enslaved Africans and their descendants. After nearly four years of violence, destruction, and approximately seven hundred thousand American deaths, the president hoped and prayed that "this mighty scourge of war would speedily pass away."[3]

(a) The Lincoln Memorial in Washington, D.C., and (b) General James Oglethorpe's statue in Chippewa Square in Savannah, Georgia, were designed by sculptor Daniel Chester French.

The cornerstone of judicial providentialism was the belief that God "rewarded or punished nations" based on "moral character and actions," which could lead to "national punishments." Oglethorpe was an early adherent of judicial providentialist thought. A small but vocal group of early eighteenth-century antislavery evangelical Christians identified the transatlantic slave trade as the source of "woe" that was afflicting the British Empire. The belief that God rewarded or punished nations based on their character became the rhetorical weapon of choice of British and American antislavery and abolitionist activists. Nearly nine decades before Lincoln surmised that slavery precipitated the Civil War, Georgia's founding father was convinced that the American Revolutionary War was a divinely ordained punishment for England's propagation of chattel slavery.[4]

By March 1865 "Lincoln had come to share the abolitionist and African American view of the Civil War as a providential, apocalyptic event that would not only end slavery but redeem the American Republic and vindicate its founding principles." The president's position diverged with William Lloyd Garrison and other radical abolitionists who believed the sole purpose of the war was to punish the nation for its sinful behavior. Lincoln countered that the Civil War would not only cleanse the United States of its original sin but also allow the American people to return to their providential purpose.[5]

Lincoln also emphasized the causal connection between legislation, adopted by the U.S. government, that prohibited the westward expansion of slavery and America's most deadly military conflict. In theory and in practice, these federal antislavery statutes bore "intriguing" similarities to Georgia's 1735 slave importation prohibition. The president then explained that slavery was the "peculiar and powerful interest" that had ignited the Civil War. He added, "To strengthen, perpetuate, and extend this interest was the object for which insurgents would rend the Union, even by war," while the U.S. government "claimed no right to do more than restrict the territorial enlargement of it."[6]

With military victory finally within his grasp, Lincoln observed that Christians in the North and the South "read the same Bible, and pray to the same God; and each invokes His aid against the other." Quoting from Proverbs in the Old Testament, the president's words were laced with mockery, irony, and humility: "It may seem strange that any men should dare to ask a just God's assistance in wringing their bread from the sweat of other men's faces; but let us judge not that we be not judged."[7]

Lincoln solemnly pledged, "if God wills," to prosecute the Civil War "until all the wealth piled by the bondsman's two hundred and fifty years of unrequited toil shall be sunk and until every drop of blood drawn by the lash, shall be paid by another drawn with the sword." Articulating providentialist themes spoken by Oglethorpe and generations of antislavery and abolition activists, the war-weary president humbly accepted the infallibility of God's will. He intoned, "The judgements of the Lord are true and righteous altogether."[8]

Lincoln ended his brief but resolute address with a frequently quoted conciliatory message: "With malice toward none; with charity for all; with firmness in the right, as God gives us to see the right; let us strive on to finish the work we are in; to bind up the nation's wounds; to care for him who shall have borne the battle, and for his widow, and his orphan—to do all which may achieve and cherish a just, and lasting peace among ourselves, and with all nations."[9]

The audience, with the probable exception of the president's soon-to-be assassin, erupted in thunderous applause as Lincoln slowly walked back to his seat. Approximately one month later, on April 9, Confederate general Robert E. Lee surrendered unconditionally to General Ulysses S. Grant at Appomattox Court House in Virginia, and within a week General Joseph E. Johnston surrendered the last rebel army still in the field to General Sherman on April 14. That evening Lincoln was shot and mortally wounded while attending a play at Ford's Theater in Washington, D.C.; at 7:22 a.m. on April 15, 1865, the fifty-six-year-old president was pronounced dead. The Civil War officially ended in Georgia on April 30, when Governor Joseph Brown surrendered the state's last ragtag regiments of Confederate troops to U.S. commanders.[10]

Lincoln's death and the long-awaited end to the military conflict elicited widespread grief amid celebrations of thanksgiving throughout the North. Abolitionists were bereaved by the shocking assassination of the "Great Emancipator" and deeply troubled by the realization that Lincoln's Emancipation Proclamation, which decreed that approximately 3.5 million enslaved Blacks living in the rebellious southern states were free, had been based solely on "military necessity." The postwar legal status of newly freed Black southerners, as well as half a million Blacks enslaved in four border states where the proclamation did not apply, remained unresolved. Resolution of the legal ambiguity required adoption of an amendment to the U.S. Constitution outlawing the institution of American slavery. The Senate had passed the Thirteenth Amendment a year earlier, on April 8, 1864, and after one failed vote and several months of intense legislative maneuvering, the House of Representatives passed the measure on January 31, 1865. The slavery abolition amendment was then transmitted to the states for ratification.[11]

Eleven months later, on December 4, the Georgia legislature convened in Milledgeville, and the first item on their postwar legislative agenda was ratification of the Thirteenth Amendment. Although there was a palpable sense of resentment and anger among the legislators, Governor Charles J. Jenkins, a lawyer from Richmond County, warned the lawmakers that Georgia could not revive slavery even if a majority voted to do so. Jenkins declared that "the ratification of this amendment . . . will remove from among us that cause of bitterness and sectional strife which has wasted our property, and deluged our land in blood." On December 6, 1865, the Georgia General Assembly voted to ratify the constitutional amendment that read in part, "Neither slavery nor involuntary servitude, except as punishment for crime . . . shall exist within the United States." Georgia became the twenty-seventh state to ratify the Thirteenth Amendment, fulfilling the federal requirement that three-quarters of the states approve the measure. The Georgia legislature's adoption of the historic amendment officially abolished chattel slavery in the United States and redeemed General James Oglethorpe's vision for a slave-free Georgia.[12]

The Oglethorpe Legacy

"The Friend of the Oppressed Negro"

HISTORICAL ARGUMENTS THAT CHALLENGE THE validity of Oglethorpe's opposition to slavery are by now familiar. Georgia's slavery prohibition, it has been argued, was solely designed to protect the morals and well-being of white colonists and lacked concern for enslaved Blacks themselves, while Oglethorpe's affiliation with the Royal African Company (RAC), the enterprise that facilitated the enslavement of tens of thousands of Africans, is frequently cited. Even his efforts to rescue Ayuba Suleiman Diallo from slavery are viewed as a singular act of generosity, not an attack against the institution of slavery itself. Following his forced exit from Georgia in 1743, Oglethorpe returned to England and, it is argued, gradually lost interest in maintaining Georgia's slavery prohibition. Implied but not stated is the assumption that he also lost interest in the fight against slavery generally.

Much debate and confusion regarding the "Oglethorpian legacy" can be attributed, as we have seen, to the conflation of the terms "antislavery" and "abolitionism," though they describe distinct political and moral perspectives. Simply stated, "antislavery" refers to individual or organized acts of resistance by enslaved Blacks such as sabotage, violent reprisals, escape, self-purchase, malingering, suicide, infanticide, learning to read and write, or military service during times of war. Also included here were efforts, primarily by white evangelical Christians and Quakers, to lessen the cruelties of enslavement through Christianization, regulation, manumission, mass boycotts, or prohibiting the spread of the institution into new territories or jurisdictions.[1]

Abolitionism, on the other hand, was the formal movement that originated in England and subsequently spread to the United States with a view toward ending the practice itself. Abolitionists were primarily divided into two philosophical camps—immediatism and gradualism—in their efforts. Whereas some abolitionists sought to gradually abolish slavery by prohibiting the transatlantic slave trade, a more ambitious group was opposed to any compromise with slaveholders and advocated for immediate abolition and granting freed Black men full citizenship rights.[2]

During the early decades of the eighteenth century, Oglethorpe was neither a gradualist nor an immediatist—little wonder, since the formal British abolitionist movement was founded more than fifty years after the Georgia colony was established in 1733. But, whatever his motives, he was an antislavery activist, and prohibiting the importation of enslaved Blacks into Georgia was a pioneer *antislavery* strategy that heralded the advent of abolitionism. Definitional distinctions notwithstanding, Oglethorpe's critics assert that his affiliation with a slave-trading company is irrefutable proof of his complicity with the traffickers of human beings.[3]

The factual basis of this accusation is accurate, but the historical record is silent regarding the specific motivation(s) that prompted him to associate with the RAC. Oglethorpe's initial purchase of RAC stock in December 1730 took place nearly two decades after the company lost its slave-trading monopoly, which had been granted by King Charles II in 1663. Political pressure exerted by an influential group of slave traders known as the Bristol Society of Merchant Ventures had forced Parliament to revoke the company's exclusive slave-trading franchise in 1712. After losing their lucrative monopoly, the RAC struggled financially and eventually shifted from trafficking African captives to primarily trading gold, ivory, and other products.[4]

In addition, according to minutes of the Bray Associates dated July 30, 1730, it was RAC officials who asked Oglethorpe, then serving as chair of the missionary society, to arrange a meeting with the group. Prior to his purchase of their stock, the businessmen assured the Bray Associates that they wanted to "be Benefactors to them [Bray Associates] for Promoting their Designs," which presumably included the Christianization of free and enslaved Black people. Unanswered questions surround the overlap of Oglethorpe's tenure as chair of the Bray Associates and his affiliation with the once-dominant slaving enterprise, and they are potentially exculpatory. Nevertheless, Oglethorpe's reputation has been broadly maligned because of his investment in and association with international slave traders.[5]

Ironically, Oglethorpe's affiliation with the RAC was a contributing factor to his coming into possession of the letter written by Ayuba Diallo describing his enslavement. Some historians have also criticized Diallo, the beneficiary of Oglethorpe's intervention, because of his family's involvement in the transatlantic slave trade. Diallo's father was a wealthy Muslim cleric who sold enslaved Africans to British traders. In fact, it was during a slave-trading mission to the African coast that the young African had been taken captive by Mandinka warriors and sold into slavery. Following his miraculous deliverance and return to Africa, one of Diallo's first acts was to purchase an enslaved woman.[6]

Despite his ambiguous behavior regarding slavery, Diallo nonetheless came to represent a significant figure in the abolition struggle. Art historians have celebrated William Hoare's 1733 painting of Diallo as the "earliest known British oil portrait of a named Black man" depicted "as an individual and an equal," and "the first of a freed slave in the history of British art." Diallo's portrait is compelling evidence of the young African's "important and lasting impact on an understanding of West African culture, black identity and the Islamic faith." His monotheism, literacy, and intelligence provided a sharp contrast to virulently racist eighteenth-century stereotypes of the "ignorant savage" and arguments that the transatlantic slave trade benefited Africans because it removed them from barbarism, heathenism, and cannibalism. Diallo's interactions with the king and queen of England and other British elites helped mollify deep-seated prejudices, which held that dark-skinned people were genetically inferior to whites.[7]

In affirming Diallo's significant role in British history and the transatlantic slave trade, modern historians are only returning to an understanding widespread among nineteenth-century abolitionists. Theodore Dwight Weld, an architect of the American abolitionist movement, recognized Diallo as an important figure who affirmed the humanity and moral rights of Black people. But Diallo's singular contributions to the fight against slavery would not have been possible if Oglethorpe had not initiated the enslaved African's deliverance from bondage. Christianization of enslaved Blacks, colonial Georgia's slavery prohibition, and Diallo's rescue were antislavery, not abolitionist activities. None of these efforts contemplated, advocated, or pursued the general abolition of slavery. However, the advocacy of Oglethorpe and other pioneer antislavery activists helped lay the moral and philosophical foundation for the movement that abolished chattel slavery throughout the British Empire and the United States of America.[8]

The most damning, and resilient, critique of Oglethorpe put forward involves his alleged ownership of or investment in a South Carolina plantation that exploited enslaved laborers. The sensational claim that Oglethorpe profited from the work of enslaved Blacks has continued to be repeated, even by prominent historians such as Judge Leon Higginbotham and David Brion Davis. Despite this seeming unanimity of opinion, however, Oglethorpe's purported enslavement of Blacks on a South Carolina plantation has never been substantiated. Moreover, the original accusation was the central element of a smear campaign devised and promoted by proslavery Georgia colonists Patrick Tailfer, Thomas Stephens, Robert Williams, and other Malcontents who realized that legalization of slavery in Georgia was dependent on the erosion of Oglethorpe's reputation and authority. More recently, historian Thomas Hart Wilkins has challenged the truthfulness of the centuries-old claim. "Because the single accusation supporting slave ownership is not direct evidence, because there is no witness to corroborate the charge, because there are no other verifiable histories, and because there were known biased motives, the veracity of the statement that James Oglethorpe owned slaves is questionable." Wilkins concludes that "the probability appears low . . . that Oglethorpe owned slaves."[9]

But if Oglethorpe's reputed exploitation of enslaved Blacks seemingly developed a life of its own, his post-Georgia advocacy against slavery has received scant attention. The death in May 1748 of John Viscount Percival, the earl of Egmont, his strongest ally among the men who served as a Georgia Trustee, and deteriorating antislavery resolve among the remaining social reformers, signaled the end of Oglethorpe's official affiliation with the Georgia experiment and its controversial slavery prohibition. He attended his last meeting of the trust on March 16, 1749.[10]

However, the general's disdain for the enslavement of Black people did not dissipate following the legalization of slavery in Georgia on January 1, 1751. To the contrary, Oglethorpe's abolitionist zeal reached its apex during the last quarter century of his long and eventful life. His journey from a growing awareness to an antislavery position to abolitionism blazed a trail that would be traced by many celebrated abolitionists after him. Included among this august group is the man known as the "Great Emancipator."

In 1936 former Oglethorpe University lecturer Amos Aschbach Ettinger attempted to place Oglethorpe's humanitarian legacy in historical context: "In urging the enactment of the . . . law, prohibiting Negro slavery in the colony,

James Oglethorpe, the Director and Deputy Governor of the Royal African Company and emancipator of Job Jalla [Diallo], became a forerunner of Abraham Lincoln." More recently, Pulitzer Prize–winning historian David Brion Davis has also argued that the sentiments raised by the Darien antislavery petition set forth in 1739, which some historians believe was written or greatly influenced by Oglethorpe, reverberated throughout the antislavery movements and culminated in President Abraham Lincoln's second inaugural address.[11]

Were these bold statements based on objective historiographical analysis, or should they be dismissed as overheated hyperbole? There are no known direct historical links between the two men; however, essential strands of Oglethorpe's antislavery and abolitionist philosophy, religious beliefs, rhetoric, and activism can be found in Lincoln's speeches and policies. With apologies to Plutarch—the Greek philosopher who compared famous Greeks and Romans—paralleling Oglethorpe's and Lincoln's meandering, sometimes ambiguous journeys from antislavery to abolitionism provides enlightenment, if not definitive answers. Both Oglethorpe and Lincoln were antislavery advocates before they embraced abolitionism, and the absence of abolitionist fervor during the early stages of their public careers has been a source of criticism and debate among historians and scholars.[12]

Prior to and immediately after the establishment of the Georgia colony in 1733, Oglethorpe did not support or advocate for the abolition of slavery. After reading a letter written by Ayuba Diallo, an enslaved African, he embarked on a moral and philosophical journey that scores of emerging abolitionists would follow. Oglethorpe's rescue of Diallo from enslavement exposed British elites to advanced African civilization, challenged long-standing racist stereotypes, and coalesced early British antislavery sentiments.

On January 17, 1739, he reminded the Trustees that legalization of slavery in Georgia would lead to the violation of the human rights of Africans. Oglethorpe's words and deeds foreshadowed, by more than half a century, key elements of ideas espoused by late eighteenth- and nineteenth-century British and American abolitionists. From 1733 to 1743 he literally cried out from the Georgia wilderness, raising a prophetic voice in opposition to the enslavement of Black people. On both sides of the Atlantic Ocean, Oglethorpe fomented a controversial, long-delayed debate over the efficacy of the institution of slavery. His strident advocacy shaped and informed the prehistory of the international abolitionist movement.[13]

Criticism that questions the sincerity of Oglethorpe's early advocacy against human bondage is understandable; however, substantial historical evidence documents his heroic fight against chattel slavery. Despite this compelling evidence, James Oglethorpe's name is rarely listed among those who advanced the abolitionist cause. For instance, in 1818 Thomas Clarkson published *The History of the Rise, Progress, and Accomplishment of the Abolition of the African Slave-Trade by the British Parliament*. Clarkson's book contained a detailed "map" or "streams" of the "forerunners and coadjutors" of the abolitionist movement. Although Clarkson celebrated Granville Sharp as the principal founder of the formal British abolitionist movement, he inexplicably omitted the name of James Oglethorpe, who was Sharp's mentor and friend.[14]

A more nuanced evaluation of the "Oglethorpian Legacy" must include the critical support he provided to emerging British abolitionists. General Oglethorpe's early antislavery activism was eclipsed by his mentorship of pioneer British abolitionists such as Olaudah Equiano, Granville Sharp, and Hannah More. Oglethorpe facilitated the initial meeting between Sharp and Equiano that led to the creation of an influential interracial partnership. The two men leveraged public outrage surrounding the *Zong* slave ship massacre to "spur" the birth of the formal abolition movement. Oglethorpe was also among the first Enlightenment thinkers to infuse judicial providentialist theology into antislavery rhetoric.[15]

General Oglethorpe's military experiences, along with an extensive knowledge of ancient African civilizations, buttressed his respect for the humanity and agency of Black people. Oglethorpe came to understand that all human beings, regardless of their race or color, possessed the God-given right to live free of bondage. He openly rejected racist stereotypes that labeled Blacks as subhuman, docile, and genetically preconditioned for perpetual servitude, while arguing that given the opportunity, enslaved Blacks would willingly sacrifice their lives for freedom.

Although enslaved Blacks were the primary agents of their ultimate liberation and the "first" abolitionists, Oglethorpe was among a small but determined interracial coalition of Quakers and evangelical Christians who aided and supported their efforts. Compelling examples of Oglethorpe's willingness to transcend racial, cultural, and religious barriers were his relationships with Mary Musgrove, the mixed-race interpreter and frontier diplomat to Native Indians, and Tomochichi, the chief of the Yamacraw Muscogee Indians; admission of Jewish colonists into Georgia; and willingness to aid Diallo and Equiano, two formerly enslaved Black men.[16]

Oglethorpe is widely acknowledged as the father of Georgia; however, traditional state histories, historical markers, and monuments have ignored or marginalized his staunch advocacy against slavery. Why or how could this glaring oversight of Oglethorpe's significant contributions to the abolitionist movement have occurred? One theory is that generations of historians who embraced the Civil War "Lost Cause" school of thought may have chosen to ignore this important but conflicting aspect of Oglethorpe's legacy. It would have been difficult, if not impossible, to rationalize his determined opposition to perpetual servitude with the idealized notion that race-based chattel slavery was a benign institution. More innocently, analysis of the general's social welfare reform strategies that focus primarily on the development and execution of the relatively short-lived Georgia plan as an assist to impoverished and persecuted whites may have undervalued the importance of his subsequent contributions to abolitionism.

Given Oglethorpe's sustained and fervent opposition to slavery, it is somewhat surprising that numerous historians have advanced, seemingly without question, the "modern consensus view" that Oglethorpe's advocacy and Georgia's slavery prohibition were solely intended to benefit white colonists. "Did the authors of the [Georgia slavery] prohibition truly believe . . . that, regardless of race, it was immoral and un-Christian to enslave any human being?" Judge Leon Higginbotham asks in his celebrated book *In the Matter of Color: Race and the American Legal Process: The Colonial Period.* The judge "sadly" concludes that Georgia's slavery ban was riddled with "inherent moral limitations" manifested in several provisions, including a "racist" fugitive slave clause. He further observes that the effectiveness of the antislavery statute was limited because it was frequently disregarded or sporadically enforced by colonial officials.[17]

Historian Gerald Horne supports the assessment that Oglethorpe and his fellow Trustees possessed no legitimate antislavery beliefs. He derides the Georgia plan as a poorly disguised, proslavery strategy that was specifically designed to fortify chattel slavery in South Carolina and the other British colonies. He asserts that Georgia's founder was an "imperfect critic of slavery" and his "all-white Georgia colony" was nothing more than a "catchment basin" for Blacks attempting to escape British enslavement. Georgia historian Douglas Grant joined the fray by asserting that "Oglethorpe had no moral or personal scruples against slavery," while historian Andrew Lannen rejects the idea that Oglethorpe's rescue of Diallo from slavery is evidence that he had "suddenly reversed his view of slavery's morality."[18]

It is quite possible that Oglethorpe's significant contributions to the struggle for human rights may have escaped detection because his opposition to chattel slavery evolved over several decades. The nineteenth-century Georgia historian Henry Bruce astutely observed that "in later life" Oglethorpe "used language which would almost make us hail him as the first prominent abolitionist." No less authority than Phinizy Spalding, a noted Oglethorpe biographer, concurred that Georgia's founder was "sincere in his antislavery stance" and honestly sought to limit the proliferation of slavery, arguing that the prevailing historical narrative needed to be revised.[19]

In 1984 historian Betty Wood initiated such a revision in a groundbreaking "reassessment" of Oglethorpe's contributions to the fight against slavery. In her carefully reasoned reevaluation, Wood discards her earlier conclusions rejecting the legitimacy of his antislavery beliefs. Based on updated research and analysis, she argues that Oglethorpe possessed a "genuine concern and compassion" for enslaved Blacks and that his desire to protect the well-being of white Georgians was "tempered" with "farsighted" appreciation of the natural rights of Black people.[20]

Wood's revised views represent an inflection point in the long-simmering debate about Oglethorpe's legacy. A "revolution of scholarship" among Georgia historians is shedding new light on the historical significance of colonial Georgia's unique slavery prohibition and has fostered a judgment that the state's antislavery legacy "played a larger role on the world stage than it has previously been given credit." Clearly, a more holistic appreciation of Oglethorpe's legacy is beginning to emerge, affirming that the political, military, religious, economic, and social ramifications of the "Georgia Plan" reverberated far beyond our state's colonial boundaries.[21]

When eighty-eight-year-old General James Oglethorpe died on June 30, 1785, a champion of liberty was lost, and a little-known but important chapter in the struggle to prohibit and abolish slavery ended. Elizabeth, Oglethorpe's beloved wife, followed him in death on October 26, 1787, and her will designated Granville Sharp, a principal founder of the formal abolitionist movement, as one of the executors of her estate. She preserved her late husband's legacy by establishing a generous trust that provided the tireless attorney with income from the profits generated by the manor of Fairstead Hall in Essex. The Oglethorpe bequest dramatically improved Sharp's finances, allowing him to devote himself full-time to the abolitionist cause.[22]

Prior to her death, Elizabeth Oglethorpe had also commissioned a memo-

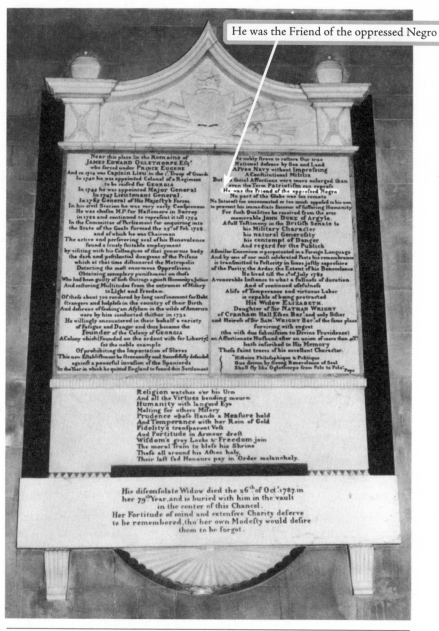

James Edward Oglethorpe Memorial Plaque erected by his wife, Elizabeth, at the Parish Church of All Saints, Cranham, England.

rial plaque erected near her husband's tomb beneath the floor of the Parish Church of All Saints, which had first captured my attention during the Oglethorpe Tercentennial observance. The obscure inscription, etched in marble, that Oglethorpe was "the Friend of the oppressed Negro" had been authored by Capel Lofft, one of Oglethorpe's close associates who shared his antislavery and abolitionist views. It was those unexpected words that inspired me to discover how General James Oglethorpe, our state's founding father, had planted seeds of abolition in Georgia's red clay.[23]

APPENDIX

Primary Documents on Enslavement and Abolition

I. KING CHARLES II OF SPAIN, ROYAL EDICT TO SPANISH FLORIDA COLONISTS INSTRUCTING THEM TO OFFER SANCTUARY TO BLACKS ENSLAVED BY THE BRITISH, NOVEMBER 7, 1693

It has been notified . . . that eight black males and two black females who had run away from the city of San Jorge [Charles Town in the Carolina colony], arrived to that presidio asking for the holy water of baptism, which they received after being instructed in the Christian doctrine. Later on, the chief sergeant of San Jorge visited the city with the intention to claim the runaways, but it was not proper to do so, because they had already become Christians. . . . As a prize for having adopted the Catholic doctrine and become Catholicized, as soon as you get this letter, set them all free and give them anything they need, and favor them as much as possible. I hope them to be an example, together with my generosity, of what others should do. I want to be notified of the following of my instructions as soon as possible.

Madrid, November 7th, 1693,
I, The King

Translation by Bruce Twyman

II. AYUBA BIN SULEIMAN DIALLO'S (JOB BEN SOLOMON) LETTER TO SOLOMON, HIS FATHER, THE SIXTH DAY OF THE MONTH OF RAMADAN, C. 1733

In the name of Allah, the most compassionate, the most merciful, and his blessings upon our Master Muhammad, the Most Generous Prophet. O Muslims in the land of Bundo, Ayuba bin Suleiman [says] peace be upon you. O Muslims, in the land of Bundo in the land of Futa in the land of Kalam, Ayuba bin Suleiman [says] peace be upon you.—O all Muslim men in the land of Bundu and all Muslim women, Ayuba bin Suleiman [says] peace be upon you. His two wives' names are Funta bin Sidiq Baas, and mother of bin Bobu Keita, her children's names are Samba bin Ayuba, Demba bin Ayuba, Fatimata bin Ayuba: O Muslim men and women in the land of Bunu, this is Ayuba in the land of the Christians. There is no good in the land of the Christians for a Muslim.—O Hamad bin Suleiman, do not worry, Ayuba prays and keeps the fast [of Ramadan], behold Muslims in the land of Bundu, this is, without doubt, Ayuba; O Muslims in the land of Bundu, [says to] his two wives, do not marry in the month of Ramadan.—O all Muslim men and women in the land of Bundu, this is Ayuba bin Suleiman Hamad bin Suleiman, no dispute and no doubt about it; O Funta bin Sidiq, O mother of bin Bubo Keita, do not marry. It is Ayuba, it is the sixth day of the month of Ramadan.

English translation of Arabic script, names and places are spelled phonetically.

III. DARIEN PETITION AGAINST THE IMPORTATION OF ENSLAVED BLACKS INTO THE GEORGIA COLONY, JANUARY 3, 1738–1739

Petition of the Inhabitants of New Inverness (Darien) to His Excellency General Oglethorpe

We are informed that our neighbors in Savannah have petitioned your excellency for the liberty of having slaves: we hope, and earnestly intreat, that before such proposals are hearkened unto, your excellency will consider our situation, and of what dangerous and bad consequences such liberty would be of to us, for many reasons.

(1) The nearness of the Spaniards, who have proclaimed freedom to all slaves who run away from their masters, makes it impossible for us to keep them, without more labor in guarding them than what we would be at to do their work.

(2) We are laborious, & know a white man may be, by the year, more usefully employed than a negroe.

(3) We are not rich, and becoming debtors for slaves, in case of their running away or dying, would inevitably ruin the poor master, and he become a greater slave to the negroe-merchant, than the slave he bought could be to him.

(4) It would oblige us to keep guard duty at least as severe as when we expected a daily invasion: and if that was the case, how miserable would it be to us, and our wives and families, to have one enemy without, and a more dangerous one in our bosoms!

(5) It is shocking to human nature, that any race of mankind and their posterity should be sentanc'd to perpetual slavery; nor in justice can we think otherwise of it, that they are thrown amongst us to be our scourge one day or other for our sins: and as freedom must be as dear to them as it is to us, what a scene of horror must it bring about! And the longer it is unexecuted, the bloody scene must be the greater.

We therefore for our own sakes, our wives and children, and our posterity, beg your consideration, and intreat, that instead of introducing slaves, you'll put us in the way to get some of our countrymen, who, with their labor in time of peace, and our vigilance, if we are invaded, with the help of those, will render it a difficult thing to hurt us, or That Part of the Province we possess. We will forever pray for your Excellency, and are with all submission, &C.

New Inverness formerly named Darien 3 Jan. 1738–9
John Mohr Mackintosh
John Mackintosh-Linvilge
John Mackintosh-Son to L. John Mackintosh-Moore
John Mackintosh-Bain
Jo. Cuthbert
James Mackay
Archibald Mcbain, his Mark Amb
Ranald Macdonald
John Macdonald
John Macklean
Jos. Burges, His Mark Be
Donald Clark-First
Alex. Clark, Son of the above
Donald Clark-Second
Donald Clark-Third, His Mark X
Hugh Morrison, His Mark Hm
Alex. Munro
Will Munro

IV. JAMES OGLETHORPE'S LETTER TO THE GEORGIA TRUSTEES OPPOSING THE LEGALIZATION OF SLAVERY IN THE GEORGIA COLONY AND EXPRESSING CONCERN FOR THE WELFARE OF ENSLAVED AFRICANS

Saint Simon's

January 17, 1739

Gentlemen,

I have wrote already a letter upon the head of Negroes and shall only add that if we allow slaves we act against the very principles by which we associated together, which was to relieve the distressed. Whereas, now we should occasion the misery of thousands in Africa, by setting men upon using arts to buy and bring into perpetual slavery the poor people who now live free there.

Instead of strengthening we should weaken the frontiers of America, give away to the owners of slaves that land which was designed as a refuge to persecuted Protestants, prevent all improvements of silk and wine and glut the markets with more of the present American commodities which already but too much interfere with the English produce. I am persuaded you will speedily reject the petition. And as soon as your resolution is known, the idle will leave the province and the industrious will fall to work, many of whom wait 'till they see the event of this application.

I have advanced a pretty deal of money for provisions and other expenses for the service of the province. I have sent over an account of what I gave to the Indians. I have also laid out money for assisting the poor, the widows and the orphans, supporting the boats that keep up the correspondence, the cattle-herders who take care of the Trustees' herds and the Trustees' servants.

I suppose before you receive this the Parliament will have decided what they will do in respect to the colony. I shall therefore say nothing further on that head, but that I hope you will first pay the certified accounts and then, if you approve of the expenses I have made, that you will order it reimbursed.—

I long to hear from you, and hope you will believe me to be, Gentlemen, your most obedient, humble servant.

V. GENERAL JAMES OGLETHORPE'S LETTER TO ANTISLAVERY ACTIVIST ATTORNEY GRANVILLE SHARP

Cranham Hall, Oct. 13, 1776

Sir,

With great pleasure I received the favour of yours of 27th September, and since, several excellent of your composing, which I have read with much satisfaction, as they all point to the great end of life, —the honour of God and love of our neighbour. You have, with great judgment, showed the threats of the prophets against the slave-owners and slave-sellers. As I have not the happiness of being known to you, it is necessary to tell you I am the person you will find mentioned in Harris's Collections (The Last Edition in two fol.), and in Smollet's, in Rolt, and all the histories of that time.

My friends and I settled the colony of Georgia, and by charter were established trustees, to make laws, &c. We determined not to suffer slavery there; but the slave-merchants, and their adherents, occasioned us not only much trouble, but at last got the then government to favour them. We would not suffer slavery (Which is against the gospel as well as the fundamental law of England) to be authorized, under our authority: we refused, as trustees, to make a law permitting such a horrid crime. The government, finding the trustees resolved firmly not to concur with what they thought unjust, took away the charter by which no law could be passed without our consent.

As you will find me in the history of those times, you will find me also in the present list of the army; and, when you come to town, I shall be very glad to see you in Grosvenor Street, where I live in London, as I do here in the country.

This cruel custom of a private man's being supported in exercising more power over the man he affirms to have bought as his slave, than the magistrate has over him the master, is a solecism in politics. This, I think, was taken from the Romans. The horrid cruelty which that proud nation showed in all they did, gave such power to the masters of slaves, that they confused even the state. Decius Brutus, by the gladiators his slaves, defended the conspirators that killed the dictator, Caesar. The cruelty of the slaveholders occasioned them to join Spartacus, who almost overturned Rome. -Their laws were so severe, and the masters' power so horrid, that (Tacitus says) four hundred slaves, entirely innocent, were put to death, because two slaves had murdered their master; and he justifies this step. A Roman threw his old and useless slaves into a pond, where he kept fish, to feed them up to an excellent taste; and their laws did not contradict it.

I find in Sir Walter Raleigh's history of the Saracens, that *their* success, and the destruction of the Grecian and Persian empires, was chiefly owing to their having vast numbers of slaves, by whom all labour and husbandry were carried on. And, on the Mahometans giving freedom to all who professed their law, the multitude in every conquered province joined them.

You mention an argument urged by Hume, that the *Africans were incapable of liberty*, and that no man capable of government was ever produced by Africa. What a historian! He must never have heard of Shishak, the great Sesostris, of Hannibal, nor of Tir-haka king of Ethiopia, whose very name frightened the mighty Assyrian monarch (2 Kings xix. 9.) Is it possible he never should have seen Herodotus, where the mighty works of the pyramids, remaining to this day, are mentioned; and, in the Θaaeia, the answer of the king of Ethiopia to Cambyses? In Leo, the African's geographical description of Africa, he would have found that Africa had produced races of heroes.

The Christian emperors would have qualified the laws for slavery; but the senate of Rome, in whom the old leaven of idolatry still prevailed, stopped such good designs. St. Augustine, in 'De Civitate Dei,' mentions that idolatry was sunk into the marrow of the Romans; —that the destruction of Rome by the Goths seemed to be a necessary dispensation of providence to root out idolatry. The Goths, and all the Northern nations, when converted to Christianity, abolished slavery. The husbandry was performed by men under the protection of the laws. Though some tenures of villeyn were too severe, yet the villeyns had the protection of laws; and their lords could not exact more than was by those laws regulated. (Bracton.)

Spain and Portugal were subdued by the moors: afterwards Portugal was recovered by the Christians. The Portuguese carried the war into Africa, discovered the sea-coast of Guinea, brought the unhappy natives away, and, looking on them as black heathens and hardly men, sold them for slaves.

The Spaniards imitated them, and declared that Moors and Turks, taken in war, might be held as slaves. But the French still hold the noble law of the Northern nations; they allow no slaves in France: but, alas! It is too true, in their plantations, where the king's will is the only law, Lewis the Fourteenth, By the 'Code-Noir,' permits and regulates slavery.

I am exceeding glad that you have entered the lists in opposition to these horrors. It is a proper time to bring these abominable abuses under consideration; and if those who have the power of legislation will be admonished, and correct them, it may save them and us from the justly-menaced destruction.

Your most obedient, &c. &c.

J. OGLETHORPE.

VI. BRITISH GENERAL SIR HENRY CLINTON'S PHILIPSBURG PROCLAMATION, JUNE 30, 1779

During the American Revolutionary War, British Army general Sir Henry Clinton declared that if "taken in arms," Black men serving in the patriot army would be purchased and forced into public service. Clinton also encouraged Black people enslaved by American patriots to escape and ally themselves with the British military.

Whereas the enemy have adopted a practice of enrolling negroes among their troops, I do hereby give notice that all negroes taken in arms, or upon any military duty, shall be purchased for the public service at a stated price; the money to be paid to the captors.

But I do most strictly forbid any person to sell or claim right over any negroe, the property of a rebel, who may take refuge with any part of this army: and I do promise to every negroe who shall desert the rebel standard, full security to follow within these lines, any occupation which he shall think proper.

Given under my hand, at Headquarters, Philipsburgh the 30th day of June, 1779.

H Clinton

VII. JAMES AND ELIZABETH OGLETHORPE MEMORIAL PLAQUES, PARISH CHURCH OF ALL SAINTS, CRANHAM, ENGLAND

The early eighteenth-century spelling convention of using the character ſ for a long S has been modified to the modern short S for readability. Final periods are only included where they are clearly intended as periods and make grammatical sense.

Near this place lie the Remains of JAMES EDWARD OGLETHORPE Esq.
who served under PRINCE EUGENE
And in 1714 was Captain Lieut. in the 1st Troop of Guards
In 1740 he was appointed Colonel of a Regiment
to be raised for Georgia
In 1745 he was appointed Major General
In 1747 Lieutenant General
In 1763 General of His Majesty's Forces
In his civil Station he was very early Conspicuous
He was chosen M.P. for Haslemere in Surrey
in 1722 and continued to represent it till 1754
In the Committee of Parliament for enquiring into
the State of the Gaols formed the 25th of Feb. 1728
and of which he was Chairman
The active and persevering zeal of his Benevolence
found a truly suitable employment
by visiting with his Colleagues of that generous body
the dark and pestilential dungeons of the Prisons
which at that time dishonored the Metropolis
Detecting the most enormous Oppressions
Obtaining exemplary punishment on those
Who had been guilty of such Outrage against Humanity & Justice

And restoring Multitudes from the extremes of Misery
to Light and Freedom.
Of these about 700 rendered by long confinement for Debt
strangers and helpless in the country of their Birth
And desirous of seeking an Asylum in the wilds of America
were by him conducted thither in 1732
He willingly encountered in their behalf a variety
of Fatigue and Danger and thus became the
Founder of the Colony of GEORGIA
A Colony which {Founded on the ardent wish for Liberty}
set the noble example
Of prohibiting the Importation of Slaves
This new Establishment he strenuously and Successfully defended
against a powerful invasion of the Spaniards
In the Year in which he quitted England to found this Settlement

He nobly strove to restore Our true
National defence by Sea and Land
A Free Navy without impressing
A Constitutional Militia
But his social Affections were more enlarged than
even the Term Patriotism can express
He was the Friend of the oppressed Negro
No part of the Globe was too remote
No interest too unconnected or too much opposed to his own
to prevent his immediate succour of suffering Humanity
For such Qualities he received from the ever
memorable JOHN DUKE OF ARGYLE
A full Testimony in the British Senate to
his Military Character
his natural Generosity
his contempt of Danger
And regard for the Publick
A similar Encomium is perpetuated in a Foreign Language
And by one of our most celebrated Poets his remembrance
is transmitted to Posterity in Lines justly expressive
Of the Purity, the Ardor, the Extent of his Benevolence
He lived till the 1st of July 1785
A venerable Instance to what a fullness of duration

And of continued usefulness
A life of Temperance and virtuous Labor
is capable of being protracted
His Widow ELIZABETH
Daughter of SIR NATHAN WRIGHT

. . .

Surviving with regret
(the with due submission to Divine Providence)
an Affectionate Husband after an union of more than 40 Ys
hath inscribed to His Memory
These faint traces of his excellent Character.
"Histoire Philosophique & Politique
One driven by strong Benevolence of Soul
Shall fly like Oglethorpe from Pole to Pole."

Pope

Religion watches o'er his Urn
And all the Virtues bending mourn
Humanity with languid Eye
Melting for others Misery
Prudence whose Hands a Measure hold
And Temperance with her Rein of Gold
Fidelity's transparent Vest
And Fortitude in Armour drest
Wisdom's grey Locks & Freedom join
The moral Train to bless his Shrine
These all around his Ashes holy
Their last sad Honours pay in Order melancholy.

Elizabeth Wright Oglethorpe Memorial Inscription

His disconsolate Widow died the 26th of Oct. 1787 in
her 79th Year, and is buried with him in the vault
in the center of this Chancel.
Her fortitude of mind and extensive Charity deserve
To be remembered, tho' her own Modesty would desire
them to be forgot.

VIII. BRITISH VICE ADMIRAL ALEXANDER COCHRANE'S PROCLAMATION OF EMANCIPATION, APRIL 2, 1814

During the War of 1812, Alexander Cochrane made an appeal to free and enslaved residents of the United States to seek the protection of "His Majesty's Ships or Vessels of War," where they would be given the option to join the British military or migrate as "Free Settlers" to other British territories.

Bermuda
April 2, 1814

A PROCLAMATION.

WHEREAS, it has been represented to me, that many Persons now resident in the UNITED STATES, have expressed a desire to withdraw therefrom, with a view of entering into His Majesty's Service, or of being received as Free Settlers into some of His Majesty's Colonies.

This is therefore to Give Notice,

That all those who may be disposed to emigrate from the UNITED STATES will, with their Families, be received on board His Majesty's Ships or Vessels of War, or at the Military Posts that may be established, upon or near the Coast of the UNITED STATES, when they will have their choice of either entering into His Majesty's Sea or Land Forces, or of being sent as FREE settlers to the British Possessions in North America or the West Indies, where they will meet with due encouragement.

Given under my Hand at Bermuda, this 2nd day of April, 1814, ALEXANDER COCHRANE.

By Command of the Vice Admiral, WILLIAM BALHETCHET. GOD SAVE THE KING.

IX. PRESIDENT ABRAHAM LINCOLN'S EMANCIPATION PROCLAMATION, JANUARY 1, 1863

During the U.S. Civil War, President Abraham Lincoln's historic proclamation declared that "all persons held as slaves within any state or designated part of a state" that is "in rebellion against the United States, shall be then, thenceforward, and forever free."

A Proclamation.

Whereas, on the twenty-second day of September, in the year of our lord one thousand eight hundred and sixty-two, a proclamation was issued by the President of the United States, containing, among other things, the following, to wit:

"That on the first day of January, in the year of our lord one thousand eight hundred and sixty-three, all persons held as slaves within any state or designated part of a state, the people whereof shall then be in rebellion against the United States, shall be then, thenceforward, and forever free; and the executive government of the United States, including the military and naval authority thereof, will recognize and maintain the freedom of such persons, and will do no act or acts to repress such persons, or any of them, in any efforts they may make for their actual freedom.

"That the executive will, on the first day of January aforesaid, by proclamation, designate the states and parts of states, if any, in which the people thereof, respectively, shall then be in rebellion against the United States; and the fact that any state, or the people thereof, shall on that day be, in good faith, represented in the Congress of the United States by members chosen thereto at elections wherein a majority of the qualified voters of such state shall have participated, shall, in the absence of strong countervailing testimony, be deemed conclusive evidence that such state, and the people thereof, are not then in rebellion against the United States.

"Now, therefore I, Abraham Lincoln, President of the United States, by virtue of the power in me vested as commander-in-chief, of the Army and Navy of the United States in time of actual armed rebellion against the authority and government of the United States, and as a fit and necessary war measure for suppressing said rebellion, do, on this first day of January, in the year of our lord one thousand eight hundred and sixty-three, and in accordance with my purpose so to do publicly proclaimed for the full period of one hundred days, from the day first above mentioned, order and designate as the states and parts of states wherein the people thereof respectively, are this day in rebellion against the United States, the following, to wit:

"Arkansas, Texas, Louisiana, (except the parishes of St. Bernard, Plaquemines, Jefferson, St. John, St. Charles, St. James Ascension, Assumption, Terrebonne, Lafourche, St. Mary, St. Martin, and Orleans, including the city of New Orleans) Mississippi, Alabama, Florida, Georgia, South Carolina, North Carolina, and Virginia, (except the forty-eight counties designated as West Virginia, and also the counties of Berkley, Accomac, Northampton, Elizabeth City, York, Princess Ann, and Norfolk, including the cities of Norfolk and Portsmouth[)], and which excepted parts, are for the present, left precisely as if this proclamation were not issued.

"And by virtue of the power, and for the purpose aforesaid, I do order and declare that all persons held as slaves within said designated states, and parts of states, are, and henceforward shall be free; and that the executive government of the United States, including the military and naval authorities thereof, will recognize and maintain the freedom of said persons.

"And I hereby enjoin upon the people so declared to be free to abstain from all violence, unless in necessary self-defense; and I recommend to them that, in all cases when allowed, they labor faithfully for reasonable wages.

"And I further declare and make known, that such persons of suitable condition, will be received into the armed services of the United States to garrison forts, positions, stations, and other places, and to man vessels of all sorts in said service.

"And upon this act, sincerely believed to be an act of justice, warranted by the constitution, upon military necessity, I invoke the considerate judgment of mankind, and the gracious favor of almighty God.

"In witness whereof, I have hereunto set my hand and caused the seal of the United States to be affixed.

"Done at the City of Washington, this first day of January, in the year of our lord one thousand eight hundred and sixty three, and of the Independence of the United States of America the eighty-seventh."

> By the President: ABRAHAM LINCOLN
> WILLIAM H. SEWARD, Secretary of State.

X. GENERAL WILLIAM T. SHERMAN'S FIELD ORDER NO. 15, JANUARY 16, 1865

Following a meeting with twenty Black preachers and lay leaders in Savannah, Georgia, on January 12, 1865, General William T. Sherman issued Field Order no. 15, which "reserved and set apart" approximately 435,000 tillable acres of land "for the settlement of the negroes now made free by the acts of war and the proclamation of the President of the United States." The temporary "license" to possess confiscated Confederate land and farm animals became popularly known as "forty acres and a mule."

Headquarters Military Division of the Mississippi,
in the Field, Savannah, Georgia, *January* 16, 1865.

1. The islands from Charleston, South, the abandoned rice fields along the rivers for thirty miles back from the sea, and the country bordering the St. Johns River, Florida, are reserved and set apart for the settlement of the negroes now made free by the acts of war and the proclamation of the President of the United States.

2. At Beaufort, Hilton Head, Savannah, Fernandina, St. Augustine and Jacksonville, the blacks may remain in their chosen or accustomed vocations—but on the islands, and in the settlements hereafter to be established, no white person whatever, unless military officers and soldiers

detailed for duty, will be permitted to reside; and the sole and exclusive management of affairs will be left to the freed people themselves, subject only to the United States Military authority and the Acts of Congress. By the laws of war, and orders of the President of the United States, the negro is free and must be dealt with as such. He cannot be subjected to conscription or forced military service, save by the written orders of the highest military authority of the department, under such regulations as the President or Congress may prescribe. Domestic servants, blacksmiths, carpenters and other mechanics, will be free to select their own work and residence, but the young and able-bodied negroes must be encouraged to enlist as soldiers in the service of the United States, to contribute their share towards maintaining their own freedom, and securing their rights as citizens of the United States.

Negroes so enlisted will be organized into companies, battalions and regiments, under the orders of the United States military authorities, and will be paid, fed and clothed according to law. The bounties paid on enlistment may, with the consent of the recruit, go to assist his family and settlement in procuring agricultural implements, seed, tools, boots, clothing, and other articles necessary for their livelihood.

3. Whenever three respectable negroes, heads of families, shall desire to settle on land, and shall have selected for that purpose an island or a locality clearly defined, within the limits above designated, the inspector of settlements and plantations will himself, or by such subordinate officer as he may appoint, give them a license to settle such island or district, and afford them such assistance as he can to enable them to establish a peaceable agricultural settlement. The three parties named will subdivide the land, under the supervision of the inspector, among themselves and such others as may choose to settle near them, so that each family shall have a plot of not more than (40) forty acres of tillable ground, and when it borders on some water channel, with not more than 800 feet water front, in the possession of which land the military authorities will afford them protection, until such time as they can protect themselves, or until Congress shall regulate their title. The quartermaster may, on the requisition of the inspector of settlements and plantations, place at the disposal of the inspector, one or more of the captured steamers, to ply between the settlements and one or more of the commercial points heretofore named in orders, to afford the settlers the opportunity to supply their necessary wants, and to sell the products of their land and labor.

4. Whenever a negro has enlisted in the military service of the United States, he may locate his family in any one of the settlements at pleasure, and acquire a homestead, and all other rights and privileges of a settler, as though present in person. In like manner, negroes may settle their families and engage on board the gunboats, or in fishing, or in the navigation of the inland waters, without losing any claim to land or other advantages derived from this system. But no one, unless an actual settler as above defined, or unless absent on government service, will be entitled to claim any right to land or property in any settlement by virtue of these orders.

5   In order to carry out this system of settlement, a general officer will be detailed as inspector of settlements and plantations, whose duty it shall be to visit the settlements, to regulate their police and general management, and who will furnish personally to each head of a family, subject to the approval of the President of the United States, a possessory title in writing, giving as near as possible the description of boundaries; and who shall adjust all claims or conflicts that may arise under the same, subject to the like approval, treating such titles altogether as possessory. The same general officer will also be charged with the enlistment and organization of the negro recruits and protecting their interests while absent from their settlements; and will be governed by the rules and regulations prescribed by the war department for such purposes.

6. Brigadier General R. Saxton is hereby appointed Inspector of Settlements and Plantations, and will at once enter on the performance of his duties. No change is intended or desired in the settlement now on Beaufort [Port Royal] Island, nor will any rights to property heretofore acquired be affected thereby.

By order of Major-General W. T. Sherman,
L. M. Dayton, Assistant Adjutant-General.

XI. ABRAHAM LINCOLN'S SECOND INAUGURAL ADDRESS, MARCH 4, 1865

President Abraham Lincoln asserts that enslaved Blacks "constituted a peculiar and powerful interest" and that "this interest was somehow the cause of the war."

Fellow-Countrymen:
At this second appearing to take the oath of the Presidential office there is less occasion for an extended address than there was at the first. Then a statement

somewhat in detail of a course to be pursued seemed fitting and proper. Now, at the expiration of four years, during which public declarations have been constantly called forth on every point and phase of the great contest which still absorbs the attention and engrosses the energies of the nation, little that is new could be presented. The progress of our arms, upon which all else chiefly depends, is as well known to the public as to myself, and it is, I trust, reasonably satisfactory and encouraging to all. With high hope for the future, no prediction in regard to it is ventured.

On the occasion corresponding to this four years ago, all thoughts were anxiously directed to an impending civil war. All dreaded it, all sought to avert it. While the inaugural address was being delivered from this place, devoted altogether to saving the union without war, insurgent agents were in the city seeking to destroy it without war—seeking to dissolve the Union, and divide effects by negotiation. Both parties deprecated war; but one of them would make war rather than let the nation survive; and the other would accept war rather than let it perish. And the war came.

One-eighth of the whole population were colored slaves, not distributed generally over the Union, but localized in the southern part of it. These slaves constituted a peculiar and powerful interest. All knew that this interest was somehow the cause of the war. To strengthen, perpetuate, and extend this interest was the object for which the insurgents would rend the Union even by war, while the Government claimed no right to do more than to restrict the territorial enlargement of it. Neither party expected for the war the magnitude or the duration which it has already attained. Neither anticipated that the cause of the conflict might cease with, or even before, the conflict itself should cease. Each looked for an easier triumph, and a result less fundamental and astounding. Both read the same Bible and pray to the same God, and each invokes His aid against the other. It may seem strange that any men should dare to ask a just God's assistance in wringing their bread from the sweat of other men's faces, but let us judge not, that we be not judged. The prayers of both could not be answered. That of neither has been answered fully. The Almighty has His own purposes. "Woe unto the world because of offenses; for it must needs be that offenses come, but woe to that man by whom the offense cometh." If we shall suppose that American slavery is one of those offenses which, in the providence of God, must needs come, but which, having continued through His appointed time, He now wills to remove, and that He gives to both North and South this terrible war as the woe due to those by whom the offense came, shall we discern therein any departure from those divine attributes which the believers in a living God always ascribe to Him? Fondly do we hope, fervently do we pray, that this mighty scourge of war may speedily pass away. Yet, if God wills that it continue until all the wealth piled by the bondsman's two hundred and fifty years of unrequited toil shall be sunk, and until every drop of blood drawn with the lash shall be paid by another drawn with the sword, as was said three thousand years ago, so still it must be said "the judgments of the Lord are true and righteous altogether."

With malice toward none, with charity for all, with firmness in the right as God gives us to see the right, let us strive on to finish the work we are in, to bind up the nation's wounds, to care for him who shall have borne the battle and for his widow and his orphan, to do all which may achieve and cherish a just and lasting peace among ourselves and with all nations.

XII. THE THIRTEENTH AMENDMENT TO THE UNITED STATES CONSTITUTION

American chattel slavery became illegal when Georgia, the twenty-seventh state to ratify the Thirteenth Amendment to the U.S. Constitution, adopted the measure, December 6, 1865.

Section 1

Neither slavery nor involuntary servitude, except as a punishment for crime whereof the party shall have been duly convicted, shall exist within the United States, or any place subject to their jurisdiction.

Section 2

Congress shall have the power to enforce this article by appropriate legislation.

September 29, 1526 (?)	Spanish explorer Lucas Vázquez de Ayllón establishes San Miguel de Gualdape, the first European settlement in what is now the United States of America along the Georgia coast near Sapelo Sound. Three months after its establishment, rebellious Africans attacked their enslavers and allied with Native Indians
1562	Captain John Hawkins undertakes the first British slaving voyage to Africa
September 8, 1565	Don Pedro Menendez establishes the St. Augustine settlement on the northeast coast of Florida
1607	Virginia becomes the first British colony founded in what is now the United States of America
August 1619	First documented arrival of enslaved Africans in British colonial America in the Virginia colony
1641	Massachusetts becomes the first British American colony to codify the enslavement of Black people
1660	The Royal African Company, a slaving enterprise, is chartered by England's King Charles II
April 1670	The Carolina colony is founded
December 22, 1696	**James Edward Oglethorpe is born in London, England**
1701	Society for the Propagation of the Gospel is founded by Doctor Thomas Bray
1701 (?)	Ayruba Sulieman Diallo is born in modern-day Senegal
March 22, 1722	**Oglethorpe is elected to the House of Commons in the British Parliament**
1724	Associates of Doctor Bray is founded to Christianize enslaved Black people
March 22, 1728	**Oglethorpe anonymously publishes *The Sailor's Advocate***

1729–1735

February 25, 1729	Oglethorpe is selected to chair Parliament's Committee on Jails
1729	Act for the Relief of Debtors is enacted by Parliament
December 1729	Deathbed meeting takes place between Oglethorpe and Doctor Thomas Bray
February 1730	Diallo is sold into slavery, transported to America, and enslaved on a Maryland colony tobacco plantation
February 15, 1730	Doctor Thomas Bray dies
March 21, 1730	Oglethorpe is elected chairman of the reorganized Bray Associates
July 30, 1730	Oglethorpe informs the Bray Associates of the Royal African Company's desire to support their missionary outreach to enslaved Africans
December 31, 1730	Oglethorpe purchases stock in the Royal African Company
June 1731	Diallo is visited by evangelist Thomas Bluett following his failed escape from bondage
January 27, 1732	Oglethorpe is elected deputy governor of the Royal African Company
April 21, 1732	King George II grants a charter establishing the Georgia colony
Summer 1732	Diallo's letter to his father is placed in Oglethorpe's possession
November 17, 1732	Oglethorpe and 114 original Georgia colonists set sail from London
December 21, 1732	Oglethorpe severs ties with the Royal African Company
February 12, 1733	Oglethorpe lands at Yamacraw Bluff and establishes the Savannah settlement
July 11, 1733	First Jewish colonists arrive in the Georgia colony
December 27, 1733	Diallo is officially manumitted

July 1734   Diallo sails from London, England

August 1, 1734   Tomochichi meets with King George II at Kensington Palace

August 8, 1734   Diallo arrives on Africa's Atlantic coast

June 1735   **Georgia Trustees officially prohibit importation of enslaved Negroes**

1736–1783

March 1736   John and Charles Wesley, Anglican missionaries, arrive in the Georgia colony

January 3, 1739   **Darien colonists issue petition opposing the legalization of slavery in Georgia**

September 9, 1739   Stono Rebellion erupts in the South Carolina colony

January 1740   **Oglethorpe leads an unsuccessful invasion of Spanish Florida, foiled in part by formerly enslaved Black militiamen at the Battle of Bloody Mose**

July 7, 1742   **Oglethorpe defeats the Spanish at the Battle of Bloody Marsh**

July 23, 1743   **Oglethorpe takes his final exit from Georgia**

September 1744   **Oglethorpe marries Elizabeth Wright**

1745?   Olaudah Equiano is born in modern-day Nigeria

March 16, 1749   **Oglethorpe attends his last meeting of the Georgia Trustees**

January 1, 1751   **Slavery is legalized in the Georgia colony**

July 1766   Olaudah Equiano purchases his freedom

1773   Diallo dies peacefully at the age of seventy-three in his native land

1773–1774   **Oglethorpe advises Equiano to hire attorney Granville Sharp to represent his friend John Annis, a formerly enslaved Black man**

September 26, 1776	Oglethorpe writes a letter of introduction to Granville Sharp
December 29, 1778	Quamino "Quash" Dolly leads British invaders through the swamps to stage a successful attack on Savannah
January/February 1779	Pioneer Black preachers George Liele, David George, and Jesse Peter arrive in war-torn Savannah
February 1779	Austin Dabney, enslaved Black Georgia patriot, fights bravely at the Battle at Kettle Creek
November 29, 1781	Approximately 142 enslaved Africans are killed during the *Zong* massacre
March 19, 1783	Equiano convinces attorney Granville Sharp to get involved in the *Zong* case

1784–1864

1784	**Oglethorpe and Hannah More become acquainted**
June 30, 1785	**Oglethorpe dies and is entombed in the Church of All Saints**
October 26, 1787	**Elizabeth Oglethorpe dies and bequeaths the profits from Fairstead Hall to Granville Sharp**
1788	Hannah More publishes *Slavery: A Poem* to coincide with the first debate over abolition in the British Parliament
1789	Equiano publishes *The Interesting Narrative of the Life of Olaudah Equiano, or Gustavus Vassa, the African*
1805	**Parliament abolishes the British transatlantic slave trade**
January 1, 1808	United States of America prohibits the importation of enslaved Blacks
January 1815	Black and white British marines occupy Cumberland Island; Admiral Sir George Cockburn enlists hundreds of formerly enslaved Black men

December 21, 1816	Robert Finley, future president of the University of Georgia, founds the American Colonization Society
August 28, 1833	**British Slavery Abolition Act given Royal Assent; more than eight hundred thousand enslaved Blacks are emancipated; slaveholders are compensated**
April 12, 1861	Confederates attack Fort Sumter in Charleston Harbor, igniting the American Civil War
January 1, 1863	**President Abraham Lincoln issues the Emancipation Proclamation authorizing the enlistment of Black men in the Union military**
September 2, 1864	General William T. Sherman telegraphs President Abraham Lincoln, "Atlanta is ours and fairly won"
November 14, 1864	General Sherman's soldiers set fire to Atlanta and commence the March to the Sea
November/December 1864	More than eighteen thousand formerly enslaved Black Georgians celebrate the Day of Jubilee by joining the march to Savannah
December 3, 1864	Hundreds of newly freed Blacks drown in rain-swollen Ebenezer Creek
December 24, 1864	**Sherman's army occupies Savannah**

1865–1996

January 12, 1865	General Sherman meets with twenty Black preachers and lay leaders at the Green-Meldrim House
January 16, 1865	General Sherman issues Field Order no. 15 creating the Sherman Reservation, a refuge for forty thousand newly freed Black colonists along the southeastern coast from Charleston, South Carolina, to Jacksonville, Florida
March 4, 1865	President Abraham Lincoln delivers his second inaugural address

James Edward Oglethorpe Tercentenary Commission, October 1996.

(Courtesy of Georgia Historical Society, Edwin Jackson Collection)

December 6, 1865   The Thirteenth Amendment to the U.S. Constitution is ratified declaring that "neither slavery nor involuntary servitude . . . shall exist within the United States, or any place subject to their jurisdiction"

November 23, 1910   James Oglethorpe statue designed by American sculptor Daniel Chester French dedicated in Chippewa Square in Savannah, Georgia. French also designed the Lincoln Memorial statue in Washington, D.C., which was dedicated in 1920

October 1923   **Dr. Thornwell Jacobs, president of Oglethorpe University, locates the lost tomb of James and Elizabeth Oglethorpe**

October 3–8, 1996   **James Edward Oglethorpe Tercentenary Commission travels to England to commemorate the three hundredth anniversary of the birth of Georgia's founding father**

NOTES

Chapter One. In the Land of Christians

1. Bluett, *Some Memoirs*, 16–17; Thaddeus Mason Harris, *Biographical Memorials of James Oglethorpe*, 24–37; Ettinger, *James Edward Oglethorpe*, 148.

2. Bluett, *Some Memoirs*, 16–17.

3. Ibid., 17.

4. Ibid., 17–18.

5. Ibid., 19–23; Trans-Atlantic Slave Trade Database, voyage 75094, http://www .slavevoyages.org.

6. Bluett, *Some Memoirs*, 21–22.

7. Ibid., 22–23; *Gentlemen's Magazine* 20 (June 1750): facing 272; Trans-Atlantic Slave Trade Database, https://www.slavevoyages.org/resources/images/category/People/1; Francis Moore, *Travels into the Inland Parts*, 320; Khan, "Muslims Arrived in America."

8. Bluett, *Some Memoirs*, 22–23.

9. Ibid.

10. Ibid.

Chapter Two. Worldly Servitude and Spiritual Freedom

1. Thomas D. Wilson, *Oglethorpe Plan*, 3, 9.

2. Baine, *Publications of James Edward Oglethorpe*, ix–x.

3. Thomas D. Wilson, *Oglethorpe Plan*, 11–13; Thomas, "James Edward Oglethorpe," 17–20.

4. *London Daily Journal* for March 27 and 29, 1722; James Oglethorpe, "To the Author of the *Daily Journal*," in Baine, *Publications of James Edward Oglethorpe*, 5–6; Thomas D. Wilson, *Oglethorpe Plan*, 14; Thomas, "James Edward Oglethorpe," 17–20; Ettinger, *Oglethorpe: A Brief Biography*, 81–83.

5. Van Horne, *Religious Philanthropy and Colonial Slavery*, 2–3.

6. Ibid., 4–6.

7. Ibid., 6; Kiersten E. Davis, "Was the Enlightenment a Force for Anti-Slavery or the Maintenance of Slavery?," AtS3614-Research Essay, 4–5, available at https://www .academia.edu/9194818.

8. Paley, Malcolmson, and Hunter, "Parliament and Slavery."

9. Van Horne, *Religious Philanthropy and Colonial Slavery*, 20.

10. Jernegan, "Slavery and Conversion," 505–506; Charles Colcock Jones, *Religious Instruction of the Negroes*, 7–9.

11. Maurice Jackson, *Let This Voice Be Heard*, 1–9; Sinha, *Slave's Cause*, 20–23.

12. Jernegan, "Slavery and Conversion," 504; Whelchel, *History and Heritage*, 82–84. The Negro spiritual "Steal Away" was a "sorrow song" believed to have been sung by generations of enslaved Black Christians. Wallace Willis, a Black man enslaved by a Choctaw Indian, composed the song prior to 1862, and it was popularized by Fisk University's Jubilee Singers.

13. Leviticus 25:10; Coffey, *Exodus and Liberation*, 6–8; Van Horne, *Religious Philanthropy and Colonial Slavery*, 9–10.

Chapter Three. "Asilum of the Unfortunate"

1. Van Horne, *Religious Philanthropy and Colonial Slavery*, 9–10; Ettinger, *James Edward Oglethorpe*, 90–91.

2. Baine, "Prison Death of Robert Castell," 38–42; Ettinger, *James Edward Oglethorpe*, 94; Betty Wood, "James Edward Oglethorpe," 71; Kenneth Coleman, "The Founding of Georgia," in Jackson and Spalding, *Forty Years of Diversity*, 7.

3. Baine, *Creating Georgia*, xiv–xv; Van Horne, *Religious Philanthropy and Colonial Slavery*, 10.

4. Baine, *Creating Georgia*, 5–6, appendix, 119–126; Van Horne, *Religious Philanthropy and Colonial Slavery*, 10–11; Pennington, "Thomas Bray's Associates," 317.

5. Baine, *Creating Georgia*, 5–6, appendix, 119–126; Van Horne, *Religious Philanthropy and Colonial Slavery*, 10–11; Pennington, "Thomas Bray's Associates," 317; Fray and Spar, *Charter of Georgia*; Georgia Historical Society, "Oglethorpe and Religion in Georgia."

6. Baine, *Creating Georgia*, 5–6, appendix, 119–126; Van Horne, *Religious Philanthropy and Colonial Slavery*, 10–11; Pennington, "Thomas Bray's Associates," 317.

7. Steiner, *Rev. Thomas Bray*, 47; Pennington, "Thomas Bray's Associates," 322; Woodson, *History of the Negro Church*, 2–6.

8. Baine, *Creating Georgia*, xiv; Van Horne, *Religious Philanthropy and Colonial Slavery*, 9–13.

9. Baine, *Creating Georgia*, 25–26.

10. Ibid., 25; Reddie, *ABOLITION!*, 88.

11. Trans-Atlantic Slave Trade Database, "Voyages Database"; Sarah Pruitt, "What was the Royal African Company?," History.com, last updated August 23, 2018, http://www.history.com/news/ask-history/what-was-the-royal-african-company; Baine, *Creating Georgia*, xiii–xxvi; Fray and Spar, *Charter of Georgia*.

12. Fray and Spar, *Charter of Georgia*; Georgia Historical Society, "Oglethorpe and Religion in Georgia."

13. Fray and Spar, *Charter of Georgia*; Georgia Historical Society, "Oglethorpe and Religion in Georgia"; Levy, "Early History of Georgia's Jews"; Georgia Historical Society, "Oglethorpe and Religion in Georgia."

14. Betty Wood, *Slavery in Colonial Georgia*, 5; Martyn, *Reasons for Establishing the Colony*, 30; Fant, "Labor Policy of the Trustees," 1–3; Phinizy Spalding, foreword to

Baine, *Publications of James Edward Oglethorpe*; Fray and Spar, *Charter of Georgia: 1732*; Fischer, *African Founders*, 392–394.

15. Anonymous, "An Appeal for the Georgia Colony," in Baine, *Publications of James Edward Oglethorpe*, 165; *London Journal*, July 29, 1732.

16. Horne, *Counter Revolution of 1776*, 91.

17. Wax, "Georgia and the Negro," 69–72; Scarborough, *Opposition to Slavery in Georgia*, 17.

18. Bluett, *Some Memoirs*, 23; letter from Ayuba Suleiman Diallo to his father, 1731?–1733, trans. Samia Abdulla, January 2017.

19. Diallo to father; Bluett, *Some Memoirs*, 23.

20. Bruce, *Life of Oglethorpe*, 132–138; Ettinger, *James Edward Oglethorpe*, 148; Oglethorpe, *British Sailor's Advocate*, 3.

21. Bruce, *Life of Oglethorpe*, 132–138.

Chapter Four. A Scene of Horror

1. Hochschild, *Bury the Chains*, 2.

2. Equiano, *Interesting Narrative*, chap. 1, 1:26–27; Francis Moore, *Travels into the Inland Parts*, 331; Allison, *Interesting Narrative of the Life*, 40–41.

3. Betty Wood, *Slavery in Colonial America*, 9–10; Mannix and Cowley, *Black Cargoes*, 50–68.

4. Inikori, *Africans and the Industrial Revolution*, 215–227.

5. Ibid., 216–227.

6. Philip Morgan, "Lowcountry Georgia," 13–47; Inikori, *Africans and the Industrial Revolution*, 216–228, 279–300.

7. Philip Morgan, "Lowcountry Georgia," 13–47.

8. Betty Wood, *Slavery in Colonial America*, 20–22; Whelchel, *History and Heritage*, 56–64.

9. Whelchel, *History and Heritage*, 63–64.

10. Ibid.; Betty Wood, *Slavery in Colonial America*, 20; Kenneth Morgan, *Slavery and the British Empire*, 60.

11. Equiano, *Interesting Narrative*, chap. 1, 1:47–50.

12. Ibid., chap. 1, 1:70–80.

13. Ibid., chap. 1, 1:78–79.

14. Walvin, *Zong*, 33–47.

15. Pearson and Richardson, "Insuring the Transatlantic Slave Trade," 417–446; "Lloyds of London Insurance."

16. Inikori, *Africans and the Industrial Revolution*, 253–266.

17. Faubert, "Granville Sharp's Manuscript Letter."

18. Newton, *Thoughts*, 11; Walvin, *Zong*, 28–29.

19. Walvin, *Zong*, 40.

20. Inikori, *Africans and the Industrial Revolution*, 253–254; Richardson, "Shipboard Revolts."

21. Inikori, *Africans and the Industrial Revolution*, 253–254; Genovese, *From Rebellion to Revolution*, xxiii, 2.

22. Betty Wood, *Slavery in Colonial America*, 17–19.

23. Trans-Atlantic Slave Trade Database; Gates, "How Many Slaves Landed?"; Douglas, "History: Slave Revolts by Sea"; Douglas, "Know Your Black History."

Chapter 5. *"The Labour of Negroes"*

1. This information came from a British website that is no longer available. For a review of that site, see Carolyn Mason, review of The Abolition of Slavery Project (website), https://worldhistorycommons.org/abolition-slavery-project.

2. William Wood, *Survey of Trade*, 179; African Merchant, *Treatise upon the Trade*, 4–5; Du Bois, *Suppression of the African Slave-Trade*, 4; Walvin, *Zong*, 29.

3. William Wood, *Survey of Trade*, 179; African Merchant, *Treatise upon the Trade*, 4–5.

4. *Slavery in America, History.com*, last updated April 20, 2021, http://www.history.com/topics/black-history/slavery.

5. Kenneth Morgan, *Slavery and the British Empire*, 26–33; Betty Wood, *Slavery in Colonial America*, 9–11.

6. Kenneth Morgan, *Slavery and the British Empire*, 26–33; Patrick Tailfer and others to the Trustees, August 27, 1735, in Lane, *General Oglethorpe's Georgia*, 2:225; Peter H. Wood, *Black Majority*, 37–42.

7. Kenneth Morgan, *Slavery and the British Empire*, 7–11; Sarikas, "13 Original Colonies."

8. John Rolfe to Sir Edwin Sandys, January 1619, quoted in Kingsbury, *Records of the Virginia Company*, 3:243; Mannix and Cowley, *Black Cargoes*, 50; Kenneth Morgan, *Slavery and the British Empire*, 21.

9. Betty Wood, *Slavery in Colonial America*, 9–12.

10. Van Horne, *Religious Philanthropy and Colonial Slavery*, 1–38.

11. Mannix and Cowley, *Black Cargoes*, 60.

12. Zielinski, "Slavery in the Colonies"; Slavery in British America, 1–7, http://cghs; Peter H. Wood, *Black Majority*, 35–62.

13. Philip Morgan, *African American Life*, 3–4; "Slavery on South Carolina Rice Plantations," Chicora Historical Society, https://docslib.org/doc/1257638/slavery-on-south-carolina-rice-plantations; Franklin and Moss, *From Slavery to Freedom*, 56–63.

Chapter 6. *"The Debatable Land"*

1. Peter H. Wood, *Black Majority*, xiv.

2. Philip Morgan, *African American Life*, 3–4; Coclanis, "Rice"; "Slavery on South Carolina Rice Plantations," Chicora Historical Society, https://docslib.org/doc/1257638/slavery-on-south-carolina-rice-plantations.

3. Peter H. Wood, "Slave Labor Camps"; Peter H. Wood, *Black Majority*, 35–62.

4. Philip Morgan, *African American Life,* 2–3; Coclanis, "Rice"; Daniel C. Littlefield, "Slave Labor."

5. Sullivan, *Georgia,* 12; Weber, *Spanish Frontier in North America,* 31; Torres-Spelliscy, "Perspective."

6. Weber, *Spanish Frontier in North America,* 31; Willie Keddell, "The Kings Edit," Hidden History Miami, Historic Lummus Park Tours with Willie Keddell, Troy Community Academy, p. 2.

7. Bolton and Ross, *Debatable Land,* xv, 138.

8. Baine, *Publications of James Edward Oglethorpe,* xi; Martyn, *Reasons for Establishing the Colony,* 30; Fant, "Labor Policy of the Trustees," 1–3; Betty Wood, *Slavery in Colonial Georgia,* 4–5; Phinizy Spalding, foreword to Blaine, *Publications of James Edward Oglethorpe.*

9. Hochschild, *Bury the Chains,* 1–3; Hammond and Mason, *Contesting Slavery,* 11–14; Martin, review of Hammond and Mason, *Contesting Slavery, What Would the Founders Think?* (blog), http://www.whatwouldthefoundersthink.com/contesting-slavery-edited-by-john-craig-hammond-and-matthew-mason-2; Sinha, *Slave's Cause,* 10.

10. Sweet, *Negotiating for Georgia,* 24–39.

11. John Musgrove to James Oglethorpe, January 24, 1735, in Lane, *General Oglethorpe's Georgia,* 1:115.

12. Patrick Tailfer, Hugh Anderson, and Da. Douglas, "A True and Historical Narrative of the Colony of Georgia in America," in Reese, *Clamorous Malcontents,* 56; Wax, "Georgia and the Negro," 69–72.

13. Levy, "Early History of Georgia's Jews," 163–178; Georgia Historical Society, "Oglethorpe and Religion in Georgia."

14. Levy, "Early History of Georgia's Jews," 163–178; Georgia Historical Society, "Oglethorpe and Religion in Georgia."

15. Levy, "Early History of Georgia's Jews," 163–178; Georgia Historical Society, "Oglethorpe and Religion in Georgia."

16. James Oglethorpe to the Trustees, May 14, 1733, in Lane, *General Oglethorpe's Georgia,* 1:15–16; James Oglethorpe to the Trustees, August 12, 1733, in Lane, *General Oglethorpe's Georgia,* 1:19–23; Betty Wood, *Slavery in Colonial Georgia,* 16.

17. James Oglethorpe to the Trustees, August 12, 1733, in Lane, *General Oglethorpe's Georgia,* 1:19–23.

Chapter 7. Diallo Is a Free Man

1. Bluett, *Some Memoirs,* 24–25, 31–32.

2. Ibid., 47–48.

3. Ibid., 12–15.

4. Ibid., 51–53.

5. Ibid., 32–33, 58.

6. Ibid., 50; National Portrait Gallery, London, News Release, "First British Portrait of a Black African Muslim and Freed Slave Goes on Display," January 19, 2011, 1–4.

7. Bluett, *Some Memoirs*, 27–30.

8. Ibid., 30; Gates, "Which Slave Wrote His Way Out?" 3; Diouf, *Servants of Allah*, 165; Richard Brent Taylor, *Islam*, 25–26.

9. Bluett, *Some Memoirs*, 32; Francis Moore, *Travels into the Inland Parts*, 320–324.

10. Bluett, *Some Memoirs*, 32; Francis Moore, *Travels into the Inland Parts*, 320–324; Harris, *Biographical Memorials of James Oglethorpe*, 28.

11. Bluett, Some *Memoirs*, 32; Francis Moore, *Travels to the Inland Parts*, 334; Harris, *Biographical Memorials of James Oglethorpe*, 28.

12. Cruickshanks, "Oglethorpes," 5.

Chapter 8. *"O God, Where Are Thy Tender Mercies?"*

1. Candler, *Colonial Records of Georgia*, 1:50–51.

2. Ibid.; Rubye Mae Jones, "Negro in Colonial Georgia," 1–8; Du Bois, *Suppression of the African Slave-Trade*, 7–8.

3. "A Petition to the Trustees," December 9, 1738, in Lane, *General Oglethorpe's Georgia*, 2:371–375; Scarborough, *Opposition to Slavery in Georgia*, 33.

4. Ettinger, *James Edward Oglethorpe*, 153–154, 169; Warren Thomas Smith, *John Wesley and Slavery*, 38–39.

5. Betty Wood, *Slavery in Colonia Georgia*, 61; Anthony, "Unindexed Official Record," 13–16.

6. Harold E. Davis, *Fledgling Province*, 149.

7. Patrick Tailfer, Hugh Anderson, and Da. Douglas, "A True and Historical Narrative of the Colony of Georgia in America," in Reese, *Clamorous Malcontents*, vii–xvi, 23.

8. Scarborough, *Opposition to Slavery in Georgia*, 69–70.

9. Ibid.; Peter H. Wood, *Black Majority*, 84.

10. Betty Wood, *Slavery in Colonial Georgia*, 66–67; David Taft Morgan Jr., "Great Awakening," 122–124.

11. Warren Thomas Smith, *John Wesley and Slavery*, 33–34.

12. Ibid., 45.

13. Frank Baker, *Works of Wesley*, 439.

14. Warren Thomas Smith, *John Wesley and Slavery*, 45.

15. Ibid., 45–46.

16. Ibid., 41–42.

17. Ibid., 46; Godwyn, *Negro's and Indians Advocate*, 9.

18. David Livingston Smith, "Essence of Evil," 1–7; Warren Thomas Smith, *John Wesley and Slavery*, 46; Godwyn, *Negro's and Indians Advocate*, 3, 167–174.

19. Warren Thomas Smith, *John Wesley and Slavery*, 47.

20. Ibid.

21. Ibid., 47–48.

22. Ibid., 48.

23. John Wesley to Captain Robert Williams, August 3, 1742, in Telford, *Letters of the Rev. John Wesley*, 2:6–8.

24. Ibid.

25. Wesley to James Hutton, April 12, 1740, in Telford, *Letters of the Rev. John Wesley*, 1:342; Wesley to Captain Robert Williams, August 3, 1742, in Telford, *Letters of the Rev. John Wesley*, 2:6–8; Wesley to Hutton, October 17, 1742, in Telford, *Letters of the Rev. John Wesley*, 1:9–11; Madron, "John Wesley on Race," 24.

26. Madron, "John Wesley on Race," 24–26; Vaux, *Memoirs of the Life*, 44; Wade, *John Wesley*, 104; Brendlinger, "John Wesley and Slavery."

Chapter 9. The Prophecy

1. "A Petition to the Trustees," December 9, 1738, in Lane, *General Oglethorpe's Georgia*, 2:374; Scarborough, *Opposition to Slavery in Georgia*, 33.

2. Oglethorpe to Trustees, January 16 and 17, 1739, in Lane, *General Oglethorpe's Georgia*, 2:387–390; Betty Wood, *Slavery in Colonial Georgia*, 31.

3. "Petition of the Inhabitants of Darien to General Oglethorpe," in Candler, *Colonial Records of Georgia*, 3:427; Wylly, *Seed That Was Sown*, 28–31; Betty Wood, *Slavery in Colonial Georgia*, 30.

The first antislavery petition written in North America is believed to be the Germantown Quaker Petition against Slavery, which was authored by Francis Daniel Pastorius and three other Pennsylvania Quakers in April 1688. The document was presented at several quarterly and annual meetings of their church, the Society of Friends, but no official action was taken. Still, the two-page antislavery petition set in motion the process that eventually led to the prohibition of slavery within the Society of Friends in 1776 and the adoption of a gradual emancipation statute by the Pennsylvania General Assembly on March 1, 1780. The prohibition of slavery by the Quakers and passage of the Pennsylvania gradual emancipation process occurred more than four decades after the Georgia Trustees officially prohibited slavery in their colony in 1735. Maurice Jackson, *Let This Voice Be Heard*, 31–52.

4. Guyatt, *Providence and the Intervention*, 14–17; Coffey, "Tremble, Britannia"; Hoare, *Memoirs of Granville Sharp*, 155–156; Scarborough, *Opposition to Slavery in Georgia*, 28, 37.

5. Inhabitants of Ebenezer to Oglethorpe, March 13, 1739, in Lane, *General Oglethorpe's Georgia*, 2:397–399; Scarborough, *Opposition to Slavery in Georgia*, 28, 37; Wylly, *Seed That Was Sown*, 36–37.

6. Trustees Letter to the Magistrates of Savannah, June 20, 1739, Candler, *Colonial Records of Georgia*, 3:431–432; Scarborough, *Opposition to Slavery in Georgia*, 38–40.

Chapter 10. The Stono Rebellion

1. James Edward Oglethorpe, "An Account of the Negroe Insurrection in South Carolina (1740)," in Baine, *Publications of James Edward Oglethorpe*, 252; Porter, *Negro on the American Frontier*, 167.

2. Oglethorpe, "Account of the Negroe Insurrection," 252; Porter, *Negro on the American Frontier*, 167; Peter H. Wood, *Black Majority*, 14–17.

3. Oglethorpe, "Account of the Negroe Insurrection," 252; Porter, *Negro on the American Frontier*, 167; Peter H. Wood, *Black Majority*, 14–17.

4. Easterby, "Report of the Committee," 83–84; Oglethorpe, "Account of the Negroe Insurrection," 252; Porter, *Negro on the American Frontier*, 167; Mark A. Smith, *Stono*, 28.

5. George Cato, "As It Come Down to Me," in Mark A. Smith, *Stono*, 55–56.

6. Oglethorpe, "Account of the Negroe Insurrection," 252; Porter, *Negro on the American Frontier*, 168.

7. Betty Wood, *Slavery in Colonia America*, 107–108; extract from "South Carolina Commons House of Assembly Report," 266–267, South Carolina Department of Archives and History; Mark A. Smith, *Stono*, 18.

8. Extract from "South Carolina Commons House of Assembly Report," 266–267, South Carolina Department of Archives and History; Mark A. Smith, *Stono*, 18.

9. Oglethorpe, "Account of the Negroe Insurrection," 253; Petition to King George II or Parliament, December 29, 1940, in Lane, *General Oglethorpe's Georgia*, 2:513–524; Porter, *Negro on the American Frontier*, 168; Ready, "Economic History of Colonial Georgia," 51; Betty Wood, *Slavery in Colonial Georgia*, 2–3; Mary Stroughton Locke, *Anti-Slavery in America*, 11–12.

10. Oglethorpe, "Account of the Negroe Insurrection," 253; Porter, *Negro on the American Frontier*, 168; McCall, *History of Georgia*, 87–88; Force, *American Archives*, 5th ser., 3:68; Candler, *Colonial Records of Georgia*, 3:80–86.

11. William Stephens, *Journal of the Proceedings*, 3:281.

12. From Hugh Anderson and others to the Trustees, December 2, 1740, in Lane, *General Oglethorpe's Georgia*, 2:491–496; Cashin, *Story of Augusta*, 12.

13. Patrick Tailfer, Hugh Anderson, Da. Douglas, and others, *A True and Historical Narrative of the Colony of Georgia in America, From the First Settlement Thereof until This Present Period* (Charles-Town: Printed by P. Timothy, 1741), 28.

14. Thomas Stephens, "The Hard Case of the Distressed People of Georgia," in Reese, *Clamorous Malcontents*, 28.

15. William Stephens, *Journal of the Proceedings*, 3:281.

16. Martyn, *Reasons for Establishing the Colony*, 30; Fant, "Labor Policy of the Trustees," 1–3; Higginbotham, *In the Matter of Color*, 226–227; Betty Wood, *Slavery in Colonial Georgia*, 5–6; Phinizy Spalding, foreword to Baine, *Publications of James Edward Oglethorpe*, 1994.

17. Higginbotham, *In the Matter of Color*, 227–232.

Chapter 11. A Fortress of Freedom

1. From Hugh Anderson and others to the Trustees, December 2, 1740, in Lane, *General Oglethorpe's Georgia*, 2:491–496; Katz and Franklin, *Proudly Red and Black*, 24–26.

2. Oglethorpe, "Account of the Negroe Insurrection," 253.

3. Ibid.

4. Ibid.; Spalding, "Oglethorpe," 65–70; Tate, *St. Augustine Expedition*, 25; Landers, *Fort Mose*, 15–16.

5. Oglethorpe, "Account of the Negroe Insurrection," 253; Spalding, "Oglethorpe," 65–70; Tate, *St. Augustine Expedition*, 25; Landers, *Fort Mose*, 15–16; Porter, *Negro on the American Frontier*, 102.

6. Ettinger, *James Edward Oglethorpe*, 234; McCall, *History of Georgia*, 104–105; Anthony, "Unindexed Official Record," 47.

7. James Oglethorpe to William Stephens, February 2, 1740, in Lane, *General Oglethorpe's Georgia*, 2:451–452; Sullivan, *Early Days*, 25.

8. Oglethorpe to Stephens, February 2, 1740, 508–510; Sullivan, *Early Days*, 25.

9. Anthony, "Unindexed Official Record," 47; McCall, *History of Georgia*, 104–105.

10. Porter, *Negro on the American Frontier*, 170; McCall, *History of Georgia*, 104–105; Ettinger, *James Edward Oglethorpe*, 237.

11. Porter, *Negro on the American Frontier*, 247, 131; Landers, *Fort Mose*, 17–19.

12. Porter, *Negro on the American Frontier*, 172; Coleman, *History of Georgia*, 33; McCall, *History of Georgia*, 124.

13. John Dobell to Egmont, August 6, 1742, in Lane, *General Oglethorpe's Georgia*, 2:644; Ettinger, *James Edward Oglethorpe*, 250–254; McCall, *History of Georgia*, 127–134.

14. Betty Wood, *Slavery in Colonial Georgia*, 77–78.

15. Thomas D. Wilson, *Oglethorpe Plan*, 195–200; McCall, *History of Georgia*, 135; Ettinger, *James Edward Oglethorpe*, 250; R. A. Roberts, *Manuscripts of the Earl*, 3:266.

Chapter 12. Ten Times Worse than Pagans

1. John Dobell to the Trustees, July 18, 1743, in Lane, *General Oglethorpe's Georgia*, 2:663–664; Scarborough, *Opposition to Slavery in Georgia*, 47.

2. Thomas D. Wilson, *Oglethorpe Plan*, 116, 194.

3. Betty Wood, *Slavery in Colonial Georgia*, 73; Fischer, *African Founders*, 404–406.

4. Pennington, "Thomas Bray Associates," 327; Lewis G. Jordan, *Negro Baptist History*, 2.

5. Thurmond, *Freedom*, 34.

6. Betty Wood, *Slavery in Colonial Georgia*, 143, 163–164.

7. Lawrence, "Religious Education of the Negro," 51; Rice, *Rise and Fall*, 143.

8. Lawrence, "Religious Education of the Negro," 143; Rice, *Rise and Fall*, 143.

9. Betty Wood, *Slavery in Colonial Georgia*, 160.

10. Pennington, "Thomas Bray Associates," 329.

11. Lawrence, "Religious Education of the Negro," 54.

12. Ibid., 44–54.

13. Ibid.; Quarles, *Negro in the American Revolution*, 180, 192; Walker, *Black Loyalists*, 5.

14. Magdol, *Right to the Land*, 139–140; Byrne, "'Uncle Billy' Sherman," 112.

Chapter 13. Arming Enslaved Soldiers

1. James Oglethorpe, *British Sailor's Advocate*, 3; Candler and Knight, *Colonial Records*, 18:102–104.

2. Candler and Knight, *Colonial Records*, 18:102–104; Anthony, "Unindexed Official Record," 48; Rubye Mae Jones, "Negro in Colonial Georgia," 45; Betty Wood, *Slavery in Colonial Georgia*, 119.

3. Candler and Knight, *Colonial Records*, 18:102–104; Anthony, "Unindexed Official Record," 48; Rubye Mae Jones, "Negro in Colonial Georgia," 45; Betty Wood, *Slavery in Colonial Georgia*, 119.

4. *Georgia Gazette*, April 1763.

5. Spalding, "Oglethorpe's Quest."

Chapter 14. A Sincere Lover of Justice

1. Thomas D. Wilson, *Oglethorpe Plan*, 116, 194.

2. Ettinger, *James Edward Oglethorpe*, 292.

3. Thomas D. Wilson, *Oglethorpe Plan*, 198–200; Betty Wood, *Slavery in Colonial Georgia*, 73.

4. Walesby, *Works of Samuel Johnson*, 6:259–262; Basker, "Johnson and Slavery," 32.

5. Equiano, *Interesting Narrative*, chap. 1, 1:5, chap. 2, 1:48–50; Allison, *Interesting Narrative of the Life*, 34–35, 47–48, 59–61.

6. Equiano, *Interesting Narrative*, chap. 3, 1:93–96, chap. 4, 1:130–170; Allison, *Interesting Narrative of the Life*, 61, 89–92.

7. Equiano, *Interesting Narrative*, chap. 5, 1:93–94, 194–195, 205–207; Allison, *Interesting Narrative of the Life*, 93; Mtubani, "Black Voice," 90.

8. Equiano, *Interesting Narrative*, chap. 5, 1:205–207; Allison, *Interesting Narrative of the Life*, 93–96.

9. Equiano, *Interesting Narrative*, chap. 7, 2:16–17; Allison, *Interesting Narrative of the Life*, 118–120.

10. Equiano, *Interesting Narrative*, chap. 9, 2:72–73; Allison, *Interesting Narrative of the Life*, 134–135, 136; Carretta, *Equiano, the African*, 109, 131–132, 165–166.

11. Exchange of letters between Granville Sharp and his niece Ann Jemima about Olaudah Equiano, 1811, Granville Sharp Papers; Equiano, *Interesting Narrative*, chap. 10, 2:119–120; Birrell, "Massacre of Slaves"; Carretta, *Equiano, the African*, 206–207.

12. Lofft, *Reports of Cases Adjudged*, 19; Ditchfield, "Lofft, Capel"; Allison, *Interesting Narrative of the Life*, 151–152; Carretta, *Equiano, the African*, 206–207.

13. Equiano, *Interesting Narrative*, chap. 10, 2:122–123; Allison, *Interesting Narrative of the Life*, 152; Carretta, *Equiano, the African*, 211.

14. Hoare, *Memoirs of Granville Sharp*, 155–156.

15. Ibid.; Thomas, "James Edward Oglethorpe," 32; Coffey, "Tremble, Britannia";

"Petition of the Inhabitants of Darien to General Oglethorpe," in Candler, *Colonial Records of Georgia*, 3:427.

16. Hoare, *Memoirs of Granville Sharp*, 155–156.

17. Ibid., 158.

18. Ibid., 157–159.

19. Ibid., 158.

20. Ibid.; Landers, *Fort Mose*, 15–16.

21. Hoare, *Memoirs of Granville Sharp*, 158.

22. Hume, *Essays*, 208, 629.

23. Hoare, *Memoirs of Granville Sharp*, 157–160; Robert Brown, *Leo Africanus*; "Tirhakah," *Easton's Bible Dictionary*, Bible Study Tools, https://www.biblestudytools.com/dictionary/tirhakah/; "Shishak," Wikipedia, https://en.wikipedia.org/wiki/Shishak; Gill, "Was Hannibal?"; 1 Kings 14:25; 2 Chronicles 12:1–12; Masonen, "Leo Africanus"; 1 Kings 14:25; 2 Chronicles 12:1–12.

24. Hoare, *Memoirs of Granville Sharp*, 158.

25. Ibid., 157–160.

26. Ibid.

27. Ibid.

28. William Roberts, *Memoirs of the Life*, 130–131, 320; Thomas D. Wilson, *Oglethorpe Plan*, 201.

29. Thomas D. Wilson, *Oglethorpe Plan*, 202; Metaxas, "Power of a Poem."

Chapter 15. "A Very Uncommon Case"

1. Exchange of letters between Granville Sharp and Ann Jemima about Equiano, 1811, Granville Sharp Papers; Hoare, *Memoirs of Granville Sharp*, 236; Equiano, *Interesting Narrative*, chap. 10, 2:122.

2. Faubert, "Granville Sharp's Manuscript Letter."

3. Hoare, *Memoirs of Granville Sharp*, 236–247; Walvin, *Zong*, 90–91, 97–103.

4. Hoare, *Memoirs of Granville Sharp*, 236–247; Walvin, *Zong*, 99.

5. Walvin, *Zong*, 99–101.

6. Ibid., 97–98; Hoare, *Memoirs of Granville Sharp*, 238.

7. Hoare, *Memoirs of Granville Sharp*, 239.

8. Ibid.; Clarkson, *History of the Rise*, 6; reported in the *Morning Chronicle and London Advertiser*, March 18, 1783; Shyllon, *Black Slaves in Britain*, 187–188.

9. Exchange of letters between Sharp and Ann Jemima about Equiano, 1811, Granville Sharp Papers; Walvin, *Zong*, 153.

10. Hoare, *Memoirs of Granville Sharp*, 242, appendix, no. 8, xvii; Walvin, *Zong*, 154–155.

11. Hoare, *Memoirs of Granville Sharp*, 242, appendix, no. 8, xvii; Walvin, *Zong*, 154–155.

12. Walvin, *Zong*, 154–155.

13. Ibid.; Hoare, *Memoirs of Granville Sharp*, 238–241.

14. Hochschild, *Bury the Chains*, 1–8; Wise, *Though the Heavens May Fall*, 217–220.

Chapter 16. "We Hold These Truths to Be Self-Evident"

1. Franklin and Moss, *From Slavery to Freedom*, 83; Locke, *First and Second Treaties*, 107–108; Ramsey, *History of the American Revolution*, 2:29; Coulter, *Short History of Georgia*, 136; Coleman, *American Revolution in Georgia*, 170–171; Wirt, *Sketches of the Life*, 124; Quarles, preface to *The Negro in the American Revolution*.

2. Lanning, *African-American Soldier*, 9.

3. Joseph T. Wilson, *The Black Phalanx*, 22; Ramsey, *History of the American Revolution*, 291; Coulter, *Short History of Georgia*, 136; Coleman, *American Revolution in Georgia*, 170–171; Franklin and Moss, *From Slavery to Freedom*, 91–92.

4. Du Bois, *Suppression of the African Slave-Trade*, 48; Coulter, *Short History of Georgia*, 136; Coleman, *American Revolution in Georgia*, 170–171; Lengyel, *Four Days in July*, 174.

5. Phillips, *American Negro Slavery*, 123–125; Walker, *Black Loyalists*, 5; Lanning, *African-American Soldier*, 15; Goodridge, "For Blacks"; Thorenz, "Substitutes, Servants and Soldiers."

6. Phillips, *American Negro Slavery*, 5; Cheek, "Quamino."

7. Walker, *Black Loyalists*, 5.

8. Woodson, "Letters Showing the Rise," 70–71; Brooks, *Silver Bluff Church*, 7.

9. Woodson, "Letters Showing the Rise," 70–71.

10. Ibid.; Sobel, *Trabelin' On*, 105–106; Ellis, "Bicentennial Celebration"; Tillman, "First African Baptist Church History."

11. Quarles, *Negro in the American Revolution*, 154; Walker, *Black Loyalists*, 5; Ellis, "Bicentennial Celebration"; Tillman, "First African Baptist Church History."

12. Quarles, *Negro in the American Revolution*, 154; Walker, *Black Loyalists*, 5; Farley, "South Carolina Negro," 75–80.

13. George D. Massey, *John Laurens*, 132; Farley, "South Carolina Negro," 79; Quarles, *Negro in the American Revolution*, 154; Walker, *Black Loyalists*, 5.

14. Jack Foner, *Blacks and the Military*, 12; George H. Moore, *Historical Notes*, 11–12; Gregory D. Massey, "Slavery and Liberty"; Farley, "South Carolina Negro," 75–80; George D. Massey, *John Laurens*, 132; "Lt. Colonel John Laurens," Valley Forge National Historical Park, National Park Service, August 9, 2019, http://www.nps.gov/vafo/learn/historyculture/johnlaurens.htm.

15. Jack Foner, *Blacks and the Military*, 12; Farley, "South Carolina Negro," 75–80; George H. Moore, *Historical Notes*, 11; George D. Massey, *John Laurens*, 132–133, 221.

16. Jack Foner, *Blacks and the Military*, 12; Farley, "South Carolina Negro," 75–80; George H. Moore, *Historical Notes*, 11; George D. Massey, *John Laurens*, 132–133, 221.

17. George H. Moore, *Historical Notes*, 8–11; Jack Foner, *Blacks and the Military*, 12; MacGregor and Nalty, *Blacks*, 49; Livermore, *Historical Research*, 139; Phillips, *American Negro Slavery*, 125; Farley, "South Carolina Negro," 75–80; George D. Massey, *John Laurens*, 132–133, 221.

18. George H. Moore, *Historical Notes*, 14.

19. Aptheker, *To Be Free*, 38; Robert Scott Davis, "Black Haitian Soldiers"; Maguire, "Haitian Soldiers"; Jordan Baker, "Shake the Earth."

20. Force, *American Archives*, 5th ser., 3:68; Candler, *Colonial Records of Georgia*, 3:80–86.

21. Grant and Grant, *Way It Was*, 15–16.

22. Coleman, *American Revolution in Georgia*, 135, 144; Woodson, *History of the Negro Church*, 43–46.

23. Bisnauth, *History of Religions*, 115–116; Quarles, *Negro in the American Revolution*, 175–177.

24. Drimmer, *Black History*, 141; Quarles, *Negro in the American Revolution*, 175–176; Coleman, *American Revolution in Georgia*, 145–146.

25. Gilmer, *Sketches*, 165; Hornsby, *Negro in Revolutionary Georgia*, 10.

26. Hornsby, *Negro in Revolutionary Georgia*, 10.

27. Ibid.

28. Cashin, *Story of Augusta*, 13–14; Brooks, *Silver Bluff Church*, 7.

29. Collier and Collier, *Decision in Philadelphia*, 185.

30. Ibid.; Bowen, *Miracle at Philadelphia*, 200–204.

31. Bowen, *Miracle at Philadelphia*, 203–204; Collier and Collier, *Decision in Philadelphia*, 219–222; Ketcham, *Anti-Federalist Papers*, 160–165.

32. Eric Foner, *Fiery Trial*, 14; "Abolition and the Abolitionists," National Geographic Society, last updated May 20, 2022, https://education.nationalgeographic.org/resource/abolition-and-abolitionists/; Stewart, *Far Cry from Freedom*, 135–139.

33. Bergman and McCarroll, *Negro in the Congressional Record*, 86–123; Grant and Grant, *Way It Was*, 19; Kaplan and Kaplan, *Black Presence*, 85; Daniel F. Littlefield Jr., *Africans and Seminoles*, 4.

34. Aptheker, *To Be Free*, 13; Grant and Grant, *Way It Was*, 19; Kaplan and Kaplan, *Black Presence*, 85; Lockley, "King of England's Soldiers," 31–37.

35. Lockley, "King of England's Soldiers," 36–41; Grant and Grant, *Way It Was*, 19; Kaplan and Kaplan, *Black Presence*, 85.

36. *Massachusetts Gazette*, October 1786; Lockley, "King of England's Soldiers," 37–38.

37. Lockley, "King of England's Soldiers," 37–38.

38. Ibid., 36–41; Grant and Grant, *Way It Was*, 19; Kaplan and Kaplan, *Black Presence*, 85.

39. Bullard, *Black Liberation on Cumberland Island* is the most comprehensive treatment of the British occupation of Cumberland Island and the evacuation of enslaved Blacks from coastal Georgia during the War of 1812.

40. Bullard, *Black Liberation on Cumberland Island*, 47–52, 55–61; Mike Bezemek, "A Chance for Freedom," National Parks Conservation Association, Spring 2021, https://www.npca.org/articles/2856-a-chance-for-freedom.

41. Bullard, *Black Liberation on Cumberland Island*, 62–66.

42. Ibid., 56–57; Mills and Weiss, "Corps of Colonial Marines"; Peters, *Florida Wars*, 40–41.

43. Bullard, *Black Liberation on Cumberland Island*, 83.

44. Ibid., 104.

45. Ibid., 113–118.

46. Act no. 508, December 19, 1816, in Lamar, *Compilation of the Laws*, 804; Riddell, "Slavery in the Maritime Provinces," 373–375; Mahon, *War of 1812*, 370–371.

47. Riddell, "Slavery in the Maritime Provinces," 373–375; Mahon, *War of 1812*, 370–371.

48. Betty Wood, *Slavery in Colonial Georgia*, 39.

49. Ibid., 127–128; Berlin, *Slaves without Masters*, 9; Candler and Knight, *Colonial Records*, 18:659.

50. Ungar, "Free Negroes," 2.

51. Ibid.

52. Aptheker, *To Be Free*, 31; Susie King Taylor, *Black Woman's Civil War Memories*, 29–30.

53. Scarborough, *Opposition to Slavery in Georgia*, 132, 134.

54. Department of Commerce, Bureau of the Census, *Negro Population*.

55. Robert Scott Davis, "Black Haitian Soldiers"; Maguire, "Haitian Soldiers at the Battle"; Jordan Baker, "Shake the Earth."

56. Berlin, *Slaves without Masters*, 48–49.

57. Scarborough, *Opposition to Slavery in Georgia*, 194–197; Finley, "Thoughts on the Colonization," 1–8.

58. Yautz, "Rev. Robert Finley."

59. Hoare, *Memoirs of Granville Sharp*, 384–385.

60. Fox, *American Colonization Society*, 47.

61. Sherwood, "Formation," 218–219.

62. Finney, "American Colonization Society"; Franklin and Moss, *From Slavery to Freedom*, 102, 109, 167–170.

63. Finley, "Thoughts on the Colonization," 334–335; Yautz, "Rev. Robert Finley."

64. Franklin and Moss, *From Slavery to Freedom*, 102, 109, 167–170.

65. Finley, "Thoughts on the Colonization," 1–8; Scarborough, *Opposition to Slavery in Georgia*, 196–200.

66. American Colonization Society, *African Repository and Georgia Journal*, 370.

67. Gilford, "Emily Tubman," 10–19.

68. Ibid.

Chapter 17. "An Act of Justice"

1. Eric Foner, "Lincoln and Colonization," in Foner, *Our Lincoln*, 135–136, 145–147; Pruitt, "5 Things"; Rhodehamel, "Forever Free," 1–5.

2. McPherson, *Ordeal by Fire*, 127–129, 140–142.

3. McPherson, *Negro's Civil War*, 19–26; Blight, *Frederick Douglass' Civil War*, 149.

4. Quarles, *Negro in the Civil War*, 127–135.

5. Philip S. Foner, *Life and Writings*, 3:225; Bennett, *Forced into Glory*, 387–388.

6. McPherson, *Negro's Civil War*, 19–26; Blight, *Frederick Douglass' Civil War*, 149.

7. Quarles, *Negro in the Civil War*, 127–135.

8. Cornish, *Sable Arm*, 94–98; McPherson, *Negro's Civil War*, 293–294.

9. Quarles, *Negro in the Civil War*, 48–50; Jack D. Foner, *Blacks and the Military*, 32–51; Lanning, *African-American Soldier*, 30–61; Cornish, *Sable Arm*, 94–111.

10. Bruun and Crosby, *Our Nation's Archive*, 425; "People and Ideas: Civil War and Reconstruction," God in America, *American Experience*, Public Broadcasting Service, https://www.pbs.org/wgbh/americanexperience/features/godinamerica-civil -war-reconstruction/.

Chapter 18. "Let My People Go!"

1. Sherman, *Memoirs*, 583; Burke Davis, *Sherman's March*, 20–21; Donald R. Shaffer, "African Americans and Sherman's March," 1–4.
2. Sherman, *Memoirs*, 583–602.
3. Ibid.
4. Sherman, *Memoirs*, 593, 598; Burke Davis, *Sherman's March,* 21.
5. Sherman, *Memoirs*, 593, 598; Burke Davis, *Sherman's March,* 21.
6. Sherman, *Memoirs*, 656–657.
7. Ibid.; Exodus 7:16.
8. Sherman, *Memoirs*, 656–657; Bennett, "Jubilee."
9. Burke Davis, *Sherman's March*, 32; Sherman, *Memoirs*, 656–657.
10. Drago, "How Sherman's March," 361–365.
11. Ibid., 363.
12. Burke Davis, *Sherman's March*, 46.
13. Du Bois, *Souls of Black Folks*, 18; Bennett, "Jubilee."

Chapter 19. Death at Ebenezer Creek

1. Sherman, *Memoirs*, 724–725; Burke Davis, *Sherman's March*, 139.
2. Drago, "How Sherman's March," 366; Mohr, *Threshold of Freedom*, 90.
3. Sherman, *Memoirs*, 664.
4. Burke Davis, *Sherman's March*, 58.
5. Ibid., 63.
6. Ibid., 63–64.
7. Hight and Stormont, *History of the Fifty-Eighth Regiment*, 426–427; Connolly, *Three Years in the Army*, 430; Conyngham, *Sherman's March*, 277; Garrison, "Sudden Death at Ebenezer Creek," 33.
8. Garrison, "Sudden Death at Ebenezer Creek," 33; Shaffer, "African Americans and Sherman's March," 1–4.
9. Cox, *Sherman's March to the Sea*, 37–38.
10. Burke Davis, Sherman's March, 92.
11. Ibid., 39; Hight and Stormont, *History of the Fifty-Eighth Regiment*, 426–427.
12. Drago, "How Sherman's March ," 370; *Ninety-Second Illinois Volunteers*, 197–198.
13. Connolly, *Three Years in the Army*, 430.
14. Burke Davis, *Sherman's March*, 92–94; Garrison, "Sudden Death at Ebenezer Creek," 33; Shaffer, "African Americans and Sherman's March," 1–4.

15. Burke Davis, *Sherman's March*, 93–94.
16. Cox, *Sherman's March to the Sea*, 37–38.
17. Burke Davis, *Sherman's March*, 139.

Chapter 20. *"Glory Be to God, We Are Free!"*

1. Records of the Office of the Secretary of War, 1791–1948, National Archives Identifier: 301637, National Archives Record Group 107.
2. Byrne, "'Uncle Billy' Sherman," 91; Simms, *First Colored Baptist Church*, 137.
3. Byrne, "'Uncle Billy' Sherman," 91–92, 97, 105.
4. Ibid., 91.
5. Ibid., 93.
6. Sherman, *Memoirs*, 728; Burke Davis, *Sherman's March*, 131.
7. Sherman, *Memoirs*, 722–725; Burke Davis, *Sherman's March*, 136.
8. Sherman, *Memoirs*, 722–725; James, "Sherman at Savannah"; *New York Tribune*, February 13, 1865.
9. James, "Sherman at Savannah"; *New York Tribune*, February 13, 1865; Sherman, *Memoirs*, 722–725; James, "Sherman at Savannah," 128–129; *New York Tribune*, February 13, 1865.
10. Sherman, *Memoirs*, 725–727; *New York Tribune*, February 13, 1865.
11. Sherman, *Memoirs*, 725–727; James, "Sherman at Savannah"; *New York Tribune*, February 13, 1865.
12. Sherman, *Memoirs*, 725–727; James, "Sherman at Savannah"; *New York Tribune*, February 13, 1865.
13. Sherman, *Memoirs*, 725–727; Burke Davis, *Sherman's March*, 137; *New York Tribune*, February 13, 1865.
14. Sherman, *Memoirs*, 725–727; Burke Davis, *Sherman's March*, 137; *New York Tribune*, February 13, 1865.
15. Sherman, *Memoirs*, 725–726; Burke Davis, *Sherman's March*, 137; *New York Tribune*, February 13, 1865.
16. Sherman, *Memoirs*, 730–732.
17. Byrne, "'Uncle Billy' Sherman," 108–109; Sherman, *Memoirs*, 726–727.
18. Byrne, "'Uncle Billy' Sherman," 108–109; Sherman, *Memoirs*, 726–727.

Chapter 21. *Lincoln's Second Inaugural Address*

1. David Brion Davis, *Problem of Slavery*, 148; "Petition of the Inhabitants of Darien to General Oglethorpe," in Candler, *Colonial Records of Georgia*, 3:427; Hoare, *Memoirs of Granville Sharpe*, 157–159; Bruun and Crosby, *Our Nation's Archive*, 437–438; White, *Lincoln's Greatest Speech*, 154–159.
2. Bruun and Crosby, *Our Nation's Archive*, 437–438; White, *Lincoln's Greatest Speech*, 154–159; "Petition of the Inhabitants of Darien to General Oglethorpe," 3:427.

3. Guyatt, *Providence and the Intervention*, 14–17; Hoare, *Memoirs of Granville Sharp*, 153–156.

4. Bruun and Crosby, *Our Nation's Archive*, 437–438; White, *Lincoln's Greatest Speech*, 157; Hoare, *Memoirs of Granville Sharp*, 153–156.

5. Sinha, "Allies for Emancipation?," 187.

6. David Brion Davis, *Problem of Slavery*, xx; Bruun and Crosby, *Our Nation's Archive*, 437–438.

7. Bruun and Crosby, *Our Nation's Archive*, 437–438; White, *Lincoln's Greatest Speech*, 144–155.

8. Bruun and Crosby, *Our Nation's Archive*, 437–438; White, *Lincoln's Greatest Speech*, 144–155; Hoare, *Memoirs of Granville Sharp*, 156.

9. Bruun and Crosby, *Our Nation's Archive*, 437–438; White, *Lincoln's Greatest Speech*, 144–155.

10. McPherson, *Ordeal by Fire*, 481–482, 484–486; Sherman, *Memoirs*, 834–835.

11. McPherson, *Ordeal by Fire*, 466–467; Bruun and Crosby, *Our Nation's Archive*, 417.

12. Conway, *Reconstruction of Georgia*, 52–54; C. Mildred Thompson, *Reconstruction in Georgia*, 156–157.

Conclusion. The Oglethorpe Legacy

1. Hochschild, *Bury the Chains*, 1–3; Hammond and Mason, *Contesting Slavery*, 11–14; Martin, review of Hammond and Mason, *Contesting Slavery*, *What Would the Founders Think?* (blog), http://www.whatwouldthefoundersthink.com/contesting-slavery-edited-by-john-craig-hammond-and-matthew-mason-2.

2. Hochschild, *Bury the Chains*, 1–3; Hammond and Mason, *Contesting Slavery*, 11–14; Martin, review.

3. Hochschild, *Bury the Chains*, 1–8; Wise, *Though the Heavens May Fall*, 217–220; Higginbotham, *In the Matter of Color*, 224.

4. Bertrand, "Downfall," 115; Ettinger, *James Edward Oglethorpe*, 147–148.

5. Baine, *Creating Georgia*, 25–26.

6. Francis Moore, *Travels into the Inland Parts*, 323; Wong, "Did We Sell Each Other."

7. Snelgrave, *New Account*, 160–161; Padgett, "1730s Portrait," 1; Barbara Wells Sarudy, "Slave Trader Muslim Ayuba Suleiman Diallo 1701–1773: Stolen from Africa Sent to Maryland to England and Back to His Wives and Children in Africa," *Women in 18C British Colonial America* (blog), March 25, 2020, https://b-womeninamericanhistory18.blogspot.com/2020/03/slave-trader-muslim-ayuba-suleiman.html; "First British Portrait of a Black African Muslim and Freed Slave Goes on Display," Art Daily, January 19, 2011, https://artdaily.cc/news/44298/First-British-Portrait-of-a-Black-African-Muslim-and-Freed-Slave-Goes-on-Display.

8. Weld, "Condition and Character," 47.

9. Wilkins, "James Edward Oglethorpe," 85, 93–94; Higginbotham, *In the Matter of Color*, 224; David Brion Davis, *Problem of Slavery*, 145.

10. Betty Wood, "The Earl of Egmont and the Georgia Colony," in Jackson and Spalding, *Forty Years of Diversity: Essays on Colonial Georgia*, 93.

11. Ettinger, *James Edward Oglethorpe*, 148; David Brion Davis, *Problem of Slavery*, 148.

12. Hochschild, *Bury the Chains*, 1–3; Hammond and Mason, *Contesting Slavery*, 11–14; Martin, review; Stewart and Long, *Plutarch's Lives*.

13. Oglethorpe to Trustees, January 16 and 17, 1739, in Lane, *General Oglethorpe's Georgia*, 2:387–390; Betty Wood, *Slavery in Colonial Georgia*, 31.

14. Clarkson, *History of the Rise*, 259–266.

15. Birrell, "Massacre of Slaves"; Faubert, "Granville Sharp's Manuscript Letter," 2.

16. Ettinger, *James Edward Oglethorpe*, 134, 137, 144–146; McCall, *History of Georgia*, 23–26, 34; Sinha, *Slave's Cause*, 10.

17. Higginbotham, *In the Matter of Color*, 227–235.

18. Horne, *Counter Revolution of 1776*, 135; Grant and Grant, *Way It Was*, 6; Lannen, "Liberty and Slavery"; Betty Wood, *Slavery in Colonial Georgia*, 4; "Betty Wood on Oglethorpe the Founder of Georgia," Africans in America, PBS, https://www.pbs.org/wgbh/aia/part1/1i3065.html.

19. Bruce, *Life of Oglethorpe*, 99; Thomas D. Wilson, *Oglethorpe Plan*, 22, 133, 193–194, 202, 206; Phinizy Spalding, foreword to Baine, *Publications of James Edward Oglethorpe*.

20. Betty Wood, "James Edward Oglethorpe," 79; Thomas, "James Edward Oglethorpe," 32.

21. Robert Scott Davis, "Wheels within Wheels," 1.

22. Will of Elizabeth Oglethorpe, 1788, William Gill Indentures, MS 2382, Hargrett Rare Book and Manuscript Library, University of Georgia Libraries; Hoare, *Memoirs of Granville Sharp*, 384–385.

23. Harris, *Biographical Memorials of James Oglethorpe*, 143–145.

BIBLIOGRAPHY

Primary Sources

American Colonization Society. *The African Repository and Georgia Journal*. Vol. 3. New York: Kraus, 1967.

Ayuba Suleiman Diallo's letter to his father, c. 1731–1733. British Library. Shelfmark: MS 20783a.

Baine, Rodney, ed. *Creating Georgia: Minutes of the Bray Associates 1730–1732 and Supplementary Documents*. Athens: University of Georgia Press, 1995.

———. *The Publications of James Edward Oglethorpe*. Athens: University of Georgia Press, 1994.

Baker, Frank, ed. *The Works of John Wesley*, vol. 25, *Letters I, 1721–1739*. Oxford: Clarendon Press, 1980.

Brown, Robert, ed. *Leo Africanus: The History and Description of Africa*. 3 vols. London: Hakluyt Society, 1896.

Bruun, Frank, and Jay Crosby, eds. *Our Nation's Archive: The History of the United States in Documents*. New York: Tess Press, 1999.

Candler, Allen, ed. *The Colonial Records of the State of Georgia*. 26 vols. Washington, D.C.: National Park Service, United States Department of the Interior, 1942.

Candler, Allen D., and Lucian Knight, eds. *The Colonial Records of the State of Georgia*. 26 vols. Atlanta, 1904–1916.

Coleman, Kenneth, and Milton L. Ready, eds. *The Colonial Records of the State of Georgia*. 7 vols. Athens: University of Georgia Press, 1968.

Conway, Alan. *The Reconstruction of Georgia*. Minneapolis: University of Minnesota Press, 1966.

Coulter, E. Merton, ed. *The Journal of William Stephens, 1741–1743*. Athens: University of Georgia Press, 1958.

Department of Commerce, Bureau of the Census. *Negro Population: 1790–1915*. Washington, D.C.: Government Printing Office, 1915.

Easterby, J. H., ed. "Report of the Committee Appointed to Enquire into the Causes of the Disappointment of Success in the Late Expedition against St. Augustine." *Journal of the Commons House of Assembly*, July 1, 1741. Columbia: Historical Commission of South Carolina, 1953.

Equiano, Olaudah. *The Interesting Narrative of the Life of Olaudah Equiano, or Gustavus Vassa, the African*. 1789. https://docsouth.unc.edu/neh/equiano1/equiano1.html.

Foner, Philip S., ed. *The Life and Writings of Frederick Douglass*. 4 vols. New York: International, 1950.

Force, Peter. *American Archives*. 5th ser., 3 vols. New York: Johnson, 1972.

Fray, William C., and Lisa A. Spar. *Charter of Georgia*, 1732. An electronic publication of the Avalon Project, Documents in Law, History and Diplomacy, Yale Law School, New Haven, Conn., 1996.

Georgia, State of. "Executive Order by the Governor, May 7, 1996." http://dlg.galileo .usg.edu/ggpd/docs/1996/ga/g600/_ps1/e9/1996_s5_h7a.con/1.pdf.

Hoare, Prince, ed. *Memoirs of Granville Sharp, Esq., Composed from His Manuscripts, and Other Authentic Documents in the Possession of His Family and of the African Institution*. Cambridge: Cambridge University Press, 1820.

Hume, David. *Essays: Moral, Political, and Literary*. Rev. ed. Edited by Eugene F. Miller. Indianapolis: Liberty Classics, 1987.

Ketcham, Ralph, ed. *The Anti-Federalist Papers and the Constitutional Convention Debates*. New York: Mentor, 1986.

Kingsbury, Susan Myra, ed. *The Records of the Virginia Company of London*. 4 vols. Washington, D.C., 1933.

Lamar, Lucius Q. *A Compilation of the Laws of the State of Georgia Passed by the Legislature since the Year 1810 to the 1819*. Augusta: T. S. Hannon, 1822.

Lane, Mills, ed. *General Oglethorpe's Georgia*. 2 vols. Savannah: Beehive Press, 1990.

Lofft, Capel. *Reports of Cases Adjudged in the Court of King's Bench, from Eastern Term 12 Geo. 3. to Michaelmas 14 Geo. S.* Dublin, 1790.

Oglethorpe, James Edward. James Edward Oglethorpe Papers, 1730–1785. Compiled by George W. DeRenne. Georgia Historical Society.

Reese, Trevor R. *The Clamorous Malcontents: Criticisms and Defenses of the Colony of Georgia, 1741–1743*. Savannah: Beehive Press, 1973.

Roberts, R. A., ed. *Manuscripts of the Earl of Egmont: Diary of Viscount Percival, Afterwards First Earl of Egmont*. 3 vols. London, 1920–1923.

Roberts, William, ed. *Memoirs of the Life and Correspondence of Mrs. Hannah More*. Vol. 1. London, 1836.

Sharp, Granville. Granville Sharp Papers from the Gloucestership Record Office. Adam Mathew Publications, D3549 13/1/s6.

———. Manuscript letter to the admiralty on the Zong massacre, 1783. DOI: 10.1080/0144039X.2016.1206285BritishLibrary.

Sherman, William Tecumseh. *Memoirs of General W. T. Sherman*. New York: Library of America, 1990.

"Slavery Abolition Act 1833." August 28, 1833. https://www.irishstatutebook.ie/eli/1833 /act/73/enacted/en/print.html.

Smith, Mark A., ed. *Stono: Documenting and Interpreting a Southern Slave Revolt*. Columbia: University of South Carolina Press, 2005.

Society for the Propagation of the Gospel. *An Abstract of the Proceedings of the Society for the Propagation of the Gospel in Foreign Parts, in the Year of Our Lord 1715*. Farmington Hills, Mich.: Gale ECCO, 2010.

South Carolina Commons House of Assembly. "South Carolina Commons House of Assembly Committee Report: A Message to the Governor's Council." *Journal of the*

Upper House 7 (November 29, 1739). In *Journal of the Commons House of Assembly*, ed. J. H. Easterby et al. Columbia: Historical Commission of South Carolina, 1953.

Steiner, Bernard C., ed. "Rev. Thomas Bray, His Life and Selected Works Relating to Maryland." Baltimore: Maryland Historical Society, 1901.

Stephens, William. *A Journal of the Proceedings in Georgia Beginning October 20, 1737*. 3 vols. London, 1742.

Tailfer, Patrick, Hugh Anderson, Da. Douglas, and others. *A True and Historical Narrative of the Colony of Georgia in America: From the First Settlement Thereof until This Present Period*. Charles-Town: P. Timothy, 1741.

Tate, John. *St. Augustine Expedition of 1740: A Report to the South Carolina General Assembly Reprinted from the Colonial Records of South Carolina*. Columbia: South Carolina Archives Department, 1954.

Taylor, Susie King. *A Black Woman's Civil War Memories*. Princeton, N.J.: Markus Wiener, 1994.

Telford, John, ed. *Letters of the Rev. John Wesley, A. M.* London: Epworth Press, 1931. Available at Wesley Center Online.

Trans-Atlantic Slave Trade Database. Edited by David Eltis and David Richardson. Emory University. http://www.slavevoyages.org.

Van Horne, John C., ed. *Religious Philanthropy and Colonial Slavery: The Correspondence of the Associates of Dr. Bray, 1717–1777*. Urbana: University of Illinois Press, 1985.

Vaux, Robert. *Memoirs of the Life of Anthony Benezet*. New York: Burt Franklin, 1817.

Walesby, F. P., ed. *The Works of Samuel Johnson*. Vol. 6. London: W. Pickering, 1825.

Woodson, Carter G., ed. "Letters Showing the Rise and Progress of the Early Negro Churches of Georgia and the West Indies." *Journal of Negro History* 1 (1916): 70–71.

Secondary Sources

"Abolition and Abolitionists." National Geographic Resource Library, May 20, 2022. https://education.nationalgeographic.org/resource/abolition-and-abolitionists/.

An African Merchant. *A Treatise upon the Trade from Great-Britain to Africa*. London, 1772.

Al-Badaai, Muna Sulaiman. "Positioning the Testimony of Job Ben Solomon, an Enslaved African American Muslim." *International Journal of Applied Linguistics and English Literature* 4, no. 6 (November 2015): 204–206.

Allison, Robert J., ed. *The Interesting Narrative of the Life of Olaudah Equiano, Written by Himself*. Boston: Bedford Books / St. Martin's Press, 1995.

Anonymous. "An Appeal for the Georgia Colony, 1732." In *The Publications of James Edward Oglethorpe*, ed. Rodney Baine, 159–166. Athens: University of Georgia Press, 1994.

Anthony, Marion Ernestine. "The Unindexed Official Record of the Negro in Georgia, 1733–1766." Master's thesis, Atlanta University, 1937.

Aptheker, Herbert. *To Be Free*. New York: First Carol, 1991.

Arnold, Calli. "No Longer Lost to History: Marker Commemorates Freed Slaves Drownings." *Effingham Herald*, May 27, 2010.

Baine, Rodney. "The Prison Death of Robert Castell and Its Effect on the Founding of Georgia." In Inscoe, *James Edward Oglethorpe*, 35–46.

Baker, Jordan. "Shake the Earth: Haitian Soldiers in the American Revolution." *East India Blogging Co.*, September 26, 2016. https://eastindiabloggingco.com /2016/09/26/haitian-soldiers-american-revolution/.

Basker, James. "Johnson and Slavery." *Harvard Library Bulletin* 20, nos. 3–4 (Fall–Winter 2009): 29–50.

Bellamy, Donnie D. "The Legal Status of Black Georgians during the Colonial and Revolutionary Eras." *Journal of Negro History* 74 (Autumn-Winter 1989): 1–10.

Bennett, Lerone, Jr. *Forced into Glory: Abraham Lincoln's White Dream*. Chicago: Johnson, 2000.

———. "Jubilee: The Making of Black America." *Ebony* 27, no. 4 (February 1972): 37–46.

Bergman, Peter M., and Jean McCarroll, comp. *Negro in the Congressional Record, 1789–1801*. New York: Bergman, 1969.

Berlin, Ira. *Slaves without Masters: The Free Negro in the Antebellum South*. New York: New Press, 1974.

Berlin, Ira, and Ronald Hoffman, eds. *Slavery and Freedom in the Age of the American Revolution*. Charlottesville: University Press of Virginia, 1983.

Berry, Daina Ramey. *The Price for Their Pound of Flesh: The Value of the Enslaved, from Womb to Grave, in the Building of a Nation*. Boston: Beacon, 2017.

Bertrand, Alicia Marie. "The Downfall of the Royal African Company on the Atlantic African Coast in the 1720's." Master's thesis, Trent University, 2011.

Birrell, Ian. "Massacre of Slaves Who Did Not Die in Vain." *Daily Mail*, September 15, 2011. https://www.dailymail.co.uk/home/books/article-2030135/Massacre-slaves-did -die-vain-THE-ZONG-BY-JAMES-WALVIN.html.

Bisnauth, Dale. *History of Religions in the Caribbean*. Kingston, Jamaica: Kingston Publishers, 1996.

Blight, David W. *Frederick Douglass' Civil War: Keeping Faith in Jubilee*. Baton Rouge: Louisiana State University Press, 1989.

Bluett, Thomas. *Some Memoirs of the Life of Job, the Son of Solomon High Priest of Boonda in Africa, Who Was a Slave about Two Years in Maryland*. London: Richard Ford, 1734.

Bolton, Herbert E., and Mary Ross. *The Debatable Land: A Sketch of the Anglo-Spanish Contest for the Georgia Country*. Berkeley: University of California Press, 1925.

Bowen, Catherine Drinker. *Miracle at Philadelphia: The Story of the Constitutional Convention, May to September 1787*. Boston: Little, Brown, 1986.

Brendlinger, Irv. "John Wesley and Slavery: Myth and Reality." Faculty Publications—College of Christian Studies, paper 116 (2006). http://digitalcommons.georgefox .edu/ccs/116.

Brooks, Walter H. *The Silver Bluff Church: A History of Negro Baptist Churches in America*. Washington, D.C.: R. L. Pendleton, 1910.

Brown, Vincent. *Tacky's Revolt: The Story of an Atlantic Slave War*. Cambridge, Mass.: Belknap Press / Harvard University Press, 2020.

Bruce, Henry. *The Life of Oglethorpe*. New York: Dodd, Meade, 1890.

Bullard, Mary R. *Black Liberation on Cumberland Island in 1815*. New Bedford, Mass.: M. R. Bullard, 1983.

Byrne, William A. "'Uncle Billy' Sherman Comes to Town: The Free Winter of Black Savannah." *Georgia Historical Quarterly* 79, no. 1 (Spring 1995): 91–116.

Carretta, Vincent. *Equiano, the African: Biography of a Self-Made Man*. Athens: University of Georgia Press, 2005.

Cashin, Edward J. *The Story of Augusta*. Spartanburg, S.C.: Reprint Company, 1991.

Cheek, Kevin J. "Quamino." *Cheek's Bay: Observations, Ruminations, and Cantankerous Notions*, February 16, 2016. https://cheeksbay.com/2016/02/16/quamino/.

Clarkson, Thomas. *The History of the Rise, Progress, and Accomplishment of the Abolition of the African Slave-Trade*. Vol. 1. New York: John S. Taylor, 1839.

Coclanis, Peter A. "Rice." *New Georgia Encyclopedia*, September 29, 2020. https://www.georgiaencyclopedia.org/articles/business-economy/rice.

Coffey, John. *Exodus and Liberation: Deliverance Politics from John Calvin to Martin Luther King*. Oxford: Oxford University Press, 2014.

———. "Tremble, Britannia!: Fear, Providence and the Abolition of the Slave Trade, 1758–1807." *English Historical Review* 127, no. 527 (August 2012): 844–881.

Coleman, Kenneth. *The American Revolution in Georgia, 1763–1789*. Athens: University of Georgia Press, 1958.

———. *Georgia History in Outline*. Rev. ed. Athens: University of Georgia Press, 1978.

———, gen. ed. *A History of Georgia*. Athens: University of Georgia Press, 1977.

Collier, Christopher, and James Collier. *Decision in Philadelphia: The Constitutional Convention of 1787*. New York: Ballantine, 1986.

Connolly, James A. *Three Years in the Army of the Cumberland: The Letters and Diary of Major James A. Connolly*. Bloomington: Indiana University Press, 1959.

Conyngham, David P. *Sherman's March through the South: With Sketches and Incidents of the Campaign*. New York: Sheldon, 1865.

Cornish, Dudley. *The Sable Arm: Black Troops in the Union Army, 1861–1865*. Lawrence: University Press of Kansas, 1956.

Coulter, E. Merton. *A Short History of Georgia*. Chapel Hill, N.C., 1933.

Cox, Jacob D. *Sherman's March to the Sea: Hood's Tennessee Campaign and the Carolina Campaigns of 1865*. Cambridge, Mass.: Da Capo, 1994.

Crane, Verner W. "The Philanthropists and the Genesis of Georgia." *American Historical Review* 27, no. 1 (October 1921): 63–69.

Cruickshanks, Eveline. "The Oglethorpes: A Jacobite Family, 1689–1760." *Royal Stuart Papers* 45 (1995).

Dabovic, Safet. "Displacement and the Negotiation of an American Identity in African Muslim Slave Narratives." PhD diss., Stony Brook University, 2009.

Davis, Burke. *Sherman's March*. New York: Vintage Books, 1980.

Davis, David Brion. *The Problem of Slavery in Western Culture*. Oxford: Oxford University Press, 1966.

———. "The Significance of Excluding Slavery from the Old Northwest in 1787." *Indiana Magazine of History* 84, no. 1 (March 1988): 75–89.

Davis, Harold E. *The Fledgling Province: Social and Cultural Life in Colonial Georgia, 1733–1776*. Chapel Hill: University of North Carolina Press, 1976.

Davis, Robert Scott. "Black Haitian Soldiers at the Siege of Savannah." *Journal of the American Revolution*, February 22, 2021. https://allthingsliberty.com/2021/02/black-haitian-soldiers-at-the-siege-of-savannah/.

———. "Wheels within Wheels: Slavery and the Framework of the Social History of the Eighteenth Century Georgia." *Journal of Backcountry Studies* 5, no. 1 (Summer 2010): 1–14.

Dillion, Merton L. *Slavery Attacked: Southern Slaves and Their Allies, 1619–1865*. Baton Rouge: Louisiana State University Press, 1990.

Diouf, Sylviane Anna. *Servants of Allah: African Muslims Enslaved in the Americas*. New York: New York University Press, 1998.

Ditchfield, G. M. "Lofft, Capel (1751–1824)." In *Oxford Dictionary of National Biography*. Oxford: Oxford University Press, 1992–.

Douglas, Nick. "Know Your Black History: Part II. Slave Revolts by Sea: Relentless Determination and the End of the Myth of the *Amistad*." *NeoGriot* (blog), October 14, 2015. https://kalamu.com/neogriot/2015/10/15/history-slave-revolts-by-sea/.

Drago, Edmund L. "How Sherman's March through Georgia Affected the Slaves." *Georgia Historical Quarterly* 57, no. 3 (1973): 361–375.

Drimmer, Melvin. *Black History: A Reappraisal*. Garden City, N.Y.: Doubleday, 1968.

Du Bois, W. E. B. *The Souls of Black Folk: Essays and Sketches*. New York: Blue Heron, 1953.

———. *The Suppression of the African Slave-Trade in the United States of America, 1638–1870*. New York: Social Science Press, 1954.

Dunkley, Daive. "RECAP: 'Anglican Evangelism and the Maintenance of Slavery in the 18th-Century Atlantic World,' Colloquium w/ MU's Daive Dunkley." Kinder Institute on Constitutional Democracy, University of Missouri. https://democracy.missouri.edu/news/recap-anglican-evangelism-and-the-maintenance-of-slavery-in-the-18th-century-atlantic-world-colloquium-w-mus-daive-dunkley.

Elliott, Fiona. "Women's Role in the Abolition of the British Slave Trade." *New Histories* 1, no. 2 (January 2010): 1–2.

Ellis, Rev. Edward L., Jr. "Bicentennial Celebration: Historic First Bryan Baptist Church." Church program, Savannah, Ga., 1988. In author's collection.

Ettinger, Amos Aschbach. *James Edward Oglethorpe: Imperial Idealist*. Oxford: Clarendon Press, 1936.

———. *Oglethorpe: A Brief Biography*. Macon, Ga.: Mercer University Press, 1984.

Ewers, Justin. "Abraham Lincoln's Great Awakenings: From Moderate to Abolitionist." *U.S. News and World Report*, February 9, 2009.

Fant, H. B. "The Labor Policy of the Trustees." *Georgia Historical Quarterly* 16, no. 1 (1932): 1–16.

Farley, M. Foster. "The South Carolina Negro in the American Revolution." *South Carolina Historical Magazine* 79, no. 2 (April 1978): 75–86.

Faubert, Michelle. "Granville Sharp's Manuscript Letter to the Admiralty on the Zong Massacre: A New Discovery in the British Library." *Slavery and Abolition* 38, no. 1 (July 2016): 1–18. DOI: 10.1080/0144039X.2016.1206285.

Finley, Robert. "Thoughts on the Colonization of Free Blacks." *African Repository and Colonial Journal* 9 (February 1834): 332–336.

Finney, Bernice E. "The American Colonization Society." *Negro History Bulletin* 12, no. 5 (February 1949): 116–118.

Fischer, David Hackett. *African Founders: How Enslaved People Expanded American Ideals*. New York: Simon & Schuster, 2022.

Foner, Eric. *The Fiery Trial: Abraham Lincoln and American Slavery*. New York: W. W. Norton, 2010.

———, ed. *Our Lincoln: New Perspectives on Lincoln and His World*. New York: W. W. Norton, 2008.

Foner, Jack. *Blacks and the Military in American History*. New York: Praeger, 1974.

Foutz, Dave. "Enlightenment, Scientific Racism and Slavery: A Historical Point." *FALSAFEH* 36, no. 3 (Autumn 2008): 5–24.

Fox, Early Lee. *The American Colonization Society, 1817–1840*. Baltimore: John Hopkins University Press, 1919.

Franklin, John Hope, and Alfred A. Moss Jr. *From Slavery to Freedom: A History of Negro Americans*. 6th ed. New York: Alfred A. Knopf, 1988.

Frey, Sylvia. *Water from the Rock: Black Resistance in a Revolutionary Age*. Princeton, N.J.: Princeton University Press, 1991.

Furstenberg, François. "Beyond Freedom and Slavery: Autonomy, Virtue, and Resistance in Early American Political Discourse." *Journal of American History* 89, no. 4 (March 2003): 1295–1330.

Garrett, Aaron. "Hume's Revised Racism Revisited." *Hume Studies* 26, no. 1 (April 2000): 171–175.

Garrison, Webb. "Sudden Death at Ebenezer Creek." *Georgia Journal* (Spring 1995): 31–34.

Gast, Phil. "Betrayal at Ebenezer Creek: Deaths of Freed Slaves in Georgia Swamp 150 Years Ago Drew Outrage." *Civil War Picket*, December 8, 2014.

Gates, Henry Louis, Jr. "How Many Slaves Landed in the U.S.?" *The African Americans: Many Rivers to Color*. PBS. https://www.pbs.org/wnet/african-americans-many-rivers-to-cross/history/how-many-slaves-landed-in-the-us/.

———. "Which Slave Wrote His Way Out of Slavery?" The Root.com, May 12, 2013.

Genovese, Eugene D. *From Rebellion to Revolution: Afro-American Slave Revolts in the Making of the Modern World*. Baton Rouge: Louisiana State University Press, 1979.

Georgia Historical Society. "Oglethorpe and Religion in Georgia." https://georgiahistory.com/education-outreach/online-exhibits/featured-historical-figures/james-edward-Oglethorpe/Oglethorpe-and-religion-in-georgia/.

Giddings, Joshua R. *The Exiles of Florida or The Crimes Committed by Our Government against the Maroons, Who Fled from South Carolina and Other Slave States, Seeking Protection under Spanish Laws.* Baltimore: Black Classic Press, 1997.

Gilford, James M. "Emily Tubman and the African Colonization Movement in Georgia." *Georgia Historical Quarterly* 59, no. 1 (Spring 1975): 10–24.

Gill, N. S. "Was Hannibal, Enemy of Ancient Rome, Black?" ThoughtCo, August 16, 2019. https://www.thoughtco.com/was-hannibal-black-118902.

Gilmer, George. *Sketches of Some of the First Settlers of Upper Georgia.* Americus, Ga.: Americus Book Company, 1926.

Godwyn, Morgan. *The Negro's & Indians Advocate, Suing for Their Admission into the Church or A Persuasive to the Instructing and Baptizing of the Negro's and Indians in Our Plantations.* London: F. D., 1680.

Goodridge, Elizabeth. "For Blacks, There Was No Clear Choice." *U.S. News and World Report,* June 27, 2008.

Grant, Donald L., and Johnathan Grant, eds. *The Way It Was in the South: The Black Experience in Georgia.* New York: Carol, 1993.

Grant, Douglas. *The Fortunate Slave.* New York: Oxford University Press, 1968.

Guyatt, Nicolas. *Providence and the Intervention of the United States, 1606–1876.* New York: Cambridge University Press, 2007.

Hammond, John Craig, and Mathew Mason, eds. *Contesting Slavery: The Politics of Bondage and Freedom in the New American Nation.* Charlottesville: University of Virginia Press, 2012.

Harris, Thaddeus Mason. *Biographical Memorials of James Oglethorpe.* Columbia, S.C.: Filiquarian, 2018.

Harris, Leslie M., and Diana Ramey Berry, eds. *Slavery and Freedom in Savannah.* Athens: University of Georgia Press, 2014.

Higginbotham, A. Leon. *In the Matter of Color: Race and the American Legal Process, the Colonial Period.* New York: Oxford University Press, 1968.

Hight, John J., and Gilbert R. Stormont, comps. *History of the Fifty-Eighth Regiment of Indiana Volunteer Infantry, Its Organization, Campaigns and Battles from 1861 to 1865.* Princeton, N.J.: Press of the Clarion, 1895.

Hochschild, Adam. *Bury the Chains: Prophets and Rebels in the Fight to Free an Empire's Slaves.* Boston: Houghton Mifflin, 2005.

Holcomb, Julie. "The Abolitionist Movement." *Essential Civil War Curriculum.* https://www.essentialcivilwarcurriculum.com/the-abolitionist-movement.html.

Horne, Gerald. *The Counter Revolution of 1776: Slave Resistance and the Origins of the United States of America.* New York: New York University Press, 2014.

Hornsby, Alton, Jr. *The Negro in Revolutionary Georgia.* Atlanta: Georgia Commission for the National Bicentennial Celebration and Georgia Department of Education, 1977.

Hoskins, Charles Lwanga. *Black Episcopalians in Georgia: Strife, Struggle and Salvation.* Savannah: self-published, 1980.

Hundley, Sarah. "Sarah Hundley's Key Passage Analysis on Hannah More's 'Slavery, A Poem." British Romantic Literature (course blog), October 27, 2014. https://

brli4.umwblogs.org/2014/10/27/sarah-hundleys-key-passage-analysis-on
-hannah-mores-slavery-a-poem/.

Hunt, Tristram. "Slavery: The Long Road to Our Historic Sorrow." *Guardian*, November 26, 2006.

Hurston, Zora Neal. *Barracoon: The Story of the Last "Black Cargo."* New York: Amistad, 2018.

Inikori, Joseph E. *Africans and the Industrial Revolution in England: A Study in International Trade and Economic Development.* Cambridge: Cambridge University Press, 2002.

Inscoe, *James*, ed. *Edward Oglethorpe: New Perspectives on His Life and Legacy, A Tercentenary Commemoration.* DeLeon Springs, Fla.: Georgia Historical Society, James Oglethorpe Tercentenary Commission and Oglethorpe University, 1997.

Isenberg, Nancy. *White Trash: The 400-Year Untold History of Class in America.* New York: Viking, 2016.

Jackson, Harvey H. "The Darien Antislavery Petition of 1739 and the Georgia Plan." *William and Mary Quarterly* 34, no. 4 (October 1, 1977): 618–631.

Jackson, Harvey H., and Phinizy Spalding, eds. *Forty Years of Diversity: Essays on Colonial Georgia.* Athens: University of Georgia Press, 1984.Jackson, Maurice. *Let This Voice Be Heard: Anthony Benezet, Father of Atlantic Abolitionism.* Philadelphia: University of Pennsylvania Press, 2009.

James, Josef C. "Sherman at Savannah." *Journal of Negro History* 39, no. 2 (April 1954): 127–137.

Jernegan, Marcus W. "Slavery and Conversion in the American Colonies." *American Historical Review* 21 (April 1916): 504–507.

"Job Ben Solomon." *Gentlemen's Magazine* 20 (1750): 35.

Johnson, Walter. "On Agency." *Journal of Social History* 37, no. 1, special issue (Autumn 2003): 113–124.

Jones, Charles Colcock. *The Religious Instruction of the Negroes in the United States.* Savannah: Thomas Purse, 1842.

Jones, Mazine D., and Kevin M. McCarthy. *Africans Americans in Florida.* Sarasota: Pineapple Press, 1993.

Jones, Ruybe Mae. "The Negro in Colonial Georgia, 1935–1805." Master's thesis, Atlanta University, 1938.

Jordan, Lewis G. *Negro Baptist History, U.S.A.* Nashville: Sunday School Publishing Board, NBC, 1930.

Jordan, Winthrop D. *White over Black: American Attitudes toward the Negro, 1550–1812.* Chapel Hill: University of North Carolina Press, 1968.

Kaplan, Sidney, and Emma Nogrady Kaplan. *The Black Presence in the Era of the American Revolution.* Amherst: University of Massachusetts Press, 1989.

Katz, William Loren, and Paula A. Franklin. *Proudly Red and Black: Stories of African and Native Americans.* New York: Atheneum, 1993.

Khan, Saeed Ahmed. "Muslims Arrived in America 400 Years Ago as Part of the Slave

Trade and Today Are Vastly Diverse." *The Conversation*, April 11, 2019. https:// theconversation.com/muslims-arrived-in-america-400-years-ago-as-part-of-the -slave-trade-and-today-are-vastly-diverse-113168.

Klingberg, Frank J. "The Evolution of the Humanitarian Spirit in Eighteenth-Century England." *Pennsylvania Magazine of History and Biography* 66, no. 3 (July 1942): 267–270.

Landers, Jane. *Fort Mose: Gracia Real de Santa Teresa de Mose, A Free Black Town in Spanish Colonial Florida*. Saint Augustine: Saint Augustine Historical Society, 1992.

———. "Gracia Real de Santa Teresa de Mose: A Free Black Town in Spanish Florida." *American Historical Review* 95, no. 1 (February 1990): 9–30.

Lannen, Andrew. "Liberty and Slavery in Colonial America, 1732–1770." *Historian* 79, no. 1 (Spring 2017): 32–55.

Lanning, Lt. Col. (Ret.) Michael Lee. *The African-American Soldier*. Secaucus, N.J.: Carol, 1997.

Lawrence, James B. "Religious Education of the Negro in the Colony of Georgia." *Georgia Historical Quarterly* 14, no. 1 (March 1930): 41–57.

Lengyel, Cornel. *Four Days in July*. Garden City, N.Y.: Doubleday, 1958.

Levy, B. H. "The Early History of Georgia's Jews." In Jackson and Spalding, *Forty Years of Diversity*, 163–178.

Littlefield, Daniel C. "Slave Labor." *South Carolina Encyclopedia*, August 23, 2022. https://www.scencyclopedia.org/sce/entries/slave-labor/.

Littlefield, Daniel F., Jr. *Africans and Seminoles, from Removal to Emancipation*. Westport, Conn.: Greenwood, 1977.

Livermore, George. *An Historical Research Respecting the Opinions of the Founders of the Republic on Negroes as Slaves, as Citizens, and as Soldiers. Read before the Massachusetts Historical Society, August 14, 1862*. Boston: Williams, 1863.

"Lloyds of London Insurance for the Slave Trade." U.S. Slave (blog), August 30, 2011. https://usslave.blogspot.com/2011/08/lloyds-of-london-insurance-for-slave.html.

Locke, John. *The First and Second Treaties of Government*. 1689; Columbia, S.C.: Pantianos, 2022.

Locke, Mary Stroughton. *Anti-Slavery in America*. Gloucester, Mass.: Radcliffe College Monographs Noll, 1965.

Lockley, Timothy. "The King of England's Soldiers: Armed Blacks in Savannah and Its Hinterlands during the Revolutionary War Era, 1778–1787." In *Slavery and Freedom in Savannah*, edited by Leslie M. Harris and Daina Ramey Berry, 26–41. Athens: University of Georgia Press, 2014.

Lowell, Carolina Grouper. *The Golden Isles of Georgia*. Boston: Little, Brown, 1932.

MacGregor, Morris J., and Barnard C. Nalty, eds. *Blacks in the United States Armed Forces: Basic Documents*. Wilmington, Del.: Scholarly Resources, 1981.

Madron, Thomas W. "John Wesley on Race: A Christian View of Equality." The United Methodist Church, General Commission on Archives and History, July 7, 1964. https://archives.gcah.org/handle/10516/1357.

Magdol, Edward. *A Right to the Land: Essays on the Freedmen's Community.* Westport, Conn.: Greenwood, 1977.

Maguire, Léa. "Haitian Soldiers at the Battle of Savannah (1779)." Black Past, January 28, 2018. https://www.blackpast.org/global-african-history/haitian -soldiers-battle-savannah-1779/.

Mahon, John K. *The War of 1812.* Gainesville: University Press of Florida, 1972.

Mannix, Daniel P., and Malcolm Cowley. *Black Cargoes: History of the Atlantic Slave Trade, 1518–1865.* New York: Viking, 1962.

Martyn, Benjamin. *Reasons for Establishing the Colony of Georgia in America.* London: W. Meadows, 1733.

Masonen, Pekka. "Leo Africanus: The Man with Many Names." *Al-Andalus Magreb* 8–9 (2001). http://www.leoafricanus.com/pictures/bibliography/Masonen /Masonen.pdf.

Massey, George D. *John Laurens and the American Revolution.* Columbia: University of South Carolina Press, 2000.

Massey, Gregory D. "Slavery and Liberty in the American Revolution, John Laurens Black Regiment Proposal." *Early America Review* 1. Available at https://www .varsitytutors.com/earlyamerica/early-america-review/volume-1/slavery-liberty -american-revolution.

McCall, Capt. Hugh. *The History of Georgia, Containing Brief Sketches of the Most Remarkable Events Up to the Present Day.* Atlanta: Cherokee, 1981.

McPherson, James. *The Negro's Civil War: How American Negroes Felt and Acted during the War for the Union.* New York: Pantheon, 1965.

———. *Ordeal by Fire: The Civil War and Reconstruction.* New York: Knopf, 1982.

Metaxas, Eric. "The Power of a Poem: Hannah More and the Abolition of the Slave Trade." *Break Point,* September 25, 2015.

Mills, T. F., and John Weiss. "Corps of Colonial Marines, Royal Marines, 1814–1816." Land Forces of Britain, the Empire, and Commonwealth. Regiments.org, last updated December 7, 2004. https://web.archive.org/web/20070920115112/http:// regiments.org/deploy/uk/reg-specf/rm3.htm.

Mohr, Clarence. *Threshold of Freedom: Masters and Slaves in Civil War Georgia.* Athens: University of Georgia Press, 1986.

Moore, Francis. *Travels into the Inland Parts of Africa: Containing a Description of the Several Nations for the Space of Six Hundred Miles up the River Gambia.* London: D. Henry and R. Cave, 1738.

Moore, George H. *Historical Notes on the Employment of Negroes in the American Army of the Revolution.* New York: C. T. Evans, 1862.

More, Hannah. *Slavery: A Poem.* London, 1788.

Morgan, David Taft, Jr. "The Great Awakening in the Carolinas and Georgia, 1740–1775." PhD diss., University of North Carolina, 1969.

Morgan, Kenneth. *Slavery and the British Empire.* Oxford: Oxford University Press, 2007.

Morgan, Philip, ed. *African American Life in the Georgia Lowcountry: The Atlantic World and the Gullah Geechee*. Athens: University of Georgia Press, 2010.

———. "Lowcountry Georgia and the Early Modern Atlantic World, 1733–ca. 1820." In Philip Morgan, *African American Life*, 13–47.

Moynihan, Lisa. "African American Agency Responses to the Contradiction of Liberalism in Early American." *Utah Historical Review* 1 (2011): 36–46.

Mtubani, Victor C. D. "The Black Voice in Eighteenth-Century Britain: African Writers against Slavery and the Slave Trade." *Phylon* 45, no. 2 (1984): 85–97.

Muhammad, Precious Rasheeda Muhammad. "Muslims and the Making of America." Muslim Public Affairs Council (2013). www.mpac.org/publications/policy-papers /muslims.

Nadelhaft, Jerome. "The Somersett Case and Slavery: Myth, Reality, and Repercussions." *Journal of Negro History* 51, no. 3 (July 1966): 193–208.

Newton, John. *Thoughts upon the African Slave Trade*. London, 1787.

Ninety-Second Illinois Volunteers. Freeport, Ill.: Journal Steam, 1875.

Oglethorpe, James. *The British Sailor's Advocate*. London: B. White, 1727–1728.

Owens, James Leggette. "The Negro in Georgia during Reconstruction, 1864–1872: A Social History." PhD diss., University of Georgia, 1975.

Padgett, Debbie, ed. "1730s Portrait of African Once Enslaved in North American Colonies Acquired for Exhibit at American Revolution Museum at Yorktown." *Dispatch: Newsletter of the Jamestown-Yorktown Foundation* 28, no. 2 (June 2014): 1–7.

Paley, Ruth, Christina Malcolmson, and Michael Hunter. "Parliament and Slavery, 1660–c. 1710." *Slavery and Abolition* 31, no. 2 (June 2010): 257–266.

Parten, Ben. "Somewhere toward Freedom: Sherman's March and Georgia's Refugee Slaves." Master's thesis, Clemson University, 2017.

Pearson, Robin, and David Richardson. "Insuring the Transatlantic Slave Trade." *Journal of Economic History* 79, no. 2 (June 2019): 417–446. DOI: 10.1017 /S0022050719000068.

Pennington, Edgar Legare. "Thomas Bray's Associates and Their Work Among the Negroes." *American Antiquarian Society* (October 1938): 311–331. https://www .americanantiquarian.org/proceedings/44806985.pdf.

Peters, Virginia Berman. *The Florida Wars*. Hamden, Conn.: Archon, 1979.

Phillips, U. B. *American Negro Slavery: A Survey of the Supply, Employment and Control of Negro Labor as Determined by the Plantation Regime*. Baton Rouge: Louisiana State University Press, 1918.

Porter, Kenneth. *The Negro on the American Frontier*. New York: Arno, 1971.

Pressly, Paul M. *On the Rim of the Caribbean: Colonial Georgia and the British Atlantic World*. Athens: University of Georgia Press, 2013.

Pruitt, Sarah. "5 Things You May Not Know about Lincoln, Slavery and Emancipation." History.com, August 19, 2019. https://www.history.com/news/5-things -you-may-not-know-about-lincoln-slavery-and-emancipation.

Quarles, Benjamin Arthur. *The Negro in the American Revolution*. New York: Da Capo Press, 1973.

———. *The Negro in the Civil War*. Boston: Little, Brown, 1953.

Ramsey, David. *The History of the American Revolution.* 2 vols. Lexington, Mass., 1815.

Ready, Milton L. "An Economic History of Colonial Georgia, 1732–1754." PhD diss., University of Georgia, 1970.

Reddie, Richard S. *ABOLITION! The Struggle to Abolish Slavery in the British Colonies.* Oxford: Gutenberg Press, 2007.

Rhodehamel, John. "Forever Free: Abraham Lincoln's Journey to Emancipation." American Library Association, March 21, 2006. https://www.ala.org/tools /programming/foreverfree/ssnbackgroundessay.

Rice, C. Duncan. *The Rise and Fall of Black Slavery.* New York: Harper & Row, 1975.

Richardson, David. "Shipboard Revolts, African Authority, and the Atlantic Slave Trade." *William and Mary Quarterly,* 3rd ser., 58, no. 1 (January 2001): 69–92.

Riddell, William Renwick. "Slavery in the Maritime Provinces." *Journal of Negro History* 5, no. 3 (July 1920): 359–375.

Salzer, James. "Georgia to Salute Its Founder, Delegation to Visit Oglethorpe's England." *Florida Times-Union* (Jacksonville), October 2, 1996. http://www .questia.com/newspaper/1G1-57502977/georgia-to-salute-its-founder-delegation -to-visit.

Sarikas, Christine. "The 13 Original Colonies: A Complete History." PrepScholar: SAT/ACT Prep Online Guides and Tips, August 27, 2019. https://blog.prepscholar .com/13-colonies.

Scarborough, Ruth. *The Opposition to Slavery in Georgia Prior to 1860.* Nashville: George Peabody College for Teachers, 1933.

Scott, Julius S. *The Common Wind: Afro-American Currents in the Age of the Haitian Revolution.* London: Verso, 2020.

Shaffer, Donald R. "African Americans and Sherman's March." *Civil War Emancipation,* December 7, 2014. http://www.civilwaralbum.com/misc5/ebenezer_pan1.htm.

Shannon, David T. *George Liele's Life and Legacy, an Unsung Hero.* Macon: Mercer University Press, 2012.

Sharp, Granville. *The Law of Retribution: A Serious Warning to Great Britain and Her Colonies, Founded on Unquestionable Examples of God's Temporal Vengeance against Tyrants, Slaveholders and Oppressors.* London: W. Richardson, 1776.

Sherwood, Henry Noble. "The Formation of the American Colonization Society." *Journal of Negro History* 2, no. 3 (July 1917): 209–228.

Shyllon, F. O. *Black Slaves in Britain.* London: Oxford University Press, 1974.

Simms, James M. *First Colored Baptist Church in North America: Constituted at Savannah, Georgia, January 20, A. D. 1788, with Biographical Sketches of the Pastors.* Philadelphia: J. B. Lippincott, 1888.

Sinha, Manisha. "Allies for Emancipation? Lincoln and Black Abolitionists." In Eric Foner, *Our Lincoln,* 167–196.

———. *The Slave's Cause: A History of Abolition.* New Haven, Conn.: Yale University Press, 2016.

Smith, David Livingston. "The Essence of Evil." *Aeon,* October 24, 2014. https://aeon .co/essays/why-is-it-so-easy-to-dehumanise-a-victim-of-violence.

Smith, Warren Thomas. *John Wesley and Slavery.* Nashville: Abingdon, 1986.

Snelgrave, William. *New Account of Some Parts of Guinea and the Slave Trade*. London: James, John, and Paul Knapton, 1734.

Sobel, Michel. *Trabelin' On: The Slave Journey to an Afro-Baptist Faith*. Princeton, N.J.: Princeton University Press, 1979.

Spalding, Phinizy. "Oglethorpe, Georgia, and the Spanish Threat." In Inscoe, *James Edward Oglethorpe*, 61–70.

———. *Oglethorpe in America*. Chicago: The University of Chicago Press, 1977.

———. "Oglethorpe's Quest for an American Zion." In Jackson and Spalding, *Forty Years of Diversity*, 60–79.

Spalding, Phinizy, and Edwin Jackson. *James Edward Oglethorpe: A New Look at Georgia's Founding Father*. Athens: Carl Vinson Institute of Government, University of Georgia, 1968.

Spalding, Phinizy, and Harvey H. Jackson, eds. *Oglethorpe in Perspective: Georgia's Founder after Two Hundred Years*. Tuscaloosa: University of Alabama Press, 1989.

Stewart, Aubrey, and George Long. *Plutarch's Lives. Translated from the Greek. With Notes and a Life of Plutarch*. Vol. 1. New York: George Bell & Sons, 1894.

Stewart, L. Lloyd. *A Far Cry from Freedom: Gradual Abolition (1799–1827)*. Bloomington, Ind.: AuthorHouse, 2006.

Sullivan, Buddy. *Early Days on the Georgia Tidewater: The Story of McIntosh County and Sapelo*. Darien, Ga.: McIntosh County Board of Commissioners, 1990.

———. *Georgia: A State History*. Charleston, S.C.: Arcadia, 2003.

Sweet, Julie Anne. "The Thirteenth Colony in Perspective: Historian's Views on Early Georgia." *Georgia Historical Quarterly* 85, no. 3 (Fall 2001): 435–460.

Sweet, Julie Anne. *Negotiating for Georgia: British-Creek Relations in the Trustee Era, 1733–1752*. Athens: University of Georgia Press, 2005.

Taylor, Richard Brent. *Islam in the African-American Experience*. Bloomington: Indiana University Press, 2003.

Thomas, Sir Keith. "James Edward Oglethorpe, Sometime Gentleman Commoner of Corpus." In Inscoe, *James Edward Oglethorpe*, 16–34.

Thompson, Angela. "African Traders of Enslaved People." *Thought Co.*, June 15, 2020, 1–4.

Thompson, C. Mildred. *Reconstruction in Georgia*. Atlanta: Cherokee, 1971.

Thorenz, Matt. "Substitutes, Servants and Soldiers: The Black Presence at New Windsor Cantonment in the Massachusetts and New Hampshire Lines." Initially presented as "Black Patriots Revealed: African-Americans in the Continental Army," February 12, 2012, at New Windsor Cantonment State Historic Site.

Thurmond, Michael L. *Freedom: Georgia's Anti-Slavery Heritage, 1733–1865*. Atlanta: Longstreet Press, 2003.

———. *A Story Untold: Black Men and Women in Athens History*. Athens, Ga.: Deeds, 2017.

Tillman, Rev. Thurmond. "The First African Baptist Church History." Church program, Savannah, Ga., 1989. In author's collection.

Torres-Spelliscy, Ciara. "Perspective—Everyone Is Talking about 1619. But That's Not Actually When Slavery in America Started." *Washington Post*, August 23, 2019.

Tucker, Ellen. "'The Starting Point' of the Abolitionist Movement: Morgan Godwyn's Plea to Evangelize Slaves." Teaching American History, August 6, 2020. https:// teachingamericanhistory.org/blog/the-starting-point-of-the-abolitionist -movement-morgan-godwyn's-plea-to-evangelize-slaves/.

Ungar, Helen. "Free Negroes in Ante-Bellum Georgia." Master's thesis, University of Georgia, 1949.

Wade, John Donald. *John Wesley*. New York: Coward-McCann, 1930.

Walker, James St. G. *The Black Loyalists: The Search for a Promised Land in Nova Scotia and Sierra Leone, 1783–1870*. New York: African Publishing Company, 1976.

Walvin, James. *The Zong, a Massacre, the Law and the End of Slavery*. New Haven, Conn.: Yale University Press, 2011.

Wax, Darold Duane. "Georgia and the Negro before the American Revolution." *Georgia Historical Quarterly* 51, no. 1 (March 1967): 63–77.

Weaver, Jace. "The Red Atlantic: Transoceanic Cultural Exchanges." *American Indian Quarterly* 53, no. 3 (January 2011): 418.

Weber, David J. *The Spanish Frontier in North America*. New Haven, Conn.: Yale University Press, 2014.

Weld, Theodore Dwight. "Condition and Character of Negroes in Africa." In *The People of Africa: A Series of Papers on Their Character, Condition, and Future Prospects*, edited by Edward W. Blyden, 43–63. New York: Anson D. F. Randolph, 1871.

Wesley, John. *Thoughts upon Slavery*. London; Reprinted in Philadelphia with notes: Sold by Joseph Crukshank, originally published 1774.

Whelchel, L. H., Jr. *The History and Heritage of African American Churches: A Way Out of No Way*. St. Paul, Minn.: Paragon House, 2011.

White, Ronald, Jr. *Lincoln's Greatest Speech: The Second Inaugural*. New York: Simon & Schuster, 2002.

Wilkins, Thomas Hart. "An Economic Interpretation of the Founding of the Colony of Georgia." Master's thesis, University of Georgia, 2002.

———. "James Edward Oglethorpe: South Carolina Slaveholder?" *Georgia Historical Quarterly* 88, no. 1 (Spring 2004): 85–94.

Wilson, Joseph T. *The Black Phalanx: African American Soldiers in the War of Independence, the War of 1812 and the Civil War*. New York: Da Capo Press, 1991.

Wilson, Thomas D. *The Oglethorpe Plan: Enlightenment Design in Savannah and Beyond*. Charlottesville: University of Virginia Press, 2015.

Wirt, William. *Sketches of the Life and Character of Patrick Henry*. Philadelphia: James Webster, 1817.

Wise, Steven M. *Though the Heavens May Fall: The Landmark Trial That Led to the End of Human Slavery*. New York: Da Capo Press, 2005.

Wong, Dwayne. "Did We Sell Each Other Into Slavery: Misconceptions about the African Involvement in the Slave Trade." *HuffPost*, December 6, 2017.

Wood, Betty. "James Edward Oglethorpe, Race, and Slavery: A Reassessment." In Spalding and Jackson, *Oglethorpe in Perspective*, 66–79.

———. *Slavery in Colonial America, 1619–1776*. Lanham, Md.: Rowman & Littlefield, 2005.

———. *Slavery in Colonial Georgia, 1730–1775*. Athens: University of Georgia Press, 1984.

Wood, Peter H. *Black Majority: Negroes in Colonial South Carolina from 1670 through the Stono Rebellion*. New York: Knopf, 1974.

———. "Slave Labor Camps in Early America: Overcoming Denial and Discovering the Gulag." In *Inequality in Early America*, edited by Carla Gardina Pestana and Sharon V. Salinger, 222–238. Hanover, N.H.: University Press of New England, 1999.

Wood, William. *A Survey of Trade, in Four Parts*. London, 1718.

Woodson, Carter Gordon. *The History of the Negro Church, 1775–1950*. Washington, D.C.: Associated Publishers, 1921; electronic ed. reprint, Chapel Hill: University of North Carolina Press, 2000.

Wylly, Charles Spalding. *The Seed That Was Sown in the Colony of Georgia: The Harvest and the Aftermath*. New York: Neale, 1910.

Yautz, Stephen. "Rev. Robert Finley: Founder of the American Colonization Society." SMY *Historical Services* (blog), November 9, 2007. http://smyhistorical.blogspot.com/2007/11/rev-robert-finley-new-jersey.html.

Zielinski, Adam E. "Slavery in the Colonies: The British Position on Slavery in the Era of Revolution." American Battlefield Trust. https://www.battlefields.org/learn/articles/slavery-in-the-colonies.

INDEX

Page numbers in italics indicate illustrations.